2000 True Type Fonts & 5000 Clip Art Images

GW00566597

Related Titles

If you like this CDROM, you'll enjoy these too!

Clipart Cornucopia™
5000 Clipart images to use in your newsletters, greeting cards, and more.

Raytrace! The Official POV-RAY CDROM
A beautiful collection of POV-Ray images, plus programs to create your own images.

Visions
500 royalty free photographs from the Preferred Stock Photo Agency.

Travel Adventure
395 royalty free photographs from around the world, color booklet included.

Fractal Frenzy
1000s of fractals including examples of all the major types from Mandelbrot to Zexpe.

Fractal Frenzy 2
A collection of 2127 images by eight renowned fractal artists.

GIFs Galore
600 MB of GIF images, categories from abstract art to Vietnam.

All of these titles are available through your local bookstore or software retailer. For more information call +1-510-674-0783.

2000 True Type Fonts & 5000 Clip Art Images

by Public Domain and Shareware Library

Walnut Creek CDROM

2000 True Type Fonts & 5000 Clipart Images
Published by Walnut Creek CDROM
1547 Palos Verdes Mall, Suite 260
Walnut Creek, CA 94596 USA

Printed in the United States of America

0   9   8   7   6   5   4   3   2   1

ISBN 1-57176-053-9

Table of Contents

Acknowledgments x

How to use this CDROM and book xi

Font and Graphics Installation xii

Font and Graphics Utility Files xiii

Font Samples

\Directory *(Description)*

\TTFCAPS (fonts with only capital letters) 2

\TTFDING (dingbats and symbols) 4

\TTFA_A 6

\TTFB_B 9

\TTFC_C 12

\TTFD_D 16

\TTFE_E 18

\TTFF_F 21

\TTFG_G 24

\TTFH_H 26

\TTFI_I 28

\TTFJ_K 29

\TTFL_M 31

\TTFN_O 36

\TTFP_Q 40

\TTFR_R 44

\TTFS_S 47

\TTFT_T 52

\TTFU_V 55

\TTFW_Z 59

Clip Art
\Directory *(Description)*

\Animals 61

\Animrept *(Reptiles)* 70

\Art 75

\Astrol *(Astrology symbols)* 82

\Birds 85

\Bookplat *(Images of old book plates)* 89

\Borders *(Decorative borders)* .90

\Building 102

\Busines1 105

\Busines2 112

\Cart1 *(Cartoons)* 119

\Cart2 *(More Cartoons)* 129

\Cats 139

\Computer 144

\Dogs 149

\Education 153

\Ethnic 160

\Fantasy 165

\Festiv *(Images related to festivity)* .174

\Fish 186

\Flowers 194

\Food 198

\Garden 211

\Graphic1 221

\Graphic2 228

\Graphsce *(Science related)* 235

\Gringrap *(The Grin Graphics Art Collection)* 241

\Ham *(Ham radio related)* 248

\Hands 253

\Holiday 258

\Home 262

\Hornback *(Hornback Clipart Collection)* 267

\Insects 274

\Jobs 281

\Maps 284

\Maps2 *(Color clip art maps, pictured in black and white)* . . .288

\Maps3 *(Color clip art maps, pictured in black and white)* . . .296

\Marine *(Marine/nautical images)* .304

\Medical 307

\Military 311

\Misc *(Assorted images)* 324

\Music 330

\Oldfas *(Old fashioned/historical)* 335

\Outdoor 338

\People1 341

\Punch *(Punch magazine cartoons)* .352

\Religion 355

\Season 367

\Sheets *(Sheets of different images)* .374

\Signs *(Signs and logos)* 378

\Space 383

\Sport 386

\Symbols 391

\Tools 395

\Transpor *(Transportation related)* 402

\Travel 411

\Trees 416

Acknowledgments

Please remember that although you own this disc, you do not own all of the programs recorded on it. Many programs on this disc are shareware. You are free to try each program for a limited time. If you are satisfied and want to continue to use the program, you should register the program. You register by sending a specified amount of money directly to the author of the program. Often the author will send you the most up-to-date version of the program and a printed manual. Please check the individual files for specific information.

Also note that the font names used by the authors of the fonts on this disc may sometimes be similar to certain commercial (not public domain or shareware) fonts. Please be aware that the fonts may differ considerably from these commercial versions.

How to Use this CDROM and book

To use this book:

This book is a reference guide to the 2000 True Type Fonts & 5000 Clipart CDROM. It includes a sample printout of each font and clip art image included on the CDROM. To find where a font/image is on the CDROM simply look directly underneath it in the book. This is the file name. At the top of each page you'll see the name of the directory where you will find the specific file.

To use this CDROM:

1. Load the CDROM into the CDROM drive.
2. Start up Windows by typing WIN at your DOS prompt.
3. From the FILE menu select RUN
4. In the COMMAND LINE box, type d:\ setup *(or substitute d:\ with the letter that identifies your CDROM drive.)*
5. Click OK to start the installation.

Font and Graphics Installation

See the following page for a list of included font and graphics utilities.

Why is everything so slow now that I've installed 100+ fonts?

Having large numbers of fonts (more than 100) installed in Windows can slow down loading of Windows itself and its applications. The method described below can help alleviate this problem.

When you install a font, Windows creates a matching FOT file, so for A0000079.TTF it would create a file called A0000079.FOT. It places this file in the Windows System Directory. If you install 100 fonts you get 200 files. This really slows things down. To fix this you must first make another sub directory somewhere on your hard disc called "FONTS" (or similar). Copy the fonts you want to install here rather than your System Directory. Go into Windows and the 'Fonts add' window. Tell windows to look in your new directory for the fonts. Make sure to disable the 'Copy fonts' button and install the fonts as before. Doing it this way removes half of the files from the Systems directory. To help things even more make a new sub directory under the Windows directory called 'FOT', i.e. \Windows\FOT. Look in your Windows system directory.

Note: All of the directories which contain PCX graphics files include graphics catalogue files which contain several thumbnail sketches of the files allowing you to view several on the screen at the same time.

FONT UTILITIES

H278(1) Ver 5.7 PRINTER'S APPRENTICE is a font management utility supporting Adobe Type Manager, Bitstream Facelift, Atech Publishers Powerpack and TrueType, although any scalable type manager should be OK. The main use of the program is as an on-line viewer of type families, with the ability to print high quality specimen sheets of keyboard layouts, ANSI charts and a general purpose reference sheet. *Bug fix & cosmetic update.* **WINDOWS[SUSA25]**

H349(1) Ver 3.3 FONT MONSTER is a TrueType and Type1 font hacker's utility allowing you to rename any font, edit other miscellaneous font data, preview Truetype fonts before installation, create font groups which you install by clicking on their Program Manager icon, print font samples, catalogues and more. *Bug fix and cosmetic update.* **WINDOWS[STAI20]**

H535(1) Ver 5.3 FONTSPEC PRO Is an excellent font handling utility providing the ability to view on-screen all your installed True-Type or Adobe font with a number of options. It will also allow you to manage your fonts in easily controlled groups. Probably its most useful feature is the ability to print out character set samples of UNINSTALLED fonts so that you can see if they are really what you want before you go to the bother of installing them. This program is fully functional except that when you print out sample fonts you also get a "nag sheet" reminding you to register. **WINDOWS[SUSA25]**

GRAPHICS UTILITIES

4016(1) Ver 0.4 RMORF is a graphics "morphing" utility which takes two images and smoothly blends them into each other. Input files must be 24-bit uncompressed Targa images or 24-bit GIFs; output files can either be 24-bit Targa files, GIF files or FLI animation files. AAPLAY FLI player also supplied to play animations. **NB. Needs minimum 938K XMS memory.** Shareware version limited to images of 320x200 resolution. *Bug fix update adds GIF format input.* **EVHOAOM[SUSA25]**

☆**4071(1) Ver 3.11** THE COMPLETE IMAGE is a command-line bitmap conversion and image processing utility. Reads, writes and converts between TGA, IMG, BMP, GIF and IPI format files, and also features complete VESA compatibility (up to 1.2 VBE), online help, user-defined variables/macros, over 100 filters built in, uses all available memory with VMM option, merge R/G/B images into one, gamma correction, contrast enhancement, generates terrain maps for POV and BOB ray tracers, plasma fractals, photo negatives, image arithmetic, "Blue-screen" effects and much more. **EAMO3SO[SUSA35]**

☆**4039(1) Ver 1.0** IMAGE COMMANDER is a bitmap graphic file cataloguing system for Windows 3.1 able to handle BMP, CLP, CUT, DIB, GIF, IFF, IMG, JAS, JIF, JPG, LBM, MAC, MSP, PCD, PIC, PCX, RAS, RLE, TGA, TIFF, WMF and WPG format files. Images can be organised into "albums" and catalogued using keywords and comments for future searches. Also scan for all images on your system, view images full screen or in a configurable slide show, activate your favourite editor to change the image or print your album as a catalogue. **WINDOWS[SUSA29]**

UPDATE ☆**3964(1) Ver 1.00** IMGFUN image enhancement and compression utility for grey and colour-mapped GIF, PCX, BMP and JPEG images. Features instant zoom and scroll images onscreen, adjust colours, brightness, contrast and cut area of images. Enables fast JPEG compression to reduce GIF images to a fraction of their original size. Also includes CHIARO SUITE v1.0 of utilities for image

format information, GIF image checking and excess character remo
val. *SCREEN THIEF moved due to size increase*
5VHO2OO[SUSA35]

3895(1) Ver 4.0 TOGETHER! is a TSR that will allow you to add
.PCX image files to text based applications. You can decide where the
picture is to be displayed on screen, horizontally, vertically, in a corner
or as an overlay. TOGETHER! should work with most graphics mode
and most DOS based applications, word processors, databases etc
*Now adds support for GIF87a format images, printing capability or
HP Laserjets and dot matrix printers, auto configuration and much
more.* **5AMOAOO[SUSA20]**

3838(1) Ver 1.46 DISP is a utility to read, write and display bitmap
images with different formats and can perform some special effects
such as rotation and dithering on them. There is no limit on image size
and the program currently supports 8, 15, 16 and 24-bit displays. Will
read bitmap files in GIF, Japan MAG/PIC/MKI, Sun RAS, JPEG
XBM, Utah RLE, PBM, PGM, PPM, PM, PCX, TIFF, Targa, XPM
MAC, GEM/IMG, IFF/LBM, BMP, QRT ray tracer, Mac PCT, VIS
PDS, Viking VIK and VICAR VIC formats and will print on HI
Laserjet and convert to GIF, SUN, JPG, XBM, PBM, PGM, PPM, PM
Tiff, Targa, XPM, MAC, IFF/LBM, BMP, PCT GEM/IMG, PCX and
VIS. Directly supports a wide range of SVGA cards plus any VESA
compatible. *Now adds GEM/IMG and PCX writing, JPEG 4 support,
FLI/FLC support plus masses of bug fixes and cosmetic improvements.*
EVHO3SO[PUSA*]

3816(1) Ver 6.0e VPIC is a file viewer for
EGA/MCGA/VGA/SVGA allowing viewing of files in the following
formats - DR Halo .CUT (with PAL if present), GIF87a and 89a,
Deluxe Paint LBM or IFF regular and enhanced, MAC, Pictor/PC
Paint PIC, ZSoft PCX (incl 256 colour), Viewpoint PIC, Color-
RIX/EGA Paint SCx files, Targa 16 or 24 TGA files, Windows 3 BMP
or BIF binary image files. Will convert to any of these except MAC,
BIF or Viewpoint PIC and will convert to GIF89a format in regular,
interlaced, inverted, mirrored or rotated 90 degrees CW or CCW. Slide
show facility with animation. *Bug fix update.* Also GIFDESK v4.5
allows multiple GIF files to be displayed on a single screen. *Now with
full GIF89a support, prints to Laserjet and adds many SVGA drivers.*
5EMOAOO[SUSA25]

H144(1) Ver 1.7 IMAGE ALCHEMY is a command-line operated
utility supporting JPEG compression and converts between 60 different graphics files formats including GIF, TIFF, Amiga IFF/LBM, PCX
(including 24-bit), Macintosh PICT, Sun RAS and RLE, HP PCL,
Encapsulated Postscript, BMP, SGI, PBM/PPM/PGM, GIF89a plus
Group III, Group IV, PICIO and SGI RLE, Vivid, MTV, DCX, QDV,
Erdas, QRT, GEM, Utah RLE, ADEX, RTL, WPG, Pictor, Autologic,
q0, BIF, Stork, XWD, Scodl, AVHRR, CALS, Cubicomp and IBM
Picture Maker, DR Halo CUT, First Publisher ART, GOES, PDS, RIX,
SPOT Image, XPM, XBM and TIFF compression types and Targa
8-32 bit images are supported. Shareware version is restricted to
640x480 and lower resolutions. *Bug fix update.* PRO-CR v2.12 is an
Optical Character Recognition program which reads several common
fonts in a range of point sizes, with no font selection required by the
user. Runs at 200 and 300dpi and allows image preview and online
correction of processed text. Supports the HP ScanJet directly and
other scanners via TIFF and PCX files. **6VHO2OO[SUSA80]**

UPDATE H164(1) Ver 1.1L GRAPHIC WORKSHOP FOR WIN-
DOWS is a utility for working with bitmapped graphics files, allowing
you to view them, convert between any two formats (with a few
restrictions), print them, dither colour images to black and white,

reverse them, rotate and flip them, scale them, reduce the number of colours and do colour dithering, crop them down to smaller files, plus other effects. Currently handles Mac, PCX up to 24-bit, GEM IMG up to 24-bit, Compuserve's GIF, TIFF (grey scale and colour), WordPerfect WPG, MS-Paint, Deluxe Paint IFF/LBM, Windows 3 .BMP, PC Paint PIC, PFS:First Publisher ART, Targa, DR Halo CUT, Kodak Photo-CD, JPEG compression, Windows WMF, FLI and FLC animation formats. *Now adds ICO, CLP and AVI support (needs Video for Windows 1.1+ for AVI support), enhanced TIFF and WMF handling and image cataloguing.* **WINDOWS[SCAN31]**

H237(1) Ver 7.0b GRAPHIC WORKSHOP is a graphics file utility allowing you to view files, convert between different formats, print to dot matrix, Laserjet Plus or Postscript laser printers and dither colour files to black and white. File formats handled are Mac, PCX (with up to 256 colours), GEM/IMG files of the sort used with Ventura Publisher, GIF files of any size and up to 256 colours, TIFF (grey scale, colour, LZW, Huffman, Group 3 & 4), WordPerfect WPG, MS-Paint, Deluxe Paint IFF/LBM, Windows 3 .BMP and RLE, Pictor/PC Paint PIC, Targa, DR Halo CUT and PFS:First Publisher ART, and can also output encapsulated PostScript files. Will use XMS/EMS/LIM memory, and features image rotation, flipping, scaling and non-dither halftoning, cropping, scanning and interactive colour adjustment. *Major rewrite now includes JPEG and complete TIFF support, expanded VESA support and image cataloguing (create composite "catalogue" files of image).* **Available on 720K format.** **5AMOAOO[SCAN31]**

UPDATE ☆**H344(1) Ver 2.01** PAINT SHOP PRO is a Windows program that will display, convert, alter and print bitmapped graphic images in 23 formats including BMP, DIB, GIF, IMG, JAS, MAC, MSP, PIC, PCX, RAS, RLE, TGA, TIFF, WPG, CLP, CUT, EPS, IFF/LBM, JIF, JPEG, PCD(Kodak Photo CD) and WMF formats. Image display includes zoom; image alteration includes rotating, resizing, resampling, trimming, fliter application, colour adjustments, brightness and contrast adjustment, colour depth adjustments, gamma correcting and greyscaling. Come with a standard set of filters, and supports applying, creating, editing and deleting user defined filters. Handles batch conversion for multiple files and allows direct scanning with any TWAIN-compliant scanner. *Bug fix update.* **Available on 720K media. WINDOWS[SUSA49]**

H463(1) Ver 2.01 GRAPHIC TOOLBOX allows viewing, modification and conversion of unusual bitmap graphics formats into more standard types. Can read BMP, PCX, ROMBO VIDI-PC .VID, RGB, Terrabase PCS, PIX, SCN, VGACAD BLD, Teletext GFX .TTX, ANI and QBASIC V00, V01, V02, V11 and V13 formats and will write RGB, BMP, V01, V02, V11 and V13. *Major update now improves PCX unpacking to include 16 and 256 colours, adds V07, V08, V09 and V12 formats and TGA unpacking module. Also includes GRAPHIC UTILITIES PACK containing converters for TTX, VID, PCS, V13, V11, V02 and V01 to BMP format, viewers for TTX, V13/11/02/01, ANI, VID and PCS format files, and BASIC source code for various utilities.* **Available on 720K media. 6VHOAOO[SUK10]**

2000
True Type Fonts

ABCDEFGHIJJKLMN
22 point (g:\ttfcaps\a0000079.ttf)

ABCDEFGHIJKLMNOPQR
22 point (g:\ttfcaps\a0000114.ttf)

ABCDEFGHIJKLMNOPQR
22 point (g:\ttfcaps\a0000138.ttf)

ABCDEFGHIJKLMNOP
22 point (g:\ttfcaps\b0000172.ttf)

ABCDEFGHIJKCMNO
22 point (g:\ttfcaps\b0000184.ttf)

ABC FHIJKL OP
22 point (g:\ttfcaps\b0000200.ttf)

ABCDEFGHIJKLMNO
22 point (g:\ttfcaps\b0000207.ttf)

ABCDEFGHIJKLMNOPQRSTUV
22 point (g:\ttfcaps\b0000281.ttf)

ABCDEFGHIJJKLM
22 point (g:\ttfcaps\c0000324.ttf)

ABCDEGEOHIIKA
22 point (g:\ttfcaps\c0000413.ttf)

ABCDEFGHJKLMNOP
22 point (g:\ttfcaps\c0000447.ttf)

ABCDEFGHIJKLMNOPQRSTUVW
22 point (g:\ttfcaps\c0000477.ttf)

ABCDEFG HIJKLMN
22 point (g:\ttfcaps\c0000483.ttf)

ABCDEFGHIJKL
22 point (g:\ttfcaps\d0000550.ttf)

ABCDEFGHIJKLMNOPQRSTUVWXYZ
22 point (g:\ttfcaps\d0000552.ttf)

ABCDEFGHIJKLMNOPQRSTUVWXYZ
22 point (g:\ttfcaps\d0000553.ttf)

ABCDEFGHIJKLMNOPQRSTUVWXYZ
22 point (g:\ttfcaps\d0000554.ttf)

(g:\ttfcaps\d0000572.ttf)

ABCDEFGHIJKLMNOPQRSTUVWX
22 point (g:\ttfcaps\d0000588.ttf)

ABCDEFGHIJKLMNOPQRSTUVWX
22 point (g:\ttfcaps\d0000594.ttf)

ABCDEFGHIJKLMNOPQR
(g:\ttfcaps\e0000608.ttf)

ABCDEFGHIJKL
22 point (g:\ttfcaps\e0000615.ttf)

ABCDEFGHIJKLMNO
22 point (g:\ttfcaps\e0000657.ttf)

ABCDEFGHIJKLMNOPQR
22 point (g:\ttfcaps\e0000670.ttf)

ABCDEFGHIJKLMNOPQR
22 point (g:\ttfcaps\e0000671.ttf)

ABCDEFGHIJKLMNO
22 point (g:\ttfcaps\g0000865.ttf)

ABCDEFGHIJKLMNOPQRSTUVWXY
22 point (g:\ttfcaps\g0000931.ttf)

ABCDEFGHIJKLMNO
22 point (g:\ttfcaps\g0000934.ttf)

ABCDEFGHIJKLMNOPQRSTU
(g:\ttfcaps\h0000946.ttf)

ABCDEFGHIJKLMNO
22 point (g:\ttfcaps\h0001016.ttf)

ABCDEFGHIJKL
22 point (g:\ttfcaps\h0001045.ttf)

ABCDEFGHIJKLMNOPQ
22 point (g:\ttfcaps\i0001048.ttf)

ABCDEFGHIJKLMNOPQR
22 point (g:\ttfcaps\i0001053.ttf)

ABCDEFGHIJKL
22 point (g:\ttfcaps\j0001087.ttf)

ABCDEFGHIJKLMNOPQRST
22 point (g:\ttfcaps\j0001088.ttf)

ABCDEFGHIJ
22 point (g:\ttfcaps\k0001130.ttf)

ABCDESGHIJKL
22 point (g:\ttfcaps\k0001131.ttf)

BCDEFGHI?
22 point (g:\ttfcaps\k0001140.ttf)

BCDEFGHIJKLMNO
22 point (g:\ttfcaps\k0001150.ttf)

BCDEFGHIJKLMNO
22 point (g:\ttfcaps\k0001152.ttf)

BCDEFGHIJKLMNO
22 point (g:\ttfcaps\l0001165.ttf)

BCDEFGHIJKLMNOPQ
22 point (g:\ttfcaps\l0001210.ttf)

BCDEFGHIJKLNOPQ
22 point (g:\ttfcaps\l0001236.ttf)

BCDEFGHIJKLMNOPQRS
22 point (g:\ttfcaps\m0001309.ttf)

BCDEFGHIJKLMNOPQ
22 point (g:\ttfcaps\m0001337.ttf)

BCDEFGHIJKLMNOPQR
22 point (g:\ttfcaps\m0001354.ttf)

BCDEFGHIJKLMNOPQR
22 point (g:\ttfcaps\m0001356.ttf)

BCDEFGHIJKLMNOPQR
22 point (g:\ttfcaps\m0001355.ttf)

BCDEFGHIJKLMN
22 point (g:\ttfcaps\m0001357.ttf)

BCDEFGHIJKL
22 point (g:\ttfcaps\m0001358.ttf)

BCDEFGHIJKLM
22 point (g:\ttfcaps\m0001359.ttf)

BCDEFGHIJKLMNOPQRST
(g:\ttfcaps\m0001364.ttf)

BCDEFGHIJKLMNOPQRS
(g:\ttfcaps\m0001413.ttf)

BCDEFGHIJKLMNOPQRSTUV
22 point (g:\ttfcaps\p0001643.ttf)

BCDEFGHIJKLMN
22 point (g:\ttfcaps\p0001708.ttf)

22 point (g:\ttfcaps\p0001723.ttf)

BO CHIKI MNOPQRS
22 point (g:\ttfcaps\p0001748.ttf)

ABCDEFGHIJKLMNOPQRSTUV
22 point (g:\ttfcaps\r0001807.ttf)

ABCDEFGHIJKLMNOPQRSTUVWXYZ
22 point (g:\ttfcaps\r0001805.ttf)

ABCDEFGHIJKLMNO
22 point (g:\ttfcaps\r0001806.ttf)

ABCDEFGHIJKLMNOPQRSTUV
22 point (g:\ttfcaps\r0001804.ttf)

ABCDEFGHIJKLMNOPQ
22 point (g:\ttfcaps\r0001808.ttf)

ABCDEFGHIJKLMNOP
22 point (g:\ttfcaps\s0001949.ttf)

ABCDEFGHIJKLMNOPQRSTUV
22 point (g:\ttfcaps\s0001990.ttf)

ABCDEFGHIJKLMNOPQRSTUVWXY
22 point (g:\ttfcaps\s0001991.ttf)

ABCDEFGHIJKLMNOP
22 point (g:\ttfcaps\t0002059.ttf)

ABCDEFGHIJKLMNOPQRSTUVW
22 point (g:\ttfcaps\t0002056.ttf)

ABCDEFGHIJKLMNOPQRS
22 point (g:\ttfcaps\t0002063.ttf)

ABCDEFGHIJK
22 point (g:\ttfcaps\t0002082.ttf)

ABCDEFGHIJKLMNOPQ
22 point (g:\ttfcaps\u0002159.ttf)

ABCDEFGHIJ
22 point (g:\ttfcaps\v0002253.ttf)

ABCDEFGHIJKLM
22 point (g:\ttfcaps\z0002358.ttf)

24 point (f:\ttfding\a0000001.ttf)

24 point (f:\ttfding\c0000321.ttf)

%‰$)(±÷×8 90145726
24 point (f:\ttfding\a0000046.ttf)

24 point (f:\ttfding\c0000327.ttf)

↑ ↑ ↑ ↑ ↑ ↑ ↗ ↗ ↗ ↗ ↗ ↗
24 point (f:\ttfding\a0000129.ttf)

24 point (f:\ttfding\c0000420.ttf)

24 point (f:\ttfding\a0000135.ttf)

24 point (f:\ttfding\c0000449.ttf)

24 point (f:\ttfding\a0000136.ttf)

24 point (f:\ttfding\p0001655.ttf)

24 point (f:\ttfding\a0000137.ttf)

24 point (f:\ttfding\d0000513.ttf)

24 point (f:\ttfding\b0000155.ttf)

24 point (f:\ttfding\d0000517.ttf)

24 point (f:\ttfding\b0000259.ttf)

24 point (f:\ttfding\d0000518.ttf)

24 point (f:\ttfding\c0000309.ttf)

24 point (f:\ttfding\d0000551.ttf)

24 point (f:\ttfding\c0000310.ttf)

24 point (f:\ttfding\d0000557.ttf)

24 point (f:\ttfding\c0000312.ttf)

24 point (f:\ttfding\d0000558.ttf)

24 point (f:\ttfding\c0000313.ttf)

24 point (f:\ttfding\f0000770.ttf)

24 point (f:\ttfding\c0000314.ttf)

24 point (f:\ttfding\g0000877.ttf)

24 point (f:\ttfding\c0000315.ttf)

24 point (f:\ttfding\g0000938.ttf)

24 point (f:\ttfding\c0000316.ttf)

24 point (f:\ttfding\i0001076.ttf)

24 point (f:\ttfding\c0000317.ttf)

24 point (f:\ttfding\l0001159.ttf)

24 point (f:\ttfding\c0000318.ttf)

24 point (f:\ttfding\l0001259.ttf)

24 point (f:\ttfding\c0000319.ttf)

⟨⟩ ← — → ↑ ↓ ↔ ↗ ↘ ≃ ⇐ ⇒ ⇑
24 point (f:\ttfding\l0001261.ttf)

AABBCCDDEEFFGGHHIJJKKL
18 point (g:\ttfa_a\a0000005.ttf)

AaBbCcDdEeFfGgHhIiJjKkLl
18 point (g:\ttfa_a\a0000009.ttf)

AaBbCcDdEeFfGgHhIiJjKkLl
18 point (g:\ttfa_a\a0000010.ttf)

AaBbCcDdEeFfGgHhIi]jRkLlMmNnOoPpQq
18 point (g:\ttfa_a\a0000011.ttf)

AaBbCcDdEeFfGgHhIi]jRkLl
18 point (g:\ttfa_a\a0000012.ttf)

AaBbCcDdEeFfGgHhIi]jRkLlMmNn
18 point (g:\ttfa_a\a0000013.ttf)

AaBbCcDdEeFfGgHhIiJjKkLlMmNnO
(g:\ttfa_a\a0000014.ttf)

AaBbCcDdEeFfGgHhIiJjKkLlMm
18 point (g:\ttfa_a\a0000015.ttf)

AaBbCcDdEeFfGgHh
18 point (g:\ttfa_a\a0000016.ttf)

AaBbCcDdEeFfGgHhIiJjKkLlMmNnO
18 point (g:\ttfa_a\a0000017.ttf)

AaBbCcDdEeFfGgHhIiJjK
18 point (g:\ttfa_a\a0000018.ttf)

AaBbCcDdEeFfGgHhIiJjKkLlM
18 point (g:\ttfa_a\a0000019.ttf)

AaBbCcDdEeFfGgHhIiJjKkLlM
18 point (g:\ttfa_a\a0000020.ttf)

AaBbCcDdEeFfGgHhIiJjKkLlMm
18 point (g:\ttfa_a\a0000021.ttf)

AaBbCcDdEeFfGgHhIiJjKkLlMmNnOoP
18 point (g:\ttfa_a\a0000022.ttf)

AaBbCcDdEeFfGgHhIiJjKkLl
18 point (g:\ttfa_a\a0000025.ttf)

AaBbCcDdEeFfGgHhIiJjKkLl
18 point (g:\ttfa_a\a0000026.ttf)

AaBbCcDdEeFfGg
18 point (g:\ttfa_a\a0000027.ttf)

AaBbCcDdEeFfGgHhIiJjKkLlMmN
18 point (g:\ttfa_a\a0000028.ttf)

AaBbCcDdEeFfGgHhIiJ
18 point (g:\ttfa_a\a0000029.ttf)

AaBbCcDdEeFfGgHhIi
18 point (g:\ttfa_a\a0000030.ttf)

AABBCCDDEEFFGGHHIIJJK
(g:\ttfa_a\a0000031.ttf)

AaBbCcDdEeFfGgHhIiJjKkLlM
18 point (g:\ttfa_a\a0000035.ttf)

AaBbCcDdEeFfGgHhIiJjKkLlM
18 point (g:\ttfa_a\a0000033.ttf)

AaBbCcDdEeFfGgHhIiJjKkLl
18 point (g:\ttfa_a\a0000032.ttf)

AaBbCcDdEeFfGgHhIiJjKkLl
18 point (g:\ttfa_a\a0000034.ttf)

AaBbCcDdEeFfGgHhIiJjKkLlM
18 point (g:\ttfa_a\a0000036.ttf)

AaBbCcDdEeFfGgHhIiJjKkLlM
18 point (g:\ttfa_a\a0000037.ttf)

AaBbCcDdEeFfGgHhIiJjKkLl
18 point (g:\ttfa_a\a0000038.ttf)

AABBCCDDEEFFGGHHIIJJKKLL
(g:\ttfa_a\a0000039.ttf)

AaBbCcDdEeFfGgHhIiJjKkLlMmNnOoPpQ
18 point (g:\ttfa_a\a0000042.ttf)

AaBbCcDdEeFfGgHhIiJjKkLlMmNnOoPpQ
18 point (g:\ttfa_a\a0000041.ttf)

AaBbCcDdEeFfGgHhIiJjKkLlMmNnOoPpQ
18 point (g:\ttfa_a\a0000040.ttf)

AABBCCDDEEFFGGHHIIJJKKLLN
18 point (g:\ttfa_a\a0000043.ttf)

AaBbCcDdEeFfGgHhIiJjKkLlMm
18 point (g:\ttfa_a\a0000045.ttf)

RaBbCcDdEeFfGgHhIiJjKkLlMmNnOoP
18 point (g:\ttfa_a\a0000047.ttf)

AaBbCcDdEeFfGgHhIiJjKkL
18 point (g:\ttfa_a\a0000048.ttf)

AaBbCcDdEeFfGgHhIiJjKk
18 point (g:\ttfa_a\a0000050.ttf)

AaBbCcDdEeFfGgHhIiJjKk
18 point (g:\ttfa_a\a0000049.ttf)

AaBbCcDdEeFfGgHhIiJjKkLlMmNnO
18 point (g:\ttfa_a\a0000051.ttf)

AaBbCcDdEeFfGgH
18 point (g:\ttfa_a\a0000052.ttf)

AaBbCcDdEeFfGgHhIi
18 point (g:\ttfa_a\a0000053.ttf)

AaBbCcDdEeFfGgHhIiJjKKkL
18 point (g:\ttfa_a\a0000054.ttf)

AaBbCcDdEeFfGgHhIiJj
18 point (g:\ttfa_a\a0000089.ttf)

AaBbCcD dEeFfAgHhJiJj
(g:\ttfa_a\a0000056.ttf)

AaBbCcDdEeFfGgHhIiJjKkLlMm
18 point (g:\ttfa_a\a0000090.ttf)

AaBbCcDdEeFfGgHhIiJjKkLl
18 point (g:\ttfa_a\a0000058.ttf)

AaBbCcDdEeFfGgHhIiJjKkLlMmNn
18 point (g:\ttfa_a\a0000091.ttf)

IaBbCcDdEeFfGgHhIiJjKkLLMmNnOoPpQqRr
18 point (g:\ttfa_a\a0000059.ttf)

AaBbCcDdEeFfGgHhIiJjKkLlMmNnOoPpQqR
18 point (g:\ttfa_a\a0000092.ttf)

AaBbCcDdEeFfGgHhliJjKKkLlMmNnOoP
18 point (g:\ttfa_a\a0000060.ttf)

ՍստՈպդգ-ՏսեՇ ԽՏՎԿՀ Հհրհ ԼՀ ՌՊԼ ՍՍ
18 point (g:\ttfa_a\a0000093.ttf)

AaBbCcDdEeFfGgHhliJjKKkLlMmNnOoP
18 point (g:\ttfa_a\a0000061.ttf)

ՍՍՈՌ ՔՏՏԵԷ ԴԿԿ ԲՒՒ ԱԿ ԿԼԼՍ
18 point (g:\ttfa_a\a0000094.ttf)

ıaBBCcɔɔ0eeFFgghhiijjkkLL
18 point (g:\ttfa_a\a0000062.ttf)

ՍՍՈՌ ՔՏՏԵԷ ԴԿԿ ԲՒՒ ԱԿ ԿԼԼՍ
18 point (g:\ttfa_a\a0000095.ttf)

AaBbCcDdEeFfGgHhIiJjKkL
18 point (g:\ttfa_a\a0000063.ttf)

AaBbCcDdEeFfGgHhIiJjKkLlMmNnOoPpQqRrSsTtUuVvWwXxYyZz
'8 point (g:\ttfa_a\a0000096.ttf)

AaBbCcDdEeFfGgHhIiJjKKLl
18 point (g:\ttfa_a\a0000064.ttf)

AaBbCcDdEeFfGgHhliJjKkLlMmNnOoP
18 point (g:\ttfa_a\a0000097.ttf)

AaBbCcDdEeFfGgHhIiJjKkLlMm
18 point (g:\ttfa_a\a0000065.ttf)

AaBbCcDdErFfGgHhliJjKkLlMmNnOoP
18 point (g:\ttfa_a\a0000098.ttf)

ıaBBCcɔ0eeFf
18 point (g:\ttfa_a\a0000066.ttf)

AABBCcDDEEFFGGHHI
18 point (g:\ttfa_a\a0000100.ttf)

AaBbCcDdEeFfGgHhliJjKkLlMmNnOo
18 point (g:\ttfa_a\a0000067.ttf)

AABBCcDDEEFFGGHHI
18 point (g:\ttfa_a\a0000099.ttf)

AABBCcDDEEFFGGHHI
18 point (g:\ttfa_a\a0000102.ttf)

AaBbCcDdEeFfGgHhIiJjKkLlMmNnOoPpQqRrSsTtUuV
18 point (g:\ttfa_a\a0000103.ttf)

a3bCcDdEeFfGgHhIiJjKkLlMmNnOoPpQqRr
18 point (g:\ttfa_a\a0000076.ttf)

AaBbCcDdEeFfGgHhIiJjKkLlMm
18 point (g:\ttfa_a\a0000081.ttf)

AaBbCcDdEeFfGgHhIiJjKkLlMm
18 point (g:\ttfa_a\a0000104.ttf)

AaBbCcDdEeFfGgHhliJjKkLlMmN
18 point (g:\ttfa_a\a0000083.ttf)

AaBbCcDdEeFfGgHhIiJjKkLl
18 point (g:\ttfa_a\a0000105.ttf)

HABBCCDDEEFFGGHHIIJJKKLLMNNNOOP
18 point (g:\ttfa_a\a0000082.ttf)

AaBbCcDdEeFfGgHhliJjK
18 point (g:\ttfa_a\a0000106.ttf)

AaBbCcDdEeFfGgHhIiJjKkLlMmNn
18 point (g:\ttfa_a\a0000084.ttf)

AaBbCcDdEeFfGgHhliJjKkLlMmNnOoPpQq
18 point (g:\ttfa_a\a0000107.ttf)

AaBbCcDdEeFfGgHhIiJjKkLl
18 point (g:\ttfa_a\a0000087.ttf)

AaBbCcDdEeFfGgHhliJjKkLlMmNnOoP
18 point - (g:\ttfa_a\a0000108.ttf)

AaBbCcDdEeFfGgHhIiJjKkLlMmN
18 point (g:\ttfa_a\a0000088.ttf)

AaBbCcDdEeFfGgHhliJjKkLlMmNnOoP
18 point (g:\ttfa_a\a0000111.ttf)

AaBbCcDdEeFfGgHhliJjKkLlMmNnOo
18 point (g:\ttfa_a\a0000109.ttf)

AaBbCcDdEeFfGgHhIiJjKkLlMmNnOo
18 point (g:\ttfa_a\a0000110.ttf)

AaBbCcDdEeFfGgHhIiJjKkLlMmNnOoPpQq
18 point (g:\ttfa_a\a0000112.ttf)

AaBbCcDdEeFfGgHhIiJjKkLlMm
18 point (g:\ttfa_a\a0000113.ttf)

AaBbCcDdEeFfGgHhIiJjKk
18 point (g:\ttfa_a\a0000115.ttf)

AaBbCcDdEeFfGgHhIiJjKk
18 point (g:\ttfa_a\a0000116.ttf)

AABBCCDDEEFFGGHHIIJJKKLL
18 point (g:\ttfa_a\a0000118.ttf)

AABBCCDDEEFFGGHHIIJJKKLLMMNNOOP
18 point (g:\ttfa_a\a0000119.ttf)

AABBCCDDEEFFGGH
18 point (g:\ttfa_a\a0000120.ttf)

AABBCCDDEEFFGGHHIIJJKKLL
18 point (g:\ttfa_a\a0000121.ttf)

AABBCCDDEEFFGGH
18 point (g:\ttfa_a\a0000122.ttf)

AABBCCDDEEFFGGHHIIJJKKLLMMNN
18 point (g:\ttfa_a\a0000123.ttf)

AABBCCDDEEFFGGHHIIJ
18 point (g:\ttfa_a\a0000124.ttf)

AABBCCDDEEFFGGHHIIJJKKLLMMNN
18 point (g:\ttfa_a\a0000125.ttf)

AABBCCDDEEFFGGHHIIJ
18 point (g:\ttfa_a\a0000126.ttf)

AaBbCcDdEeFfGgHhIiJjKkLlM
18 point (g:\ttfa_a\a0000127.ttf)

AaBbCcDdEeFfGgHhIiJjKkLlMm
ArnoldBoecklin-ExtraBold, 18 point (g:\ttfa_a\a0000128.ttf)

AaBbCcDdEeFfGgHhIiJjKkLlMmNnOoPpQ
18 point (g:\ttfa_a\a0000130.ttf)

AaBbCcDdEeFfGgHhIiJjKkLlMmNnOoPpQ
18 point (g:\ttfa_a\a0000131.ttf)

AaBbCcDdEeFfGgHhIiJjKkLlMm
18 point (g:\ttfa_a\a0000132.ttf)

AaBbCcDdEeFfGgHhIiJjKkLlMmNnO
18 point (g:\ttfa_a\a0000133.ttf)

AaBbCcDdEeFfGgHhIiJjKkLlMmNnOoP
18 point (g:\ttfa_a\a0000134.ttf)

AaBbCcDdEeFfGgHhIiJjKkLlMmNnOoP
18 point (g:\ttfa_a\a0000139.ttf)

AaBbCcDdEeFfGgHhIiJjKkLlM
18 point (g:\ttfa_a\a0000142.ttf)

AaBbCcDdEeFfGgHhIiJjKkLlM
18 point (g:\ttfa_a\a0000141.ttf)

AaBbCcDdEeFfGgHhIiJjKkLlM
18 point (g:\ttfa_a\a0000140.ttf)

AaBbCcDdEeFfGgHhIiJjKkLl
18 point (g:\ttfa_a\a0000143.ttf)

AaBbCcDdEeFfGgHhIiJjKkLlMmNnO
18 point (g:\ttfa_a\a0000144.ttf)

AaBbCcDdEeFfGgHhIiJj
18 point (g:\ttfa_a\a0000145.ttf)

AaBbCcDdEeFfGgHhIiJjKkLlM
18 point (g:\ttfa_a\a0000146.ttf)

AaBbCcDdEeFfGgHhIiJjKkLlMmN
18 point (g:\ttfa_a\a0000147.ttf)

AaBbCcDdEeFfGgHhIiJj
18 point (g:\ttfa_a\a0000057.ttf)

Pa3bCcDdEeFfGgHhIiJjKkLlMmNnOoPpQqRr
18 point (g:\ttfa_a\a0000072.ttf)

Pa3bCcDdEeFfGgHhIiJjKkLlMmNnOoPpQqRr
18 point (g:\ttfa_a\a0000075.ttf)

Pa3bCcDdEeFfGgHhIiJjKkLlMmNnOoPpQqRrSsTtUuVvWwX
18 point (g:\ttfa_a\a0000073.ttf)

Pa3bCcDdEeFfGgHhIiJjKkLlM
18 point (g:\ttfa_a\a0000074.ttf)

AaBbCcDdEeFfGgHhI
24 point   (g:\ttfb_b\b0000148.ttf)

AaBbCcDdEeFfGgH
24 point   (g:\ttfb_b\b0000149.ttf)

AaBbCcDdEeFfGgHh
24 point   (g:\ttfb_b\b0000150.ttf)

AABBCCDDEEFFGGHHIIJ
24 point   (g:\ttfb_b\b0000151.ttf)

AaBbCcDdEeFfGgHh
24 point   (g:\ttfb_b\b0000152.ttf)

AaBbCcDdEeFfGgHhIiJiKkLlM
24 point   (g:\ttfb_b\b0000153.ttf)

AaBbCcDdEeFfGg Hh IiJj
24 point   (g:\ttfb_b\b0000154.ttf)

AABBCCDDEEFFGGHHI
24 point   (g:\ttfb_b\b0000156.ttf)

AaBbCcDdEeFfGgHhIiJj
24 point   (g:\ttfb_b\b0000157.ttf)

AabbccddEeFfJubggjKkLlM
24 point   (g:\ttfb_b\b0000158.ttf)

AaBbCcDdEeffGgHhIiJjKkLl
24 point   (g:\ttfb_b\b0000162.ttf)

AaBbCcDdEeffGgHhIiJjKkLl
24 point   (g:\ttfb_b\b0000160.ttf)

AaBbCcDdEeffGgHhIiJjK
24 point   (g:\ttfb_b\b0000159.ttf)

AaBbCcDdEeffGgHhIiJjK
24 point   (g:\ttfb_b\b0000161.ttf)

AaBbCcDdEeffGgHhIiJjKk
24 point   (g:\ttfb_b\b0000163.ttf)

AABBCCDDEEFFGGHHIIJJK
24 point   (g:\ttfb_b\b0000164.ttf)

AaBbCcDdEeFfGs
24 point   (g:\ttfb_b\b0000165.ttf)

AaBbCcDdEeFfGgHhIi
24 point   (g:\ttfb_b\b0000166.ttf)

AaBbCcDdEeFfGgHhIiJ
24 point   (g:\ttfb_b\b0000167.ttf)

AaBbCcDdEeFfGgHhIiJj
24 point   (g:\ttfb_b\b0000168.ttf)

AABBCCDDEEFFGGHHIIJJ
24 point   (g:\ttfb_b\b0000169.ttf)

AABBCCDDEEFFGG
24 point   (g:\ttfb_b\b0000170.ttf)

AABBCCDDEEF
24 point   (g:\ttfb_b\b0000171.ttf)

AABBCCDDEEFFG
24 point   (g:\ttfb_b\b0000173.ttf)

AaBbCcDdEeFfGgHhIiJiKkL
24 point   (g:\ttfb_b\b0000177.ttf)

AaBbCcDdEeFfGgHhIi
24 point   (g:\ttfb_b\b0000179.ttf)

AaBbCcDdEeFfGgHhIiJ
24 point   (g:\ttfb_b\b0000181.ttf)

AaBbCcDdEeFfGgHhIi
24 point   (g:\ttfb_b\b0000182.ttf)

AaBbCcDdEeFfGgHhIiJjKk
24 point   (g:\ttfb_b\b0000187.ttf)

AaBbCcDdEeFfGgHhIiJjKk
24 point   (g:\ttfb_b\b0000185.ttf)

AaBbCcDdEeFfGgHhIiJj
24 point   (g:\ttfb_b\b0000188.ttf)

AaBbCcDdEeFfGgHhIiJj
24 point   (g:\ttfb_b\b0000186.ttf)

AaBbCcDdEeFfGgHhIiJj
24 point   (g:\ttfb_b\b0000189.ttf)

AaBbCcDdEeFfGgHhIiJjKkLl
24 point   (g:\ttfb_b\b0000190.ttf)

AaBbCcDdEeFfGgHhIiJjK
24 point   (g:\ttfb_b\b0000193.ttf)

AaBbCcDdEeFfGgHhIiJ
24 point   (g:\ttfb_b\b0000194.ttf)

AaBbCcDdEeFfGgHhIiJjK
24 point (g:\ttfb_b\b0000195.ttf)

AABBCCDDEEFFGGHHII
24 point (g:\ttfb_b\b0000196.ttf)

AaBbCcDdEeFfGgHhIiJjK
24 point (g:\ttfb_b\b0000198.ttf)

AaBbCcDdEeFfGgHhIiJj
24 point (g:\ttfb_b\b0000202.ttf)

AaBbCcDdEeFfGgHhIiJjKkLLMmNnO
24 point (g:\ttfb_b\b0000204.ttf)

AaBbCcDdEeFfGgHhIi
24 point (g:\ttfb_b\b0000205.ttf)

AaBbCcDdEeFfGgHhIiJj
24 point (g:\ttfb_b\b0000206.ttf)

AaBbCcDdEeFfGgHhIiJjK
24 point (g:\ttfb_b\b0000211.ttf)

AaBbCcDdEeFfGgHhIiJjKkLlM
24 point (g:\ttfb_b\b0000212.ttf)

AaBbCcDdEeFfGgHhIiJjKkLlM
24 point (g:\ttfb_b\b0000213.ttf)

AaBbCcDdEeFfGgHhI
24 point (g:\ttfb_b\b0000214.ttf)

AaBbCcDdEeFfGgHhI
24 point (g:\ttfb_b\b0000215.ttf)

AaBbCcDdEeFfGgHhIiJjK
24 point (g:\ttfb_b\b0000216.ttf)

AaBbCcDdEeFfGgHhIiJjKkLl
24 point (g:\ttfb_b\b0000217.ttf)

AaBbCcDdEeFfGgHhIi
24 point (g:\ttfb_b\b0000218.ttf)

aabbccddeeffgghhiijj
24 point (g:\ttfb_b\b0000219.ttf)

AaBbCcDdEeFfGgHhIiJi
24 point (g:\ttfb_b\b0000220.ttf)

AaBbCcDdEeFfGgHhIiJjK
24 point (g:\ttfb_b\b0000221.ttf)

AaBbCcDdEeFfGgHhIiJjKkLlMmNnOoPp
24 point (g:\ttfb_b\b0000222.ttf)

AaBbCcDdEeFfGgHhIiJjKkLlMmNnOoPp
24 point (g:\ttfb_b\b0000223.ttf)

AaBbCcDdEeFfGgHh
24 point (g:\ttfb_b\b0000224.ttf)

AaBbCcDdEeFfGgHhIiJjK
24 point (g:\ttfb_b\b0000230.ttf)

AaBbCcDdEeFfGgHhIiJjK
24 point (g:\ttfb_b\b0000228.ttf)

AaBbCcDdEeFfGgHhIiJj
24 point (g:\ttfb_b\b0000229.ttf)

AaBbCcDdEeFfGgHhIiJj
24 point (g:\ttfb_b\b0000226.ttf)

AaBbCcDdEeFfGgHhIiJj
24 point (g:\ttfb_b\b0000231.ttf)

AaBbCcDdEeFfGgHhIiJj
24 point (g:\ttfb_b\b0000232.ttf)

AaBbCcDdEeFfGgH
24 point (g:\ttfb_b\b0000233.ttf)

AaBbCcDdEeFfGgHhIiJjKkL
24 point (g:\ttfb_b\b0000234.ttf)

AaBbCcDdEeFfGgHhIiJj
24 point (g:\ttfb_b\b0000235.ttf)

AaBbCcDdEeFfGgHhIiJj
24 point (g:\ttfb_b\b0000236.ttf)

AaBbCcDdEeFfGgHhIiJjKk
24 point (g:\ttfb_b\b0000237.ttf)

AaBbCcDdEeFfGgHhI
24 point (g:\ttfb_b\b0000238.ttf)

24 point (g:\ttfb_b\b0000239.ttf)

AaBbCcDdEeFfGgHhIiJj
24 point (g:\ttfb_b\b0000240.ttf)

AaBbCcDdEeFfGgHhIiJjK
24 point (g:\ttfb_b\b0000243.ttf)

AaBbCcDdEeFfGgHhIiJ
24 point (g:\ttfb_b\b0000241.ttf)

AaBbCcDdEeFfGgHhIiJj
24 point (g:\ttfb_b\b0000242.ttf)

AaBbCcDdEeFfGgHhIiJjKKL
(g:\ttfb_b\b0000244.ttf)

AaBbCcDdEeFfGgHhIi
24 point (g:\ttfb_b\b0000248.ttf)

AaBbCcDdEeFfGgHhIi
24 point (g:\ttfb_b\b0000246.ttf)

AaBbCcDdEeFfGgHhI
24 point (g:\ttfb_b\b0000245.ttf)

AaBbCcDdEeFfGgHhI
24 point (g:\ttfb_b\b0000247.ttf)

AaBbCcDdEeFfGgHhIi
24 point (g:\ttfb_b\b0000249.ttf)

AaBbCcDdEeFfGgHhI
24 point (g:\ttfb_b\b0000250.ttf)

AaBbCcDdEeFfGgHhIi
24 point (g:\ttfb_b\b0000251.ttf)

AaBbCcDdEeFfGgHhIi
24 point (g:\ttfb b\b0000252.ttf)

aBbCcDdEeFfGgHhIiJjK
24 point (g:\ttfb_b\b0000254.ttf)

aBbCcDdEeFfGgHhIiJjK
24 point (g:\ttfb_b\b0000253.ttf)

aBbCcDdEeFfGgHhIiJjK
24 point (g:\ttfb_b\b0000256.ttf)

AaBbCcDdEeFfGgHhIiJjK
24 point (g:\ttfb b\b0000257.ttf)

AaBbCcDdEeFfGgHhIiJj
24 point (g:\ttfb_b\b0000258.ttf)

AaBbCcDdEeFfGgHhIiJj
24 point (g:\ttfb b\b0000260.ttf)

AaBbCcDdEeFfGgHh
24 point (g:\ttfb b\b0000261.ttf)

AaBbCcDdEeFfGgHhIiJj
24 point (g:\ttfb_b\b0000262.ttf)

AaBbCcDdEeFfGg
24 point (g:\ttfb_b\b0000263.ttf)

AaBbCcDdEeFfGg
(g:\ttfb_b\b0000264.ttf)

AaBbCcDdEeFfGgHhIiJjKkLlMmNn
24 point (g:\ttfb_b\b0000265.ttf)

AaBbCcDdEeffGgHhIiJjKkLl
24 point (g:\ttfb_b\b0000269.ttf)

AaBbCcDdEeFfGgHhIiJjKkLl
24 point (g:\ttfb_b\b0000267.ttf)

AaBbCcDdEeffGgHhIiJjK
24 point (g:\ttfb_b\b0000266.ttf)

AaBbCcDdEeffGgHhIiJjK
24 point (g:\ttfb_b\b0000268.ttf)

AaBbCcDdEeffGgHhIiJjKk
24 point (g:\ttfb_b\b0000271.ttf)

AaBbCcDdEeFfGgHhIiJjKkLlM
24 point (g:\ttfb_b\b0000272.ttf)

AaBbCcDdEeFf
24 point (g:\ttfb_b\b0000273.ttf)

AaBbCcDdEeFfGgHhIiJj
24 point (g:\ttfb_b\b0000275.ttf)

AABBCCDDEEFFGG
24 point (g:\ttfb_b\b0000276.ttf)

AaBbCcDdEeFfGgHhIi
24 point (g:\ttfb_b\b0000277.ttf)

AaBbCcDdEeFfGgHhIi
24 point (g:\ttfb_b\b0000278.ttf)

AaBbCcDdEeFfGgHhI
24 point (g:\ttfb_b\b0000279.ttf)

AaBbCcDdEeFfGgHhIiJjKkLlM
18 point (g:\ttfc_c\c0000283.ttf)

AaBbCcDdEeFfGgHhIiJjKkLlMm
18 point (g:\ttfc_c\c0000284.ttf)

AaBbCcDdEeFfGgHhIiJjKkLlMm
18 point (g:\ttfc_c\c0000285.ttf)

AaBbCcDdEeFfGgHhIiJjKkLlMm
18 point (g:\ttfc_c\c0000286.ttf)

AaBbCcDdEeFfGgHhIiJjKkLl
18 point (g:\ttfc_c\c0000287.ttf)

AaBbCcDdEeFfGgHhIiJjKkLlM
18 point (g:\ttfc_c\c0000288.ttf)

AaBbCcDdEeFfGgHhIiJjKkLl
18 point (g:\ttfc_c\c0000289.ttf)

AABBCCDDEEFFGGHH
18 point (g:\ttfc_c\c0000290.ttf)

AaBbCcDdEeFfGgHhIiJjKkLlMmNnOoPpQqRr
18 point (g:\ttfc_c\c0000291.ttf)

AaBbCcDdEeFfGgHhIiJjKkLlMmNnO
18 point (g:\ttfc_c\c0000292.ttf)

AaBbCcDdEeFfGgHhIiJjKkLlMmNn
18 point (g:\ttfc_c\c0000293.ttf)

AaBbCcDdEeFfGgHhIiJjKk
18 point (g:\ttfc_c\c0000298.ttf)

AaBbCcDdEeFfGgHhIiJjKkLlMmN
18 point (g:\ttfc_c\c0000299.ttf)

AaBbCcDdEeFfGgHhIiJjKkLlN
18 point (g:\ttfc_c\c0000301.ttf)

AaBbCcDdEeFfGgHh
18 point (g:\ttfc_c\c0000302.ttf)

AaBbCcDdEeFfGgHhIiJjKkLl
18 point (g:\ttfc_c\c0000303.ttf)

AaBbCcDdEeFfGgHhIiJjKkLlMmNnOoPpQ
18 point (g:\ttfc_c\c0000304.ttf)

AaBbCcDdEeFfGgHhIiJjKkLlMmN
18 point (g:\ttfc_c\c0000305.ttf)

AaBbCcDdEeFfGgHhIi
18 point (g:\ttfc_c\c0000306.ttf)

AaBbCcDdEeFfGgHhIiJjKk
18 point (g:\ttfc_c\c0000307.ttf)

AaBbCcDdEeFfGgHhIiJjKkLl
18 point (g:\ttfc_c\c0000325.ttf)

ALT A SHIFT B CTRL C P D ENTER E CTRL F
18 point (g:\ttfc_c\c0000326.ttf)

AABBCCDDEEFFGGHHIIJJK
18 point (g:\ttfc_c\c0000332.ttf)

AABBCCDDEEFFGGHHIIJJKKLLMMNNO
18 point (g:\ttfc_c\c0000333.ttf)

AaBbCcDdEeFfGgHhIiJjKkLlMmNnOoPp
18 point (g:\ttfc_c\c0000334.ttf)

AaBbCcDdEeFfGgHhIiJjKkLlMmNnOoPpQqRrSsTtUuVvWwX
18 point (g:\ttfc_c\c0000335.ttf)

AaBbCcDdEeFfGgHhIiJjKkLlMmNnOoPp
18 point (g:\ttfc_c\c0000337.ttf)

AaBbCcDdEeFfGgHhIiJjKk
18 point (g:\ttfc_c\c0000339.ttf)

AaBbCcDdEeFfGgHhIiJjKkLlM
18 point (g:\ttfc_c\c0000343.ttf)

AaBbCcDdEeFfGgHhIiJjKkLlMmNn
18 point (g:\ttfc_c\c0000344.ttf)

AaBbCcDdEeFfGgHhIiJjKkLlMmNn
18 point (g:\ttfc_c\c0000345.ttf)

AaBbCcDdEeFfGgHhIiJjKkLlMmNn
18 point (g:\ttfc_c\c0000346.ttf)

AaBbCcDdEeFfGgHhIiJjKkLl
18 point (g:\ttfc_c\c0000340.ttf)

AaBbCcDdEeFfGgHhIiJjKkLl
18 point (g:\ttfc_c\c0000342.ttf)

AaBbCcDdEeFfGgHhIiJjKkLlMmNn
18 point (g:\ttfc_c\c0000348.ttf)

AaBbCcDdEeFfGgHhIiJjKkLlMmNn
18 point (g:\ttfc_c\c0000349.ttf)

AaBbCcDdEeFfGgHhIiJjKkLlMm
18 point (g:\ttfc_c\c0000350.ttf)

AaBbCcDdEeFfGgHhIiJjKkLlMmN
18 point (g:\ttfc_c\c0000351.ttf)

AaBbCcDdEeFfGgHhIiJjKkLlM
18 point (g:\ttfc_c\c0000355.ttf)

AaBbCcDdEeFfGgHhIiJjKkLlM
18 point (g:\ttfc_c\c0000353.ttf)

AaBbCcDdEeFfGgHhIiJjKkLl
18 point (g:\ttfc_c\c0000352.ttf)

AaBbCcDdEeFfGgHhIiJjKkLl
18 point (g:\ttfc_c\c0000354.ttf)

aBbCcDdEeFfGgHhIiJjKkLlMmNnOoPpQqRrSsTtUuVvWwXxY
18 point   (g:\ttfc_c\c0000356.ttf)

aBBCCDDEeFfGgHhJJJJRRLLm
18 point   (g:\ttfc_c\c0000357.ttf)

ABBCCDDEEFFGGHHIIJJKKLLMMN
18 point   (g:\ttfc_c\c0000359.ttf)

AaBbCcDdEeFfGgHhIiJjK
18 point   (g:\ttfc_c\c0000360.ttf)

AaBbCcDdEeFfGgHh
18 point   (g:\ttfc_c\c0000361.ttf)

AaBbCcDdEeFfGgHhIiJjKkL
18 point   (g:\ttfc_c\c0000363.ttf)

AaBbCcDdEeFfGgHhIiJjKkLl
18 point   (g:\ttfc_c\c0000362.ttf)

AaBbCcDdEeFfGgHhIiJjKkLlMm
18 point   (g:\ttfc_c\c0000365.ttf)

AaBbCcDdEeFfGgHhIiJjKkLlMmN
18 point   (g:\ttfc_c\c0000366.ttf)

AaBbCcDdEeFfGgHhIiJjKkLlMmN
18 point   (g:\ttfc_c\c0000368.ttf)

AaBbCcDdEeFfGgHhIiJjKkLlM
18 point   (g:\ttfc_c\c0000369.ttf)

AaBbCcDdEeFfGgHhIiJjKkLlMmNnO
18 point   (g:\ttfc_c\c0000371.ttf)

ABBCCDDEEFFGGHHIIJJK
18 point   (g:\ttfc_c\c0000372.ttf)

ABBCCDDEEFFGGHHIIJJ
18 point   (g:\ttfc_c\c0000373.ttf)

AaBbCcDdEeFfGgHhIiJjKkLlMmNn
18 point   (g:\ttfc_c\c0000374.ttf)

AaBbCcDdEeFfGgHhIiJjKkLlMm
18 point   (g:\ttfc_c\c0000375.ttf)

AaBbCcDdEeFfGgHhIiJjKkLlM
18 point   (g:\ttfc_c\c0000377.ttf)

AaBbCcDdEeFfGgHhIiJjKkLl
18 point   (g:\ttfc_c\c0000379.ttf)

BbCcDdEeFfGgHhIiJjKkLlMmNnOoPpQqRrSsTtUuUuWwXxYyZz
18 point   (g:\ttfc_c\c0000384.ttf)

AaBbCcDdEeFfGgHhIiJjKkClM
18 point   (g:\ttfc_c\c0000385.ttf)

AaBbCcDdEeFfGgHhIiJjKkLlM
18 point   (g:\ttfc_c\c0000386.ttf)

AaBbCcDdEeFfGgHhIiJjKkLlM
18 point   (g:\ttfc_c\c0000387.ttf)

AaBbCcDdEeFfGgHhIiJjKkLlMmNn
18 point   (g:\ttfc_c\c0000388.ttf)

AaBbCcDdEeFfGgHhIiJjKkLlMmN
18 point   (g:\ttfc_c\c0000392.ttf)

AaBbCcDdEeFfGgHhIiJjKkLlM
18 point   (g:\ttfc_c\c0000389.ttf)

AaBbCcDdEeFfGgHhIiJjKkLlM
18 point   (g:\ttfc_c\c0000391.ttf)

AaBbCcDdEeFfGgHhIiJjKkLlMmNnO
18 point   (g:\ttfc_c\c0000393.ttf)

AaBbCcDdEeFfGgHhIiJjKkLlMmNnOoP
18 point   (g:\ttfc_c\c0000395.ttf)

AaBbCcDdEeFfGgHhIiJjKkLlMmNnO
18 point   (g:\ttfc_c\c0000396.ttf)

AaBbCcDdEeFfGgHhIiJjKkLlMmNnOoP
18 point   (g:\ttfc_c\c0000397.ttf)

iDGⱭⱭꞴB ⱴ✝Ⱦ ꓭ WOⱯⱸ ⊖
18 point   (g:\ttfc_c\c0000398.ttf)

AaBbCcDdEeFfGgHhIiJjKkLl
18 point   (g:\ttfc_c\c0000399.ttf)

AaBbCcDdEeFfGgHhIiJjKkLlMmNnOoPpQqRrSsTtUuVvWwX
18 point   (g:\ttfc_c\c0000400.ttf)

AaBbCcDdEeFfGgHhIiJjKkLlMmN
18 point   (g:\ttfc_c\c0000402.ttf)

AaBbCcDdEeFfGgHhIiJjKkLlMmNnOoPpQq
18 point   (g:\ttfc_c\c0000403.ttf)

AaBbCcDdEeFfGgHhIiJjKkLl
18 point   (g:\ttfc_c\c0000404.ttf)

AaBbCcDdEeFfGgHhIiJjKkLl
18 point   (g:\ttfc_c\c0000405.ttf)

AaBbCcDdEeFfGgHhIiJjKkLlMmNnOoPpQq
18 point   (g:\ttfc_c\c0000406.ttf)

AaBbCcDdEeFfGgHhIiJjKkLlMmN
18 point   (g:\ttfc_c\c0000407.ttf)

AaBbCcDdEeFfGgHhIiJjKkLlM
18 point   (g:\ttfc_c\c0000408.ttf)

AaBbCcDdEeFfGgHhIiJjKkLlM
18 point   (g:\ttfc_c\c0000410.ttf)

AaBbCcDdEeFfGgHhIiJjK
18 point   (g:\ttfc_c\c0000409.ttf)

AaBbCcDdEeFfGgHhIiJjKkLlM
18 point (g:\ttfc_c\c0000411.ttf)

AaBbCcDdEeFfGgHhIiJjKkLlMmNnOoPp
18 point (g:\ttfc_c\c0000414.ttf)

AaBbCcDdEeFfGgHhIiJjKkLlMmNnO
18 point (g:\ttfc_c\c0000415.ttf)

AaBBCcDdEeFFGgHHIiJJK
18 point (g:\ttfc_c\c0000416.ttf)

AaBbCcDdEeFfGgHhIiJjKkLlMmNnOoPpQqRrSsTt
Cindybob Normal, 18 point (g:\ttfc_c\c0000417.ttf)

AaBbCcDdEeFfGgHhIiJjKkUMmn
18 point (g:\ttfc_c\c0000418.ttf)

AaBbCcDdEeFfGgHhIiJjKkLlMmNnOo
18 point (g:\ttfc_c\c0000421.ttf)

AaBbCcDdEeFfGgHhIiJjKkLlMmNnOoPpQqRr
18 point (g:\ttfc_c\c0000422.ttf)

AaBbCcDdEeFfGgHhIiJjKkLlMmNnOoPpQq
18 point (g:\ttfc_c\c0000423.ttf)

AaBbCcDdEeFfGgHhIiJjKkLlMmNnO
18 point (g:\ttfc_c\c0000424.ttf)

AaBbCcDdEeFfGgHhIiJjKkLlMmNnOoPp
18 point (g:\ttfc_c\c0000425.ttf)

AaBbCcDdEeFfGgHhIiJjKkLlMmNn
18 point (g:\ttfc_c\c0000426.ttf)

AaBbCcDdEeFfGgHhIiJjKk
18 point (g:\ttfc_c\c0000427.ttf)

AaBbCcDdEeFfGgHhIiJjKkLl
18 point (g:\ttfc_c\c0000428.ttf)

A a B b C c D d E e F f G g H h I i J j
18 point (g:\ttfc_c\c0000430.ttf)

A a B b C c D
18 point (g:\ttfc_c\c0000431.ttf)

A a B b C c D d E e F f G g H h I i J j
18 point (g:\ttfc_c\c0000432.ttf)

AaBbCcDdEeFfGgHhIiJjKkLlMm
18 point (g:\ttfc_c\c0000436.ttf)

AaBbCcDdEeFfGgHhIiJjKkLlMmNn
18 point (g:\ttfc_c\c0000437.ttf)

AaBbCcDdEeFfGgHhIiJjKkLlMmN
18 point (g:\ttfc_c\c0000439.ttf)

AaBbCcDdEeFfGgHhIiJjKkLlMmNn
18 point (g:\ttfc_c\c0000441.ttf)

AaBbCcDdEeFfGgHhIiJj
18 point (g:\ttfc_c\c0000444.ttf)

AaBbCcDdEeFfGgHhIiJjKkL
Collegiate-Norm, 18 point (g:\ttfc_c\c0000446.ttf)

AABBCCDDEEFFGGHHIIJJK
18 point (g:\ttfc_c\c0000448.ttf)

AaBbCcDdEeFfGgHhIiJjKkLlMm
18 point (g:\ttfc_c\c0000450.ttf)

AaBbCcDdEeFfGgHhIiJjKkl
18 point (g:\ttfc_c\c0000453.ttf)

AaBbCcDdEeFfGgHhIiJjKkLl
18 point (g:\ttfc_c\c0000454.ttf)

AaBbCcDdEeFfGgHhIiJjK
18 point (g:\ttfc_c\c0000456.ttf)

AaBbCcDdEeFfGgHhIiJjKkLlMm
18 point (g:\ttfc_c\c0000457.ttf)

AaBbCcDdEeFfGgHhIiJjKkLlMm
18 point (g:\ttfc_c\c0000459.ttf)

AaBbCcDdEeFfGgHhIiJjK
18 point (g:\ttfc_c\c0000461.ttf)

□a□Bǯξʌ□єчφбгϩнïï
16 point (g:\ttfc_c\c0000463.ttf)

AaBbCcDdEeFfGgHhIiJjKkLlMmNnOoPp
18 point (g:\ttfc_c\c0000464.ttf)

AaBbCcDdEeFfGgHhIiJjK
18 point (g:\ttfc_c\c0000465.ttf)

AaBbCcDdEeFfGgHhIiJjK
18 point (g:\ttfc_c\c0000467.ttf)

AaBbCcDdEeFfGgHhIiJjKkLlMmNnOoPp
18 point (g:\ttfc_c\c0000468.ttf)

AaBbCcDdEeFfGgHhIiJjKkLlMmNnOoPp
18 point (g:\ttfc_c\c0000468.ttf)

AABBCCDDEEFFGGHHIIJJKKLL
18 point (g:\ttfc_c\c0000469.ttf)

AaBbCcDdEeFfGgHhIiJjKkLl
18 point (g:\ttfc_c\c0000470.ttf)

AaBbCcDdEeFfGgHhIiJjKkLl
18 point (g:\ttfc_c\c0000471.ttf)

AaBbCcDdEeFfGgHhIiJjKkLl
18 point (g:\ttfc_c\c0000472.ttf)

AaBbCcDdEeFfGgHhIiJjKkLl
18 point (g:\ttfc_c\c0000473.ttf)

BbCcDdEeFfGgHhIiJjKkLl
18 point (g:\ttfc_c\c0000474.ttf)

BbCcDdEeFfGgHhIiJjKkLl
18 point (g:\ttfc_c\c0000475.ttf)

(illegible decorative script)
18 point (g:\ttfc_c\c0000476.ttf)

bCcDdEeF fGgHhIiJjKkLlMmNnOoPpQqRrSsT
18 point (g:\ttfc_c\c0000478.ttf)

BbCcDdEeFfGgHhIiJjKkLlM
18 point (g:\ttfc_c\c0000480.ttf)

BbCcDdEeFjG gHhIiJjKkLlM mNnO
18 point (g:\ttfc_c\c0000481.ttf)

BbCcDdEeFjG gHhIiJjKkLlM mN
8 point (g:\ttfc_c\c0000482.ttf)

aBbCcDdEeFjG gHhIiJj
18 point (g:\ttfc_c\c0000484.ttf)

BbCcDdEeFjG gHhIiJjKkLlMmNnO
18 point (g:\ttfc_c\c0000485.ttf)

BbCcDdEeFjGgHhIiJjKkLlMmNnO
18 point (g:\ttfc_c\c0000486.ttf)

bCcDdEeFfGgHhIiJjKkLlMmNnOoPpQqRrSsTtUu
18 point (g:\ttfc_c\c0000488.ttf)

BbCcDdEeFfGgHhIiJjKkLlMmNnOoPpQq
18 point (g:\ttfc_c\c0000489.ttf)

BbCcDdEeFfGgHhIiJjKkLlMmNnOoPp
18 point (g:\ttfc_c\c0000490.ttf)

BBCCDDEEFFGGHHIIJJKKLL
18 point (g:\ttfc_c\c0000491.ttf)

BbCcDdEeFfGgHhIiJjKkLlMmNnOoP
18 point (g:\ttfc_c\c0000492.ttf)

BbCcDdEeFfGgHhIiJjKkLlMmNn
18 point (g:\ttfc_c\c0000493.ttf)

BBCCDDEEFFGGHHIIJJKK
18 point (g:\ttfc_c\c0000494.ttf)

BBCCDDEEFFGGHHIIJJKKLL
18 point (g:\ttfc_c\c0000495.ttf)

BACCDdEeFfGgHhIiJjKkLlMmNnOoPpQq
18 point (g:\ttfc_c\c0000496.ttf)

BACCDdEeFfGgHhIiJjKkLlMmNnOoPpQq
18 point (g:\ttfc_c\c0000498.ttf)

BACCDdEeFfGgHhIiJjKkLlMmNnOoPp
18 point (g:\ttfc_c\c0000499.ttf)

AaBbCcDdEeFfGgHhIiJjKkLl
18 point (g:\ttfc_c\c0000500.ttf)

AaBbCcDdEeFfGgHhIiJjKkLl
18 point (g:\ttfc_c\c0000501.ttf)

AaBbCcDdEeFfGgHhIiJjKkLlMmNnOoPpQqR
18 point (g:\ttfc_c\c0000502.ttf)

AaBbCcDdEeFfGgHhIiJjKkLlMmNn
18 point (g:\ttfc_c\c0000504.ttf)

AaBbCcDdEeFfGgHhIi
18 point (g:\ttfc_c\c0000505.ttf)

AaBbCcDdEeFfGgHhIiJjKkLl
18 point (g:\ttfc_c\c0000506.ttf)

AaBbCcDdEeFfGgHhIiJj
18 point (g:\ttfc_c\c0000507.ttf)

АаБбЦцДдЕеОфГгХхИиЖжКкЛлМм
18 point (g:\ttfc_c\c0000508.ttf)

АаБбЦцДдЕеОфГгХхИиЖжКкЛл
18 point (g:\ttfc_c\c0000509.ttf)

ФфИиСсВвУуАаПпРрШшОоЛлД
18 point (g:\ttfc_c\c0000510.ttf)

ФфИиСсВвУуАаПпРрШшО
18 point (g:\ttfc_c\c0000511.ttf)

ФфИиСсВвУуАаПпРрШшОоЛлДдЬ
18 point (g:\ttfc_c\c0000512.ttf)

AaBbCcDdEeFfGgHhIiJjKkLlMmNn
18 point (g:\ttfc_c\c0000294.ttf)

AaBbCcDdEeFfGgHhIiJjKkLlMmNnOoPpQ
18 point (g:\ttfc_c\c0000296.ttf)

AaBbCcDdEeFfGgHhIiJjKkLl
18 point (g:\ttfc_c\c0000297.ttf)

AABBCCDDEEFFGGHHIIJJKKLLMMNN
18 point (g:\ttfc_c\c0000358.ttf)

AaBbCcDdEeFfGgHhIiJjKkLlMmNnOoPpQqRrSsTtUuVvWwXxYyZz
18 point (g:\ttfc_c\c0000380.ttf)

AaBbCcDdEeFfGgHhIiJjKkLlMmNnOoPpQqRrSsTtUuVvWwXxYyZz
18 point (g:\ttfc_c\c0000383.ttf)

AaBbCcDdEeFfGgHhIiJjKkLlMmNnOoPpQqRrSsTt
18 point (g:\ttfc_c\c0000382.ttf)

A a B b C c D d E e F f G g H h I i J j
18 point (g:\ttfc_c\c0000434.ttf)

A a B b C c D d E e F f G g H h I i J j
18 point (g:\ttfc_c\c0000435.ttf)

24 point (g:\ttfd_d\d0000515.ttf)

AaBbCcDdEeFfGgHhliJjKkLlM
24 point (g:\ttfd_d\d0000546.ttf)

24 point (g:\ttfd_d\d0000519.ttf)

AaBbCcDdEeFfGgf
24 point (g:\ttfd_d\d0000547.ttf)

AaBbCcDdEeFfGgHhIiJjKkLlMmN
24 point (g:\ttfd_d\d0000526.ttf)

AaBbCcDdEeFfGgHhliJj
24 point (g:\ttfd_d\d0000548.ttf)

AaBbCcDdEeFfGgHhIiJjK
24 point (g:\ttfd_d\d0000527.ttf)

AaBbCcDdEeFfGgHhliJjKkLl
24 point (g:\ttfd_d\d0000549.ttf)

AaBbCcDdEeFfGgHhIiJjKkLlMmNnOoP
24 point (g:\ttfd_d\d0000528.ttf)

AaBbCcDdEeffGgH
24 point (g:\ttfd_d\d0000556.ttf)

aaBBCCDDeeFFGGHHi
24 point (g:\ttfd_d\d0000528.ttf)

AaBbCcDdEeFfGgHhliJ
24 point (g:\ttfd_d\d0000559.ttf)

aaBBCCDDeeF
24 point (g:\ttfd_d\d0000529.ttf)

AaBbCcDdEeFfGgHhli
24 point (g:\ttfd_d\d0000562.ttf)

aaBBCCDDeeFFG
24 point (g:\ttfd_d\d0000530.ttf)

AaBbCcDdEeFfGgHhliJjKkLlM
24 point (g:\ttfd_d\d0000560.ttf)

AaBbCcDdEeFfGgHhliJ
24 point (g:\ttfd_d\d0000531.ttf)

AaBbCcDdEeFf
24 point (g:\ttfd_d\d0000561.ttf)

AaBbCcDdEeFfGgHh
24 point (g:\ttfd_d\d0000532.ttf)

AaBbCcDdEeFfGg
24 point (g:\ttfd_d\d0000563.ttf)

AaBbCcDdEeFfGgHhIiJjKkLlMmNnOoPpQqRrSsTtUuVvWwXxYyZz
24 point (g:\ttfd_d\d0000533.ttf)

AaBbCcDdEeFfGgBhdi Jj
24 point (g:\ttfd_d\d0000565.ttf)

AABBCCDDEEFFGG
24 point (g:\ttfd_d\d0000534.ttf)

AaBbCcDdEeFfG
24 point (g:\ttfd_d\d0000566.ttf)

JjBbCcQaJlPpGgqtfOoQ
24 point (g:\ttfd_d\d0000536.ttf)

AaBbCcDdEeFfGgBhdi JjK
24 point (g:\ttfd_d\d0000564.ttf)

RrBbCcDdEeFfGgHhIiJj
24 point (g:\ttfd_d\d0000537.ttf)

AaBbCcDdEeFfGgBhc
24 point (g:\ttfd_d\d0000567.ttf)

AaBbCcDdEeFfGgHhIiJjKkLlMm
24 point (g:\ttfd_d\d0000542.ttf)

AABBCCDDEEFFGGHHIIJ
24 point (g:\ttfd_d\d0000568.ttf)

AaBbCcDdEeFfGcHhliJj
24 point (g:\ttfd_d\d0000543.ttf)

AaBbCcDdEeFfGgHhliJjKkLl
24 point (g:\ttfd_d\d0000569.ttf)

AaBbCcDdEeFfGgHhIiJjKk
24 point (g:\ttfd_d\d0000544.ttf)

AaBbCcDdEeFfGgHhliJ
24 point (g:\ttfd_d\d0000570.ttf)

AaBbCcDdEeFfGgH
24 point (g:\ttfd_d\d0000545.ttf)

AaBbCcDdEeFfGgHhIiJjKkLlMmNnO
24 point (g:\ttfd_d\d0000571.ttf)

BbCcDdEeFfGgHhIiJjKkLlM
24 point (g:\ttfd_d\d0000573.ttf)

BbCcDdEeFfGgHhIiJjKkLlMmNnOoPp
24 point (g:\ttfd_d\d0000574.ttf)

BbCcDdEeFfGgHhIiJjKkLlMmNnOoPp
24 point (g:\ttfd_d\d0000575.ttf)

AaBbCcDdEeFf
24 point (g:\ttfd_d\d0000577.ttf)

AaBbCcDdE
24 point (g:\ttfd_d\d0000576.ttf)

AaBbCcD
24 point (g:\ttfd_d\d0000578.ttf)

BbCcDdEeFfGgHhIiJjKkLlMmN
24 point (g:\ttfd_d\d0000580.ttf)

BbCcDdEeFfGgHhIiJjKkLl
24 point (g:\ttfd_d\d0000581.ttf)

BbCcDd Ee FfGg Hh Ii Jj KkL
24 point (g:\ttfd_d\d0000582.ttf)

ABBCCDDEEFFGGHHIIJJKKL
24 point (g:\ttfd_d\d0000586.ttf)

ABBCCDDEEFFGGHHIIJJK
24 point (g:\ttfd_d\d0000584.ttf)

BBCCDDEEFFGGHHIIJJKKLLMMNNOO
24 point (g:\ttfd_d\d0000585.ttf)

ABBCCDDEEFFGGHHIIJJKKL
24 point (g:\ttfd_d\d0000583.ttf)

ABBCCDDEEFFGGHHI
24 point (g:\ttfd_d\d0000587.ttf)

ABBCCDDEEFFGG
24 point (g:\ttfd_d\d0000589.ttf)

ABBCCDDEEFFGGHHIIJJKKL
24 point (g:\ttfd_d\d0000590.ttf)

ABBCCDDEEFFGGHHIIJJKKLLMM
24 point (g:\ttfd_d\d0000591.ttf)

ABBCCDDEEFFGGHHIIJ
24 point (g:\ttfd_d\d0000592.ttf)

AABBCCDDEEFFGGHHIIJJKKL
24 point (g:\ttfd_d\d0000593.ttf)

AABBCCDDEEFFGGHHIIJJKKLLMM
24 point (g:\ttfd_d\d0000595.ttf)

AaBbCcDdEeffGgHhIi
24 point (g:\ttfd_d\d0000520.ttf)

AaBbCcDdEef
24 point (g:\ttfd_d\d0000522.ttf)

AaBbCcDdEeffGgHhIiJjK
24 point (g:\ttfd_d\d0000523.ttf)

AaBbCcDdEeffG
24 point (g:\ttfd_d\d0000524.ttf)

AaBbCcDdEeFfGgHhIiJjKkLlMm
24 point (g:\ttfd_d\d0000538.ttf)

AaBbCcDdEeFfGgHhIi
24 point (g:\ttfd_d\d0000540.ttf)

AaBbCcDdEeFfGgHhIiJjKk
4 point (g:\ttfd_d\d0000541.ttf)

ABCDEFGHIJKLMNOPQRSTUVWXYZ
18 point (g:\ttfe_e\e0000597.ttf)

ABCDEFGHIJKLMNOPQRSTUVWX
18 point (g:\ttfe_e\e0000596.ttf)

ABCDEFGHIJKLMNOPQRSTUVWXYZ
18 point (g:\ttfe_e\e0000598.ttf)

ABCDEFGHIJKLMNOPQR
18 point (g:\ttfe_e\e0000599.ttf)

ABCDEFGHIJKLMNOPQRSTU
18 point (g:\ttfe_e\e0000600.ttf)

ABCDEFGHIJKLMNOPQRSTUVWXYZABCDEFGHIJKL
18 point (g:\ttfe_e\e0000601.ttf)

ABCDEFGHIJKLMNOPQRSTUVW
18 point (g:\ttfe_e\e0000602.ttf)

ABCDEFGHIJKLMNOPQRSTUVW
18 point (g:\ttfe_e\e0000606.ttf)

ABCDEFGHIJKLMNOPQRSTUVWXYZabcdeig
18 point (g:\ttfe_e\e0000603.ttf)

ABCDEFGHIJKLMNOPQRSTUVWXYZabcdeig
18 point (g:\ttfe_e\e0000604.ttf)

ABCDEFGHIJKLMNO
18 point (g:\ttfe_e\e0000605.ttf)

ABCDEFGHIJKLMNOPQRS
18 point (g:\ttfe_e\e0000607.ttf)

ABCDEFGHIJKLMNOPQRST
18 point (g:\ttfe_e\e0000609.ttf)

ABCDEFGHIJKLMNOPQRSTUVWXYZa
18 point (g:\ttfe_e\e0000610.ttf)

ABCDEFGHIJKLMH
18 point (g:\ttfe_e\e0000611.ttf)

ABCDEFGHIJKLMNOP
18 point (g:\ttfe_e\e0000612.ttf)

ABCDEFGHIJKLMNOPQRSTUVWXYZABCDEFGHIJKLMNOPQRSTUVWXYZ
18 point (g:\ttfe_e\e0000613.ttf)

ABCDEFGHIJKLMNOPQR
18 point (g:\ttfe_e\e0000614.ttf)

ABCDEFGHIJKLMNOPQRSTU
18 point (g:\ttfe_e\e0000619.ttf)

ABCDEFGHIJKLMNOPQRST
18 point (g:\ttfe_e\e0000618.ttf)

ABCDEFGHIJKLMNOPQRSTUVWXYZ
18 point (g:\ttfe_e\e0000620.ttf)

ABCDEFGHIJKLMN
18 point (g:\ttfe_e\e0000621.ttf)

ABCDEFGHIJKLMNOPQRSTUVW
18 point (g:\ttfe_e\e0000622.ttf)

ABCDEFGHIJKLMNOP
18 point (g:\ttfe_e\e0000623.ttf)

ABCDEFGHIJKLMNOPQRS
18 point (g:\ttfe_e\e0000624.ttf)

ABCDEFGHIJKLMNOPQRSTUVWX
18 point (g:\ttfe_e\e0000625.ttf)

ABCDEFGHIJKLM
18 point (g:\ttfe_e\e0000626.ttf)

ABCDEFGHIJKLMNOPQRSTUV
18 point (g:\ttfe_e\e0000627.ttf)

ABCDEFGHIJKLMNOPQRSTU
18 point (g:\ttfe_e\e0000629.ttf)

ABCDEFGHIJKLMNOPQ
18 point (g:\ttfe_e\e0000630.ttf)

ABCDEFGHIJKLMNOPQRSTUVW
18 point (g:\ttfe_e\e0000631.ttf)

ABCDEFGHIJKLMNOPQRSTUVWXYZabcdeig
18 point (g:\ttfe_e\e0000632.ttf)

ABCDEFGHIJKLMNOP
18 point (g:\ttfe_e\e0000633.ttf)

ABCDEFGHIJKLMNOPQRSTUVW
18 point (g:\ttfe_e\e0000634.ttf)

ABCDEFGHIJKLMNOPQRS
18 point (g:\ttfe_e\e0000635.ttf)

ABCDEFGHIJKLMNOPQRST
18 point (g:\ttfe_e\e0000636.ttf)

ABCDEFGHIJKLMNOPQR
18 point (g:\ttfe_e\e0000637.ttf)

ABCDEFGHIJKLMNOPQRSTUVWXY
18 point (g:\ttfe_e\e0000638.ttf)

ABCDEFGHIJKL
18 point (g:\ttfe_e\e0000639.ttf)

ABCDEFGHIJKLMNO
18 point (g:\ttfe_e\e0000640.ttf)

ABCDEFGHIJKLMNOPQRS
18 point (g:\ttfe_e\e0000641.ttf)

ABCDEFGHIJKLMNOPQRSTU
18 point (g:\ttfe_e\e0000643.ttf)

BCDEFGHIJKLMNOPQR
18 point   (g:\ttfe_e\e0000667.ttf)

BCDEFGHIJKLM
18 point   (g:\ttfe_e\e0000668.ttf)

ABCDEFGH
18 point   (g:\ttfe_e\e0000669.ttf)

BCDEFGHIJKLMNOPQRSTUVWXY
18 point   (g:\ttfe_e\e0000672.ttf)

BCDEFGHIJKLMNOPQRSTUVWXYZabc
18 point   (g:\ttfe_e\e0000676.ttf)

BCDEFGHIJKLMNOPQRSTUVWXYZ
18 point   (g:\ttfe_e\e0000677.ttf)

ABCDEFGHIJKLMNO
18 point   (g:\ttfe_e\e0000678.ttf)

BCDEFGHIJKLMNOPQRSTUVWX
18 point   (g:\ttfe_e\e0000679.ttf)

BCDEFGHIJKLMNOPQRSTUVW
18 point   (g:\ttfe_e\e0000680.ttf)

BCDEFGHIJKLMNOPQRSTUVW
18 point   (g:\ttfe_e\e0000681.ttf)

CDEFGHIJKLMNOPQRSTUVWXYZa
18 point   (g:\ttfe_e\e0000682.ttf)

BCDEFGHIJKLMNOPQRSTUVWXYZabcd
18 point   (g:\ttfe_e\e0000683.ttf)

BCDEFGHIJKLMNOPQRSTUVWX
18 point   (g:\ttfe_e\e0000684.ttf)

BCDEFGHIJKLMNOPQRSTUVWXYZab
18 point   (g:\ttfe_e\e0000685.ttf)

CDEFGHIJKLMNOPQRSTUVWXYZabcdefghijk
18 point   (g:\ttfe_e\e0000686.ttf)

BCDEFGHIJKLMNOPQRSTUV
18 point   (g:\ttfe_e\e0000687.ttf)

BCDEFGHIJKLMNOPQRSTUVWXYZabc
18 point   (g:\ttfe_e\e0000688.ttf)

BCDEFGHIJKLMNOPQRSTUV
18 point   (g:\ttfe_e\e0000689.ttf)

BCDEFGHIJKLMNOPQRS
18 point   (g:\ttfe_e\e0000690.ttf)

ABCDEFGHIJKLM
18 point   (g:\ttfe_e\e0000691.ttf)

BCDEFGHIJKLMNOPQRSTUV
18 point   (g:\ttfe_e\e0000692.ttf)

ABCDEFGHIJKLMNOPQRSTUVWXYZABC
18 point   (g:\ttfe_e\e0000645.ttf)

ABCDEFGHIJKLMNO
18 point   (g:\ttfe_e\e0000646.ttf)

ABCDEFGHIJKLMNOPQRSTUV
18 point   (g:\ttfe_e\e0000644.ttf)

ABCDEFGHIJKLMNOPQR
18 point   (g:\ttfe_e\e0000647.ttf)

ABCDEFGHIJKLMNOPQRSTUVWXY
18 point   (g:\ttfe_e\e0000649.ttf)

ABCDEFGHIJKLMNOPQ
18 point   (g:\ttfe_e\e0000648.ttf)

ABCDEFGHIJKLMNOPQRSTUVWXYZA
18 point   (g:\ttfe_e\e0000651.ttf)

ABCDEFGHIJKLMN
18 point   (g:\ttfe_e\e0000652.ttf)

ABCDEFGHIJKLMNOPQRST
18 point   (g:\ttfe_e\e0000654.ttf)

ABCDEFGHIJKLMNOPQRSTUVWX
18 point   (g:\ttfe_e\e0000655.ttf)

ABCDEFGHIJKLMNOP
18 point   (g:\ttfe_e\e0000656.ttf)

ABCDEFGHIJKLMΓ OPQRS
18 point   (g:\ttfe_e\e0000658.ttf)

ABCDEFGHIJKLMNOPQRSTU
18 point   (g:\ttfe_e\e0000659.ttf)

ABCDEFGHIJKLMNOPQR
18 point   (g:\ttfe_e\e0000660.ttf)

ABCDEFGHIJKLMNOPQ
18 point   (g:\ttfe_e\e0000661.ttf)

ABCDEFGHIJKLMNOPQRSTUVWXYZab
18 point   (g:\ttfe_e\e0000673.ttf)

ABCDEFGHIJKLMNOPQRSTU
18 point   (g:\ttfe_e\e0000674.ttf)

ABCDEFGHIJKLMNOPQRSTUV
18 point   (g:\ttfe_e\e0000662.ttf)

ABCDEFGHIJKLMNOPQRSTUVWXYZabcde
18 point   (g:\ttfe_e\e0000664.ttf)

ABCDEFGHIJKLMNO
18 point   (g:\ttfe_e\e0000665.ttf)

ABCDEFGHIJKLMNOPQRSTUVWXYZab
18 point   (g:\ttfe_e\e0000666.ttf)

ABCDEFGHIJKLMNO
18 point   (g:\ttfe_e\e0000693.ttf)

ABCDEFGHIJKLNOPQRST
18 point   (g:\ttfe_e\e0000694.ttf)

ABCDEFGHIJKLMNOPQRSTUVWXYZabc
18 point   (g:\ttfe_e\e0000695.ttf)

ABCDEFGHIJKLMNOPQRSTUVWX
18 point   (g:\ttfe_e\e0000696.ttf)

ABCDEFGHIJKLMNOPQRSTUVW
18 point   (g:\ttfe_e\e0000697.ttf)

ABCDEFGHIJKLMNOPQRSTUVWXYZabcd
18 point   (g:\ttfe_e\e0000699.ttf)

ABCDEFGHIJKLMNOPQRSTUVWXYZab
18 point   (g:\ttfe_e\e0000700.ttf)

ABCDEFGHIJKLMNOPQRSTUV
18 point   (g:\ttfe_e\e0000701.ttf)

ABCDEFGHIJKLMNOPQRSTUVW
18 point   (g:\ttfe_e\e0000702.ttf)

ABCDEFGHIJKLMNOPQRSTUVWXY
8 point   (g:\ttfe_e\e0000703.ttf)

ABCDEFGHIJKLM
18 point   (g:\ttfe_e\e0000704.ttf)

ABCDEFGHI JKLMNOPQRS
18 point   (g:\ttfe_e\e0000706.ttf)

ABCDEFGHI
18 point   (g:\ttfe_e\e0000707.ttf)

ABCDEFGHI JKLMNOPQ
18 point   (g:\ttfe_e\e0000708.ttf)

ABCDEFGHI JK
18 point   (g:\ttfe_e\e0000709.ttf)

ABCDEFGHIJKLMNOPQRST
18 point   (g:\ttfe_e\e0000710.ttf)

ABCDEFGHIJKLM
18 point   (g:\ttfe_e\e0000711.ttf)

ABCDEFGHIJKLMNOPQRSTUVW
18 point   (g:\ttfe_e\e0000712.ttf)

ABCDEFGHIJKLMNOP
18 point   (g:\ttfe_e\e0000713.ttf)

ÍÎÏÌÏÏÌJ̧ĴĶĹĽĻŁŃÑŅÒÓŐÔÕŐ
18 point   (g:\ttfe_e\e0000714.ttf)

ABCDEFGHIJKLMNOPQRSTUV
18 point   (g:\ttfe_e\e0000715.ttf)

ABCDEFGHIJKLMNOPQRSTUVW
18 point   (g:\ttfe_e\e0000716.ttf)

ABCDEFGHIJKLMNOPQRSTUVWX
18 point   (g:\ttfe_e\e0000717.ttf)

ABCDEFGHIJKLMNOP
18 point   (g:\ttfe_e\e0000718.ttf)

ABCDEFGHIJKLMNOPQRSTUVW
18 point   (g:\ttfe_e\e0000719.ttf)

ABCDEFGHIJKLMNOPQRSTUVWX
18 point   (g:\ttfe_e\e0000720.ttf)

ABCDEFGHIJKLMNOPQRSTUVW
18 point   (g:\ttfe_e\e0000721.ttf)

ABCDEFGHIJKLMNOPQRSTUVWXY
18 point   (g:\ttfe_e\e0000722.ttf)

ABCDEFGHIJKLMNOPQRSTUVW
18 point   (g:\ttfe_e\e0000723.ttf)

ABCDEFGHIJKLMNOPQRSTUVW
18 point   (g:\ttfe_e\e0000726.ttf)

ABCDEFGHIJKLMNOPQRSTUVWXYZabcdefc
18 point   (g:\ttfe_e\e0000724.ttf)

ABCDEFGHIJKLMNO
18 point   (g:\ttfe_e\e0000725.ttf)

ABCDEFGHIJKLMNOPQRSTUVWXYZ.
18 point   (g:\ttfe_e\e0000727.ttf)

ABCDEFGHIJKLMNOPQR
18 point   (g:\ttfe_e\e0000728.ttf)

ABCDEFGHIJKLMNOPQRSTUVWXY
18 point   (g:\ttfe_e\e0000729.ttf)

ABCDEFGHIJKLMNOPQRSTUVWX.
18 point   (g:\ttfe_e\e0000731.ttf)

ABCDEFGHIJKLMNOPQRSTUVWXYZabcdefghi
18 point   (g:\ttfe_e\e0000730.ttf)

ABCDEFGHIJKLMNOPQRS.
18 point   (g:\ttfe_e\e0000732.ttf)

ABCDEFGHIJKLMNOPQRSTUVWX
18 point   (g:\ttfe_e\e0000642.ttf)

BCDEFGHIJKLMNOPQRST
24 point (g:\ttff_f\0000733.ttf)

BCDEFGHIJKLMNOPQRST
24 point (g:\ttff_f\0000735.ttf)

BCDEFGHIJKLMNOP
24 point (g:\ttff_f\0000734.ttf)

BCDEFGHIJKLMNOPQRST
24 point (g:\ttff_f\0000736.ttf)

BCDEFGHIJKLMNOPQRSTUV
24 point (g:\ttff_f\0000737.ttf)

BCDEFGHIJKLMNOP
24 point (g:\ttff_f\0000738.ttf)

BCDEFGHIJKLMNO
24 point (g:\ttff_f\0000739.ttf)

BCDEFGHIJKLM
24 point (g:\ttff_f\0000740.ttf)

BCDEFGHIJKLMNOPQRSTU
24 point (g:\ttff_f\0000741.ttf)

Iᴛᴍ⋀()ᴊᴜᴛᴜʀᴜᴢ ⌐ɪᴊ (((()))){ʬ{{}}}ᵐⁱⁱ
24 point (g:\ttff_f\0000742.ttf)

BCDEFGHIJKLMMN
24 point (g:\ttff_f\0000743.ttf)

BCDEFGHIJKLMNOP
24 point (g:\ttff_f\0000744.ttf)

BCDEFGHIJKLM
24 point (g:\ttff_f\0000745.ttf)

BCDEFGHIJKLMNOPD
24 point (g:\ttff_f\0000746.ttf)

BCDEFGHIJKLMNO
24 point (g:\ttff_f\0000747.ttf)

CDEFGHIJKLMNOPQRSTUVWXYZab
24 point (g:\ttff_f\0000748.ttf)

BCDEFGHIJKLMNOPQR
24 point (g:\ttff_f\0000749.ttf)

BCDEFGHIJKLMNOPQRS
24 point (g:\ttff_f\0000751.ttf)

ABCDEFGHIJKLMNOPQRSTU
24 point (g:\ttff_f\0000752.ttf)

ABCDEFGHIJKLMNOPQRSTUVWXYZa
24 point (g:\ttff_f\0000753.ttf)

ABCDEFGHIJKLMNOPQRSTUVWXYZa
24 point (g:\ttff_f\0000754.ttf)

ABCDEFGHIJKLMNOPQRSTUVWXYZabcd
24 point (g:\ttff_f\0000755.ttf)

ABCDEFGHIJKLMNOPQR
24 point (g:\ttff_f\0000757.ttf)

ABCDEFGHIJKLMNOPQRS
24 point (g:\ttff_f\0000760.ttf)

ABCDEFGHIJKLM
24 point (g:\ttff_f\0000761.ttf)

ABCDEFGHIJKLMNO
24 point (g:\ttff_f\0000762.ttf)

ABCDEFGHIJKLMNOPQRST
24 point (g:\ttff_f\0000763.ttf)

ABCDEFGHIJKLM
24 point (g:\ttff_f\0000764.ttf)

ABCDEFGHIJKLMN
24 point (g:\ttff_f\0000765.ttf)

ABCDEFGHIJKLMNOPQR
24 point (g:\ttff_f\0000766.ttf)

ABCDEFGHIJKLM
24 point (g:\ttff_f\0000767.ttf)

ABCDEFGHIJKLMNOPQRSTU
24 point (g:\ttff_f\0000768.ttf)

ABCDEFGHIJKLMNOPQRSTUVWXY
24 point (g:\ttff_f\0000769.ttf)

ABCDEFGHIJKLMNOP
24 point (g:\ttff_f\0000771.ttf)

ABCDEFGHIJKLMNOP
24 point (g:\ttff_f\0000772.ttf)

ABCDEFGHIJKLMNOP
24 point (g:\ttff_f\0000773.ttf)

ABCDEFGHIJKLMNOPQRST
24 point (g:\ttff_f\0000774.ttf)

ABCDEFGHIJKLMNO
24 point (g:\ttff_f\0000775.ttf)

ABCDEFGHIJ
24 point (g:\ttff_f\0000776.ttf)

ABCDEFGHIJKL
24 point (g:\ttff_f\0000777.ttf)

ABCDEFGHIJKLMNOPQR
24 point (g:\ttff_f\0000778.ttf)

ABCDEFGHIJKLMNOPQRSTUVW
24 point (g:\ttff_f\0000779.ttf)

ABCDEFGHIJKL
24 point (g:\ttff_f\0000780.ttf)

ABCDEFGHIJKLMNOPQR
24 point (g:\ttff_f\0000781.ttf)

ABCDEFGHIJKLMN
24 point (g:\ttff_f\0000782.ttf)

ABCDEFGHIJKLMNOPQ
24 point (g:\ttff_f\0000783.ttf)

ABCDEFGHIJKLMNOPQRS
24 point (g:\ttff_f\0000785.ttf)

ABCDEFGHIJKLMNOPQ
24 point (g:\ttff_f\0000786.ttf)

ABCDEFGHIJKLMNOPQRST
24 point (g:\ttff_f\0000787.ttf)

ABCDEFGHIJKLMNOP
24 point (g:\ttff_f\0000788.ttf)

ABCDEFGHIJKLMNOPQR
24 point (g:\ttff_f\0000789.ttf)

ABCDEFGHIJKLMNOPQRSTUVWX
24 point (g:\ttff_f\0000790.ttf)

ABCDEFGHIJKLMNOPQRSTUV
24 point (g:\ttff_f\0000791.ttf)

ABCDEFGHIJKLMNOPQ
24 point (g:\ttff_f\0000792.ttf)

ABCDEFGHIJKLMNOPQRSTUVWX
24 point (g:\ttff_f\0000793.ttf)

ABCDEFGHIJKLMNO
24 point (g:\ttff_f\0000794.ttf)

ABCDEFGHIJKLMNOPQRSTUVWX
24 point (g:\ttff_f\0000795.ttf)

ABCDEFGHIJKLMNOPQRSTUV
24 point (g:\ttff_f\0000796.ttf)

ABCDEFGHIJKLMNOPQRS
24 point (g:\ttff_f\0000797.ttf)

ABCDEFGHIJKLMNOPQR
24 point (g:\ttff_f\0000799.ttf)

ABCDEFGHIJKLMNOPQ
24 point (g:\ttff_f\0000800.ttf)

ABCDEFGHIJKLMNOPQR
24 point (g:\ttff_f\0000801.ttf)

ABCDEFGHIJKLMNOPQ
24 point (g:\ttff_f\0000802.ttf)

ABCDEFGHIJKLMNOPQRST
24 point (g:\ttff_f\0000803.ttf)

ABCDEFGHIJKLMNOPQR
24 point (g:\ttff_f\0000804.ttf)

ABCDEFGHIJKLMNOPQR
24 point (g:\ttff_f\0000805.ttf)

ABCDEFGHIJKLMNOPQRS
24 point (g:\ttff_f\0000806.ttf)

ABCDEFGHIJKLMNOPQRS
24 point (g:\ttff_f\0000807.ttf)

ABCDEFGHIJKLMNOPQRS
24 point (g:\ttff_f\0000808.ttf)

ABCDEFGHIJKLMNOPQRSTUVWXYZa
24 point (g:\ttff_f\0000809.ttf)

ABCDEFGHIJKLMNOPQRSTUVWXYZa
24 point (g:\ttff_f\0000810.ttf)

ABCDEFGHIJKLMNOPQRSTUVWXYZa
24 point (g:\ttff_f\0000811.ttf)

CDEFGHIJKLMN
24 point (g:\ttff_f\0000812.ttf)

BCDEFGHIJKLMNOPQ
24 point (g:\ttff_f\0000813.ttf)

CDEFGHIJKLMNOPQRS
24 point (g:\ttff_f\0000814.ttf)

BCDEFGHIJKLMN
4 point (g:\ttff_f\0000815.ttf)

BCDEFGHIJKLMNOP
24 point (g:\ttff_f\0000816.ttf)

BCDEFGHIJKLMNOP
24 point (g:\ttff_f\0000817.ttf)

BCDEFGHIJKLMNOPQ
24 point (g:\ttff_f\0000818.ttf)

CDEFGHIJKLMNOPQRSTUV
24 point (g:\ttff_f\0000819.ttf)

CDEFGHIJKLMNOPQRSTUV
24 point (g:\ttff_f\0000820.ttf)

CDEFGHIJKLMNOPQRSTUVWXYZa
24 point (g:\ttff_f\0000821.ttf)

CDEFGHIJKLMNOPQRSTUVWXYZa
24 point (g:\ttff_f\0000822.ttf)

DEFGHIJKLMNOPQRSTUVWXYZabc
24 point (g:\ttff_f\0000824.ttf)

DEFGHIJKLMNOPQRSTUVWXYZabc
24 point (g:\ttff_f\0000825.ttf)

DEFGHIJKLMNOPQRSTUVWXYZabcdefgh
24 point (g:\ttff_f\0000826.ttf)

BCDEFGHIJKLMNOPQR
24 point (g:\ttff_f\0000827.ttf)

BCDEFGHIJKLMNOPQR
24 point (g:\ttff_f\0000828.ttf)

CDEFGHIJKLMNOPQRSTUV
24 point (g:\ttff_f\0000829.ttf)

BCDEFGHIJKLMNOPQRS
24 point (g:\ttff_f\0000832.ttf)

ABCDEFGHIJKLMNOPQR
24 point (g:\ttff_f\0000830.ttf)

ABCDEFGHIJKLMNOPQR
24 point (g:\ttff_f\0000831.ttf)

ABCDEFGHIJKLMNOPQRSTU
24 point (g:\ttff_f\0000833.ttf)

ABCDEFGHIJKLMN
24 point (g:\ttff_f\0000834.ttf)

ABCDEFGHIJKLMN
24 point (g:\ttff_f\0000835.ttf)

ABCDEFGHIJKLMNOPQ
24 point (g:\ttff_f\0000836.ttf)

ABCDEF GHIJKLMNO
24 point (g:\ttff_f\0000837.ttf)

ABCDEFGHIJKLMNOPQRS
24 point (g:\ttff_f\0000838.ttf)

ABCDEFGHIJKLMNOPQRS
, 24 point (g:\ttff_f\0000839.ttf)

ABCDEFGHIJKLMNOPQRS
24 point (g:\ttff_f\0000758.ttf)

ABCDEFGHIJKLMNOPQRSTUVW
18 point (g:\ttfg_g\g0000841.ttf)

ABCDEFGHIJKLMNOPQRSTUVW
18 point (g:\ttfg_g\g0000843.ttf)

᛫᛫᛫ ᛫᛫᛫ ᛫᛫᛫ ᛫᛫᛫ ᛫᛫᛫
18 point (g:\ttfg_g\g0000844.ttf)

ABCDEFGHIJKLMNOPQRSTUVWXYZabcdefg
18 point (g:\ttfg_g\g0000845.ttf)

ABCDEFGHIJKLMNOPQRSTUVWXYZabcdefghijklmnopqr
18 point (g:\ttfg_g\g0000846.ttf)

ABCDEFGHIJKLMNOPQRSTUVWXYZ
18 point (g:\ttfg_g\g0000847.ttf)

ABCDEFGHIJKLMNOP
18 point (g:\ttfg_g\g0000848.ttf)

ABCDEFGHIJKLMNOPQRSTUVW
18 point (g:\ttfg_g\g0000849.ttf)

ABCDEFGHIJKLMNOPQRSTUV
18 point (g:\ttfg_g\g0000850.ttf)

ABCDEFGHIJKLMNOPQRSTUV
18 point (g:\ttfg_g\g0000853.ttf)

ABCDEFGHIJKLMNOPQRSTUVW
18 point (g:\ttfg_g\g0000857.ttf)

ABCDEFGHIJKLMNOPQRSTUVW
18 point (g:\ttfg_g\g0000856.ttf)

ABCDEFGHIJKLMNOPQRSTUV
18 point (g:\ttfg_g\g0000854.ttf)

ABCDEFGHIJKLMNOPQRSTUVWXYZabcdefgh
18 point (g:\ttfg_g\g0000858.ttf)

ABCDEFGHIJKLMNOPQRSTUVWXYZabcdefgh
18 point (g:\ttfg_g\g0000861.ttf)

ABCDEFGHIJKLMNOPQRSTUVWXYZabcde
18 point (g:\ttfg_g\g0000859.ttf)

ABCDEFGHIJKLMNOPQRSTUVWXYZabcde
18 point (g:\ttfg_g\g0000860.ttf)

ABCDEFGHIJKLMNOPQRSTUVWXYZab
18 point (g:\ttfg_g\g0000862.ttf)

ABCDEFGHIJKLMNOPQRSTUVWXYZ
18 point (g:\ttfg_g\g0000863.ttf)

ABCDEFGHIJKLMNOPQRSTUVW
18 point (g:\ttfg_g\g0000864.ttf)

ABCDEFGHIJKLMNOPQRSTUVWX
18 point (g:\ttfg_g\g0000866.ttf)

ABCDEFGHIJKLMNOPQRSTUV
18 point (g:\ttfg_g\g0000867.ttf)

ABCDEFGHIJKLMNOF
18 point (g:\ttfg_g\g0000868.ttf)

ABCDEFGHIJKLMNOPQF
18 point (g:\ttfg_g\g0000869.ttf)

ABCDEFGHIJKLMNOPQRSTUVW
18 point (g:\ttfg_g\g0000870.ttf)

ABCDEFGHIJKLMNOPQRSTUVW
18 point (g:\ttfg_g\g0000871.ttf)

ABCDEFGHIJKLMN
18 point (g:\ttfg_g\g0000872.ttf)

ABCDEFGHIJKLMNOPQRSTUVW
18 point (g:\ttfg_g\g0000873.ttf)

ABCDEFGHIJKLMNOPQRSTUVW
18 point (g:\ttfg_g\g0000875.ttf)

ABCDEFGHIJKLMNOPQRSTUV
18 point (g:\ttfg_g\g0000874.ttf)

ABCDEFGHIJKLMNOPQRSTUVW
18 point (g:\ttfg_g\g0000876.ttf)

ABCDEFGHIJKLMNOPQRSTU
18 point (g:\ttfg_g\g0000878.ttf)

ABCDEFGHIJKLMNOPQRS
18 point (g:\ttfg_g\g0000879.ttf)

ABCDEFGHIJKLMNOPQRSTUVW
18 point (g:\ttfg_g\g0000880.ttf)

ABCDEFGHIJKLMNOPQ
18 point (g:\ttfg_g\g0000881.ttf)

ABCDEFGHIJKLMNOPQR
18 point (g:\ttfg_g\g0000882.ttf)

ABCDEFGHIJKLMNOPQRSTUVWXYZ
18 point (g:\ttfg_g\g0000883.ttf)

ABCDEFGHIJKLMNOPQ
18 point (g:\ttfg_g\g0000884.ttf)

ABCDEFGHIJKLMNOPQRSTUV
18 point (g:\ttfg_g\g0000885.ttf)

ABCDEFGHIJKLMNOPQRS
18 point (g:\ttfg_g\g0000886.ttf)

ABCDEFGHIJKLMNOPQRSTU
18 point (g:\ttfg_g\g0000887.ttf)

ABCDEFGHIJKLMNO
18 point (g:\ttfg_g\g0000888.ttf)

BCDEFGHIJKLMNOPQR
18 point   (g:\ttfg_g\0000889.ttf)

CDEFGHIJKLMNOPQRSTUVWXYZ
18 point   (g:\ttfg_g\0000890.ttf)

UDEFGHIJKLMNOPQRSTUVWXYZAB
point   (g:\ttfg_g\0000891.ttf)

CDEFGHIJKLMNOPQRSTUVWX
18 point   (g:\ttfg_g\0000892.ttf)

BCDEFGHIJKLMNOPQRSTUVWX
18 point   (g:\ttfg_g\0000894.ttf)

BCDEFGHIJKLMNOP
18 point   (g:\ttfg_g\0000893.ttf)

BCDEFGHIJKLMNOPQRS
18 point   (g:\ttfg_g\0000895.ttf)

CCDEFGHIJKLMNOPQRS
18 point   (g:\ttfg_g\0000896.ttf)

CDEFGHIJKLMNOPQRSTUVW
18 point   (g:\ttfg_g\0000900.ttf)

BCDEFGHIJKLMNOPQRSTU
18 point   (g:\ttfg_g\0000897.ttf)

BCDEFGHIJKLMNOPQRSTUV
18 point   (g:\ttfg_g\0000898.ttf)

CDEFGHIJKLMNOPQRSTUVW
18 point   (g:\ttfg_g\0000901.ttf)

CCDEFGHIJKLMNOPQRS
18 point   (g:\ttfg_g\0000902.ttf)

BCDEFGHIJKLMNOPQRSTU
18 point   (g:\ttfg_g\0000903.ttf)

CDEFGHIJKLMNOPQRSTUVWXY
18 point   (g:\ttfg_g\0000905.ttf)

CDEFGHIJKLMNOPQRSTUVWXY
18 point   (g:\ttfg_g\0000906.ttf)

BCDEFGHIJKLMNOPQR
18 point   (g:\ttfg_g\0000907.ttf)

CDEFGHIJKLMNOPQRSTUVWXYZabcdefghijk
18 point   (g:\ttfg_g\0000908.ttf)

CDEFGHIJKLMNOPQRSTUV
18 point   (g:\ttfg_g\0000915.ttf)

BCDEFGHIJKLMNOPQRST
18 point   (g:\ttfg_g\0000916.ttf)

CDEFGHIJKLMNOPQRSTUVW
18 point   (g:\ttfg_g\0000917.ttf)

ABCDEFGHIJKLMNOPQRSTUV
18 point   (g:\ttfg_g\0000914.ttf)

ABCDEFGHIJKLMNOPQRSTU
18 point   (g:\ttfg_g\0000918.ttf)

ABCDEFGHIJKLMNOPQRSTU
18 point   (g:\ttfg_g\0000919.ttf)

ABCDEFGHIJKLMNOPQRSTUVW
18 point   (g:\ttfg_g\0000920.ttf)

ABCDEFGHIJKLMNOPQRSTUVW
18 point   (g:\ttfg_g\0000921.ttf)

ABCDEFGHIJKLMNOPQRSTUVWXY
18 point   (g:\ttfg_g\0000922.ttf)

ABCDEFGHIJKLMNOPQRSTUVWXY
18 point   (g:\ttfg_g\0000923.ttf)

ABCDEFGHIJKLMNOPQRST
18 point   (g:\ttfg_g\0000925.ttf)

ABCDEFGHIJKLMNOPQRSTU
18 point   (g:\ttfg_g\0000926.ttf)

ABCDEFGHIJKLMNOPQRSTUVWX
18 point   (g:\ttfg_g\0000927.ttf)

ABCDEFGHIJKLMNOPQRSTUVWXYZABCDEFGHI
18 point   (g:\ttfg_g\0000928.ttf)

ABXΔEΦΓHIωKΛMNOΠΘPΣTYηΩΞ
18 point   (g:\ttfg_g\0000930.ttf)

ABCDEFGHIJKLMNOPQRSTU
18 point   (g:\ttfg_g\0000940.ttf)

ਅਭਡਪੈਰਖੀੲੴਖਏੲੱਟੰਫਉੲੲੲੲੑਬਰਦੇਤਗਾਜ
18 point   (g:\ttfg_g\0000941.ttf)

ABCDEFGHIJKLMNOPQRSTUVWXYZabcdefghijk
18 point   (g:\ttfg_g\0000909.ttf)

ABCDEFGHIJKLMNOPQRSTUVWXYZabcdefghijk
18 point   (g:\ttfg_g\0000912.ttf)

ABCDEFGHIJKLMNOPQRSTUVWXYZabcdefghijklmnopqrstuvw
18 point   (g:\ttfg_g\0000910.ttf)

ABCDEFGHIJKLMNOPQRSTUV
18 point   (g:\ttfg_g\0000911.ttf)

ABCDEFGHIJKLMNOPQRSTUVWXYZab
18 point   (g:\ttfg_g\0000913.ttf)

abcdefghijklmnopqrstuuwx
18 point (g:\ttfh_h\0000942.ttf)

abcdefghijklmnopqrstuuwx
8 point (g:\ttfh_h\0000944.ttf)

abcdefghijklmnop
18 point (g:\ttfh_h\0000943.ttf)

abcdefghijklmnopqrst
18 point (g:\ttfh_h\0000945.ttf)

ABCDEFGHIJKLMNOPQRSTUVWXYZabcdefghijklmnopqrstuvwxyz
18 point (g:\ttfh_h\0000947.ttf)

ABCDEFGHIJKLMNOPQ
18 point (g:\ttfh_h\0000948.ttf)

ABCDEFGHIJKL
18 point (g:\ttfh_h\0000949.ttf)

ABCDEFGHIJKLM
18 point (g:\ttfh_h\0000950.ttf)

ABCDEFGHIJKLMNOPQRSTU
18 point (g:\ttfh_h\0000951.ttf)

ABCDEFGHIJKLMNOPQRSTU
18 point (g:\ttfh_h\0000954.ttf)

ABCDEFGHIJKLMNOPQRSTUVWXYZab
18 point (g:\ttfh_h\0000952.ttf)

ABCDEFGHIJKLMN
18 point (g:\ttfh_h\0000953.ttf)

ABCDEFGHIJKLMNOPQ
18 point (g:\ttfh_h\0000955.ttf)

ABCDEFGHIJKLMNOPQRSTUV
18 point (g:\ttfh_h\0000956.ttf)

ABCDEFGHIJKLMN P RSTUV
18 point (g:\ttfh_h\0000957.ttf)

ABCDEFGHIJKLMNOPQR
18 point (g:\ttfh_h\0000958.ttf)

ABCDEFGHIJKL
18 point (g:\ttfh_h\0000959.ttf)

ABCDEFGHIJKLMNOPQRSTUVWXY
18 point (g:\ttfh_h\0000960.ttf)

ABCDEFGHIJKLMNOPQRSTUVWXY
18 point (g:\ttfh_h\0000963.ttf)

ABCDEFGHIJKLMNOPQRSTUVWXYZabcdefghijkl
18 point (g:\ttfh_h\0000961.ttf)

ABCDEFGHIJKLMNOPQ
18 point (g:\ttfh_h\0000962.ttf)

ABCDEFGHIJKLMNOPQRSTUVWX
18 point (g:\ttfh_h\0000964.ttf)

ABCDEFGHIJKLMNOPQRST
18 point (g:\ttfh_h\0000965.ttf)

ABCDEFGHIJKLMNOPQRSTUVW
*9 point (g:\ttfh_h\0000967.ttf)

ABCDEFGHIJKLMNOPQRSTUVWXYZabcdef
18 point (g:\ttfh_h\0000968.ttf)

ABCDEFGHIJKLMNOPQRST
18 point (g:\ttfh_h\0000970.ttf)

ABCDEFGHIJKLMNOPQRST
18 point (g:\ttfh_h\0000969.ttf)

ABCDEFGHIJKLMNOPQRS
18 point (g:\ttfh_h\0000971.ttf)

ABCDEFGHIJKLMNOPQRSTUVWX
!8 point (g:\ttfh_h\0000972.ttf)

ABCDEFGHIJKLMNOPQRSTUV
18 point (g:\ttfh_h\0000973.ttf)

ABCDEFGHIJKLMNOPQRSTUVWXYZ
18 point (g:\ttfh_h\0000974.ttf)

ABCDEFGHIJKLMNOPQR
18 point (g:\ttfh_h\0000975.ttf)

ABCDEFGHIJKLMNOPQRSTU
18 point (g:\ttfh_h\0000976.ttf)

ABCDEFGHIJKLMNOPQRST
18 point (g:\ttfh_h\0000978.ttf)

ABCDEFGHIJKLMNOPQRS
18 point (g:\ttfh_h\0000979.ttf)

ABCDEFGHIJKLM
18 point (g:\ttfh_h\0000980.ttf)

ABCDEFGHIJKLMNOPQRSTU
18 point (g:\ttfh_h\0000981.ttf)

ABCDEFGHIJKLMNOPQRSTU
18 point (g:\ttfh_h\0000982.ttf)

ABCDEFGHIJKLMNOPQRSTUVWXYZabc
18 point (g:\ttfh_h\0000983.ttf)

ABCDEFGHIJKLMNOPQRSTUVWXYZabcdefg
18 point (g:\ttfh_h\0000985.ttf)

ABCDEFGHIJKLMNOPQRSTUVWXYZabc
18 point (g:\ttfh_h\0000987.ttf)

ABCDEFGHIJKLMNOPQRSTUVWXYZabc
(g:\ttfh_h\0000990.ttf)

CDEFGHIJKLMNOPQRSTUVWXY
18 point (g:\ttfh_h\h0000991.ttf)

CDEFGHIJKLMNOPQRSTUVWXYZ
18 point (g:\ttfh_h\h0000992.ttf)

CDEFGHIJKLMNOPQRSTUVWXYZ
18 point (g:\ttfh_h\h0000994.ttf)

CDEFGHIJKLMNOPQRSTUVWXYZ
18 point (g:\ttfh_h\h0000995.ttf)

CDEFGHIJKLMNOPQRSTUV
18 point (g:\ttfh_h\h0000996.ttf)

DEFGHIJKLMNOPQRSTUVWXYZabc
18 point (g:\ttfh_h\h0000999.ttf)

CDEFGHIJKLMNOPQR
18 point (g:\ttfh_h\h0001008.ttf)

cderfghijklmnopq
8 point (g:\ttfh_h\h0001009.ttf)

CDEFGHIJKLMNOPQRSTUVW
point (g:\ttfh_h\h0001010.ttf)

CDEFGHIJKLMNO
18 point (g:\ttfh_h\h0001011.ttf)

CDEFGHIJKLMNOPQRSTUVW
18 point (g:\ttfh_h\h0001012.ttf)

CDEFGHIJKLMNOPQR
18 point (g:\ttfh_h\h0001013.ttf)

CDEFGHIJKLMNOPQRSTUVWX
18 point (g:\ttfh_h\h0001014.ttf)

BCDEFGHIJKLMNOPQ
8 point (g:\ttfh_h\h0001015.ttf)

CDEFGHIJKLMNOPQRS
18 point (g:\ttfh_h\h0001017.ttf)

DEFGHIJKLMNOPQRSTUVWXYZ
18 point (g:\ttfh_h\h0001020.ttf)

CDEFGHIJKLMNOPQ
18 point (g:\ttfh_h\h0001021.ttf)

CDEFGHIJKLMNOPQRSTU
18 point (g:\ttfh_h\h0001022.ttf)

CDEFGHIJKLMNOPQRSTUV
18 point (g:\ttfh_h\h0001023.ttf)

BCDEFGHIJKLMNO
18 point (g:\ttfh_h\h0001024.ttf)

BCDEFGHIJKLMNOPQR
18 point (g:\ttfh_h\h0001025.ttf)

ABCDEFGHIJKLMNOPQRSTUV
18 point (g:\ttfh_h\h0001026.ttf)

ABCDEFGHIJKLMNOPQRSTUVW
18 point (g:\ttfh_h\h0001028.ttf)

ABCDEFGHIJKLMNOPQRS
18 point (g:\ttfh_h\h0001027.ttf)

ABCDEFGHIJKLMNOPQRSTU
18 point (g:\ttfh_h\h0001029.ttf)

ABCDEFGHIJKLMNOPQRSTUVWXYZabcdefghijkl
18 point (g:\ttfh_h\h0001030.ttf)

ABCDEFGHIJKLMNOPQRSTUVWXYZabcdefghijklm
18 point (g:\ttfh_h\h0001031.ttf)

ABCDEFGHIJKLMNOPQRSTUVWXYZabcd
18 point (g:\ttfh_h\h0001032.ttf)

ABCDEFGHIJKLMNOPQRSTUVWXYZabcdefg
18 point (g:\ttfh_h\h0001033.ttf)

ABCDEFGHIJKLMNOPQ
18 point (g:\ttfh_h\h0001037.ttf)

ABCDEFGHIJKLMNOPQRSTUVWX
18 point (g:\ttfh_h\h0001035.ttf)

ABCDEFGHIJKL
18 point (g:\ttfh_h\h0001036.ttf)

ABCDEFGHIJKLM
18 point (g:\ttfh_h\h0001038.ttf)

ABCDEFGHIJKLMNOP
18 point (g:\ttfh_h\h0001039.ttf)

ABCDEFGHIJKLMNOPQ
18 point (g:\ttfh_h\h0001040.ttf)

ABCDEFGHIJKLMNOPQRSTUVWXYZABCDEFGHIJKLMNOPQRSTUVWXYZ
18 point (g:\ttfh_h\h0001041.ttf)

ABCDEFGHIJKLMNOPQR
18 point (g:\ttfh_h\h0001042.ttf)

ABCDEFGHIJKLMNOPQR
18 point (g:\ttfh_h\h0001044.ttf)

ABCDEFGHIJKL
18 point (g:\ttfh_h\h0001043.ttf)

ABCDEFGHIJKLMNOPQRSTUV
18 point (g:\ttfh_h\h0000977.ttf)

ABCDEFGHIJKLM
22 point (g:\ttfi_i\0001046.ttf)

ABCDEFGHIJKLMN
22 point (g:\ttfi_i\0001049.ttf)

ABCDEFGHIJKLMNOPQRSTUV
22 point (g:\ttfi_i\0001050.ttf)

ABCDEFGHIJKLMNOPQRSTUV
22 point (g:\ttfi_i\0001052.ttf)

ABCDEFGHIJKLMNOPQRSTUVWXYZABC
22 point (g:\ttfi_i\0001051.ttf)

ABCDEFGHIJKLMNOPQRSTUV
22 point (g:\ttfi_i\0001054.ttf)

ABCDEFGHIJKLMNOP
22 point (g:\ttfi_i\0001055.ttf)

ABCDEFGHIJKLMNOP
22 point (g:\ttfi_i\0001059.ttf)

ABCDEFGHIJKLMNOP
22 point (g:\ttfi_i\0001057.ttf)

ABCDEFGHIJK
22 point (g:\ttfi_i\0001058.ttf)

ABCDEFGHIJKLMNOP
22 point (g:\ttfi_i\0001056.ttf)

ABCDEFGHIJKLM
22 point (g:\ttfi_i\0001060.ttf)

ABCDEFGHIJKLMNOPQRSTU
22 point (g:\ttfi_i\0001062.ttf)

ABCDEFGHIJKLMNOPQRSTU
22 point (g:\ttfi_i\0001066.ttf)

ABCDEFGHIJKLMNOPQRS
22 point (g:\ttfi_i\0001063.ttf)

ABCDEFGHIJKLMNOPQRSTUVWXYZab
22 point (g:\ttfi_i\0001064.ttf)

ABCDEFGHIJKLMN
22 point (g:\ttfi_i\0001065.ttf)

ABCDEFGHIJKLMNOPQ
22 point (g:\ttfi_i\0001067.ttf)

abcdefghijklmnopqrstuvwx
22 point (g:\ttfi_i\0001068.ttf)

ABCDEFGHIJKLMNOP
22 point (g:\ttfi_i\0001069.ttf)

ABCDEFGHIJKLMNOPQRSTUVWXYZa
22 point (g:\ttfi_i\0001070.ttf)

ABCDEFGHIJKLMNOPQRSTUVWXYZab
(g:\ttfi_i\0001071.ttf)

ABCDEFGHIJKLMNOPQRSTUVWXYZa
22 point (g:\ttfi_i\0001072.ttf)

ABCDEFGHIJKLMNOPQRSTUV
22 point (g:\ttfi_i\0001073.ttf)

ABCDEFGHIJKLMNOPQR
22 point (g:\ttfi_i\0001074.ttf)

ABCDEFGHIJKLMNOPQRSTU
22 point (g:\ttfi_i\0001075.ttf)

ᔕᐊᐃᐃᒍᔕᐁᐊᒼᒡᐃᒍᐃᐸᐳᑫᑕᐅ
22 point (g:\ttfi_i\0001077.ttf)

ABCDEFGHIJKLMNOPQRSTUVWXYZABCDEFGHIJK
22 point (g:\ttfi_i\0001078.ttf)

ABCDEFGHIJKLMNOPQRSTUVWXYZABC
22 point (g:\ttfi_i\0001079.ttf)

ABCDEFGHIJKLMNOPQRSTUVW
(g:\ttfi_i\0001080.ttf)

CDEFGHIJKLMNOPQRST
22 point   (g:\ttfj_k\j0001089.ttf)

EFGHIJKLMNOPORSTUVWXYZABCDEFGHI
22 point   (g:\ttfj_k\j0001090.ttf)

DEFGHIJKLMNOPORSTUVWXYZABCDEFGHI
22 point   (g:\ttfj_k\j0001093.ttf)

EFGHIJKLMNOPORSTUVWXYZABCDE
22 point   (g:\ttfj_k\j0001091.ttf)

CDEFGHIJKLMNOPORSTUVW
22 point   (g:\ttfj_k\j0001092.ttf)

DEFGHIJKLMNOPORSTUVWXYZA
22 point   (g:\ttfj_k\j0001094.ttf)

22 point   (g:\ttfj_k\j0001095.ttf)

3 DEFGH IJKLMNOPORSTU
22 point   (g:\ttfj_k\j0001098.ttf)

3 DEFGH IJKLMNOPORS
22 point   (g:\ttfj_k\j0001096.ttf)

BCDEFGH IJK
22 point   (g:\ttfj_k\j0001097.ttf)

BFUYPSELXOZWHRMCVT
22 point   (g:\ttfj_k\j0001100.ttf)

BFUYPSELXOZWHRMCVT
22 point   (g:\ttfj_k\j0001099.ttf)

CDEFGHIJKLMNOPORSTUVW
22 point   (g:\ttfj_k\j0001101.ttf)

CDEFGHIJKLMNOPORSTUVW
22 point   (g:\ttfj_k\j0001102.ttf)

CDEFGHIJKLMNOPORST
22 point   (g:\ttfj_k\j0001103.ttf)

BCDEFGHIJKLMNOP
22 point   (g:\ttfj_k\k0001104.ttf)

BCDEFGHIJKLMNOP
22 point   (g:\ttfj_k\k0001105.ttf)

CDEFGHIJKLMNOPQRST
(g:\ttfj_k\k0001106.ttf)

CDEFGHIJKLMNOP2RSTU
22 point   (g:\ttfj_k\k0001108.ttf)

BCDEFGHIJKLMNOPORSTUVWXYZabc
22 point   (g:\ttfj_k\k0001109.ttf)

ABCDEFGHIJKLMNO
22 point   (g:\ttfj_k\k0001110.ttf)

ABCDEFGHIJKLMNO
22 point   (g:\ttfj_k\k0001111.ttf)

ABCDEFGHIJKLMNOP2RSTU
22 point   (g:\ttfj_k\k0001112.ttf)

ABCDEFGHIJKLMNOP2RSTUU
22 point   (g:\ttfj_k\k0001113.ttf)

ABCDEFGHIJKLMNOP2R
22 point   (g:\ttfj_k\k0001114.ttf)

ABCDEFGHIJKLMNOP2RSTUVWXYZ
22 point   (g:\ttfj_k\k0001115.ttf)

ABCDEFGHIJKLMNO
22 point   (g:\ttfj_k\k0001116.ttf)

ABCDEFGHIJKLMNO
22 point   (g:\ttfj_k\k0001117.ttf)

ABCDEFGHIJKLMNOPQRST
22 point   (g:\ttfj_k\k0001118.ttf)

A B C D E F G H I
22 point   (g:\ttfj_k\k0001119.ttf)

A B C D E F G H I J K L M
22 point   (g:\ttfj_k\k0001120.ttf)

A B C D E F
22 point   (g:\ttfj_k\k0001121.ttf)

A B C D E F G H I
22 point   (g:\ttfj_k\k0001122.ttf)

A B C D E F G
22 point   (g:\ttfj_k\k0001123.ttf)

A B C D E F G H I J K L
22 point   (g:\ttfj_k\k0001124.ttf)

ABCDEFGHIJKLMNOPORST
22 point   (g:\ttfj_k\k0001127.ttf)

ABCDEFGHIJKLMNOPORST
22 point   (g:\ttfj_k\k0001128.ttf)

A B C D E F G H I J K L M
22 point   (g:\ttfj_k\k0001129.ttf)

ABCDEFGHIJKLMNOP2RSTUV
22 point (g:\ttfj_k\k0001133.ttf)

ABCDEFGHIJKLMNOP2R
22 point (g:\ttfj_k\k0001134.ttf)

ABCDEFGHIJKLMNOPQRSTUVW
22 point (g:\ttfj_k\k0001136.ttf)

ABCDEFGHIJKLMNOPQRST
22 point (g:\ttfj_k\k0001137.ttf)

ABCDEFGHIJ
22 point (g:\ttfj_k\k0001138.ttf)

ABCDEFGHIJKLMNOPQRST
22 point (g:\ttfj_k\k0001141.ttf)

ABCDEFGHIJKLMNOPQRS
22 point (g:\ttfj_k\k0001142.ttf)

ABCDEFGHIJKLMNOPQRST
22 point (g:\ttfj_k\k0001143.ttf)

ABCDEFGHIJKLMNOPQ
22 point (g:\ttfj_k\k0001144.ttf)

ABCDEFGHIJKLMNOPQ
22 point (g:\ttfj_k\k0001145.ttf)

ABCDEFGHIJKLMNOPQR
22 point (g:\ttfj_k\k0001146.ttf)

ABCDEFGHIJKLMN
22 point (g:\ttfj_k\k0001147.ttf)

ABCDEFGHIJKLMNOPQ
22 point (g:\ttfj_k\k0001148.ttf)

ABCDEFGHIJKLMNOPQR
22 point (g:\ttfj_k\k0001149.ttf)

ABCDEFGHIJKLMNOP
22 point (g:\ttfj_k\k0001154.ttf)

ABCDEFGHIJKLMNOP
22 point (g:\ttfj_k\k0001153.ttf)

ABCDEFGHIJKLM
22 point (g:\ttfj_k\k0001155.ttf)

ABCDEFGHIJKLMN
22 point (g:\ttfj_k\k0001156.ttf)

ABCDEFGHIJKLMNOP
22 point (g:\ttfj_k\k0001157.ttf)

Alt   Ctrl Del Esc Tab
22 point (g:\ttfj_k\k0001125.ttf)

A B C D E A B C D E F
22 point (g:\ttfj_k\k0001126.ttf)

ABCDEFGHIJKLMNOPQRS
22 point (g:\ttfj_k\j0001082.ttf)

ABCDEFGHIJKLMNOPQRS
22 point (g:\ttfj_k\j0001084.ttf)

ABCDEFGHIJKL
22 point (g:\ttfj_k\j0001083.ttf)

ABCDEFGHIJKLMNO
22 point (g:\ttfj_k\j0001085.ttf)

ABCDEFGHIJKLM
18 point   (g:\ttfl_m\0001160.ttf)

ABCDEFGHI
18 point   (g:\ttfl_m\0001161.ttf)

ABCDEFGHI
18 point   (g:\ttfl_m\0001162.ttf)

BCDEFGHIJKLMNOPQRSTUVWXYZabcdefgh
18 point   (g:\ttfl_m\0001164.ttf)

ABCDEFGHIJKLMNOPQRS
18 point   (g:\ttfl_m\0001166.ttf)

ABCDEFGHIJKLMNOPQRS
(g:\ttfl_m\0001167.ttf)

BCDEFGHIJKLMNOPQRSTUVW
(g:\ttfl_m\0001169.ttf)

BCDEFGHIJKLMNOPQRS
(g:\ttfl_m\0001170.ttf)

ABCDEFGHIJKLMNOPQRS
18 point   (g:\ttfl_m\0001171.ttf)

BCDEFGHIJKLMNOPQRSTUVWX
18 point   (g:\ttfl_m\0001172.ttf)

ABCDEFGHIJKLMNOP
18 point   (g:\ttfl_m\0001173.ttf)

BCDEFGHIJKLMNOPQRS
18 point   (g:\ttfl_m\0001175.ttf)

BCDEFGHIJKLMNOPQRSTUVWX
18 point   (g:\ttfl_m\0001176.ttf)

BCDEFGHIJKLMNOPQRSTUVWX
18 point   (g:\ttfl_m\0001177.ttf)

ABCDEFGHIJKLMNOP
18 point   (g:\ttfl_m\0001178.ttf)

BCDEFGHIJKLMNOPQRSTUVWXYZabc
18 point   (g:\ttfl_m\0001180.ttf)

BCDEFGHIJKLMNOPQRSTUVWXYZabcdefghi
18 point   (g:\ttfl_m\0001181.ttf)

BCDEFGHIJKLMNOPQRSTUVWXYZabcdefghi
18 point   (g:\ttfl_m\0001182.ttf)

BCDEFGHIJKLMNOPQRSTUVWXYZabcdefghij
18 point   (g:\ttfl_m\0001183.ttf)

BCDEFGHIJKLMNOPQRSTUVWXYZ
18 point   (g:\ttfl_m\0001184.ttf)

ABCDEFGHIJKLMNOPQRSTUVWXYZ
18 point   (g:\ttfl_m\0001186.ttf)

ABCDEFGHIJKLMNOPQ
18 point   (g:\ttfl_m\0001185.ttf)

ABCDEFGHIJKLMNOPQRSTU
18 point   (g:\ttfl_m\0001187.ttf)

ABCDEFGHIJKLMNOPQRSTUVWXYZABCDEFG
(g:\ttfl_m\0001188.ttf)

ABCDEFGHIJKLMNOPQRSTUVWXYZABCDEFG
18 point   (g:\ttfl_m\0001191.ttf)

ABCDEFGHIJKLMNOPQRSTUVWXYZABCD
18 point   (g:\ttfl_m\0001189.ttf)

ABCDEFGHIJKLMNOPQRSTUV
18 point   (g:\ttfl_m\0001190.ttf)

ABCDEFGHIJKLMNOPQRSTUVWXYZ
18 point   (g:\ttfl_m\0001192.ttf)

ABCDEFGHIJKLMNOPQRST
18 point   (g:\ttfl_m\0001193.ttf)

abcdefghijklmnopqr
18 point   (g:\ttfl_m\0001194.ttf)

ABCDEFGHIJKLMNOPQRSTUVWXY
18 point   (g:\ttfl_m\0001195.ttf)

ABCDEFGHIJK
18 point   (g:\ttfl_m\0001196.ttf)

ABCDEFGHIJK
18 point   (g:\ttfl_m\0001200.ttf)

ABCDEFG
18 point   (g:\ttfl_m\0001197.ttf)

ABCDEFGHIJK
18 point   (g:\ttfl_m\0001198.ttf)

ABCDEFGHIJK
18 point   (g:\ttfl_m\0001199.ttf)

ABCDEFGHI
18 point   (g:\ttfl_m\0001201.ttf)

ABCDEFGHIJKLMNOPQRSTUVWX
18 point   (g:\ttfl_m\0001202.ttf)

ABCDEFGHIJKLMNOPQRSTUV
18 point   (g:\ttfl_m\0001204.ttf)

ABCDEFGHIJKLMNOP
18 point   (g:\ttfl_m\0001205.ttf)

ABCDEFGHIJKLMNOPQRSTUVWX
18 point   (g:\ttfl_m\0001203.ttf)

ABCDEFGHIJKLMNOPQRS
18 point   (g:\ttfl_m\0001158.ttf)

ABCDGFGHIJKLM NOPQR
18 point (g:\ttfl_m\0001239.ttf)

A BCDGFGHIJ KL
18 point (g:\ttfl_m\0001240.ttf)

ABCDEFGHIJKLMNOP
18 point (g:\ttfl_m\0001242.ttf)

abcdefghijklmnopqrstuvwxyzabcdefghijk
18 point (g:\ttfl_m\0001243.ttf)

abcdefghijklmnopqrstuvwx
18 point (g:\ttfl_m\0001244.ttf)

abcdefghijklmnopqrstuvwxyzabc
18 point (g:\ttfl_m\0001245.ttf)

ABCDEFGHIJKLMNOPQRSTUV
18 point (g:\ttfl_m\0001246.ttf)

ABCDEFGHIJKLMNOPQRSTUV
18 point (g:\ttfl_m\0001247.ttf)

ABCDEFGHIJKLMNOPQRSTUV
18 point (g:\ttfl_m\0001250.ttf)

ABCDEFGHIJKLMNO
18 point (g:\ttfl_m\0001249.ttf)

ABCDEFGHIJKLMNOPQRSTUV
18 point (g:\ttfl_m\0001251.ttf)

ABCDEFGHIJKLMNOPQRSTUVWXYZab
18 point (g:\ttfl_m\0001253.ttf)

ABCDEFGHIJKLMN
18 point (g:\ttfl_m\0061254.ttf)

ABCDEFGHIJKLM
18 point (g:\ttfl_m\0001230.ttf)

ABCDEFGHIJKLM NOPQRSTUV
18 point (g:\ttfl_m\0001231.ttf)

ABCDEFGHIJKLM NOP
18 point (g:\ttfl_m\0001232.ttf)

ABCDEFGHIJKLMNOPQRSTU
18 point (g:\ttfl_m\0001234.ttf)

ABCDEFGHIJKLMNOPQRSTUVWXYZₐᵦ𝒸□ₑ□
18 point (g:\ttfl_m\0001235.ttf)

ABCDEFGHIJKLMNOPQRST
18 point (g:\ttfl_m\0001237.ttf)

ABCDEFGHIJKLMNOPQRST
18 point (g:\ttfl_m\0001238.ttf)

ABCDEFGHIJKLMNOPQRST
18 point (g:\ttfl_m\0001241.ttf)

ABCDEFGHIJKLMNOPQRSTUVW
18 point (g:\ttfl_m\0001207.ttf)

ABCDEFGHIJKLMNOPQRSTUVW
18 point (g:\ttfl_m\0001206.ttf)

ABCDEFGHIJKLMNOPQRS
18 point (g:\ttfl_m\0001208.ttf)

ABCDEFGHIJKLMNOPQRSTUV
18 point (g:\ttfl_m\0001209.ttf)

ABCDEFGHIJKLMNOPQRSTUV
18 point (g:\ttfl_m\0001213.ttf)

ABCDEFGHIJKLMNO
18 point (g:\ttfl_m\0001212.ttf)

ABCDEFGHIJKLMNOPQRST
18 point (g:\ttfl_m\0001214.ttf)

ABCDEFGHIJKLMNOPQRSTUVWXYZabcdef
18 point (g:\ttfl_m\0001216.ttf)

ABCDEFGHIJKLMNOPQRSTUVWXYZabcdef
18 point (g:\ttfl_m\0001218.ttf)

ABCDEFGHIJKLMNOPQRST
18 point (g:\ttfl_m\0001217.ttf)

ABCDEFGHIJKLMNOPQRS
18 point (g:\ttfl_m\0001219.ttf)

ABCDEFGHIJKLMNOPQRSTUVWX
18 point (g:\ttfl_m\0001220.ttf)

ABCDEFGHIJKLI
18 point (g:\ttfl_m\0001221.ttf)

ABCDEFGHIJKLMNOPQRSTU
18 point (g:\ttfl_m\0001222.ttf)

ABCDEFGHIJKLMNO
18 point (g:\ttfl_m\0001223.ttf)

ABCDEFGHIJKLMNOPQRST
18 point (g:\ttfl_m\0001224.ttf)

ABCDEFGHIJKLMNO
18 point (g:\ttfl_m\0001225.ttf)

ABCDEFGHIJKLMNOPQRSTUVWXYZabcde
18 point (g:\ttfl_m\0001226.ttf)

ABCDEFGHIJKLMNOPQRSTU
18 point (g:\ttfl_m\0001227.ttf)

ABCDEFGHIJKLMNOPQRSTUVWX
18 point (g:\ttfl_m\0001228.ttf)

ABCDEFGHIJKLM NOPQRS
18 point (g:\ttfl_m\0001229.ttf)

ABCDEFGHIJKLMNOP
18 point (g:\ttfl_m\0001255.ttf)

BCDEFGHIJKLMNOPQRSTU
18 point (g:\ttfl_m\0001256.ttf)

BCDEFGHIJKLMNOPQRST
18 point (g:\ttfl_m\0001257.ttf)

BCDEFGHIJKLMNOPQRSTUV
18 point (g:\ttfl_m\0001258.ttf)

ψωεϑϖϱςφ——→·‹›▷◁01
18 point (g:\ttfl_m\0001260.ttf)

ABCDEFGHIJKLMNOPQR
18 point (g:\ttfl_m\0001262.ttf)

BCDEFGHIJKLMNOPQRSTUV
18 point (g:\ttfl_m\0001264.ttf)

BCDEFGHIJKLMNOPQRSTUV
18 point (g:\ttfl_m\0001263.ttf)

BCDEFGHIJKLMNOPQRST
18 point (g:\ttfl_m\0001266.ttf)

BCDEFGHIJKLMNOPQRSTUVW
18 point (g:\ttfl_m\0001271.ttf)

BCDEFGHIJKLMNOPQRSTUVW
18 point (g:\ttfl_m\0001268.ttf)

BCDEFGHIJKLMNOPQRSTUVWX
18 point (g:\ttfl_m\0001273.ttf)

BCDEFGHIJKLMNOPQRSTUVWX
18 point (g:\ttfl_m\0001275.ttf)

abcdefghijklmnopqrstuvwxyzabcdefghijklmnopqrstuvwxyz
18 point (g:\ttfl_m\0001285.ttf)

abcdefghijklmnopqrstuvwxyzabcdefghijklmnopqrstuvwxyz
18 point (g:\ttfl_m\0001282.ttf)

abcdefghijklmnopqrstuvwxyzabcdefghijklmnop
(g:\ttfl_m\0001283.ttf)

abcdefghijklmnopqrstuvwxyzabcdefghijklmnopqrstuvwxyz
18 point (g:\ttfl_m\0001284.ttf)

abcdefghijklmnopqrstuvwxyzabcdefghijklmnopqrstuvwx
(g:\ttfl_m\0001286.ttf)

BCDEFGHIJKLMNOPQRSTUV
18 point (g:\ttfl_m\0001287.ttf)

BCDEFGHIJKLMNOPQRSTUVWXYZABCD
18 point (g:\ttfl_m\0001288.ttf)

BCDEFGHIJKLMNOPQRSTUVWXYZABCDEFGHIJ
18 point (g:\ttfl_m\0001289.ttf)

ABCDEFGHIJKLMNOPQRSTUVWXYZABCD
18 point (g:\ttfl_m\m0001290.ttf)

ABCDEFGHIJKLMNOPQRST
18 point (g:\ttfl_m\m0001291.ttf)

ABCDEFGHIJKLMNOPQRSTUVWX
18 point (g:\ttfl_m\m0001292.ttf)

ABCDEFGHIJKLMNOPQRSTUVWXYZABCDEFGHIJKLMNOP
18 point (g:\ttfl_m\m0001293.ttf)

ABCDEFGHIJKLMNOPQRSTUV
18 point (g:\ttfl_m\m0001295.ttf)

ABCDEFGHIJKLMNOPQRSTUV
18 point (g:\ttfl_m\m0001294.ttf)

ABCDEFGHIJKLMNOPQRSTUVWXYZa
18 point (g:\ttfl_m\m0001296.ttf)

ABCDEFGHIJKLMNOPQRSTU
18 point (g:\ttfl_m\m0001297.ttf)

ABCDEFGHIJKLMNOPQRSTUV
18 point (g:\ttfl_m\m0001299.ttf)

ABCDEFGHIJKLMNOPQRSTUVWX
18 point (g:\ttfl_m\m0001312.ttf)

ABCDEFGHIJKLMNOPQRSTUVWX
18 point (g:\ttfl_m\m0001313.ttf)

ABCDEFGHIJKLMNOPQRST
18 point (g:\ttfl_m\m0001314.ttf)

ABCDEFGHIJKLMNOPQRSTUVWXY
18 point (g:\ttfl_m\m0001315.ttf)

ABCDEFGHIJKLMNOPQRSTUVWXYZabcd
18 point (g:\ttfl_m\m0001316.ttf)

ABCDEFGHIJKLMNOPQRSTUV
18 point (g:\ttfl_m\m0001317.ttf)

ABCDEFGHIJKLMNOPQRSTUVWXYZab
18 point (g:\ttfl_m\m0001318.ttf)

ABCDEFGHIJKLMNOPQRSTUVWXYZabcdefghijklmnopq
18 point (g:\ttfl_m\m0001321.ttf)

ABCDEFGHIJKLMNOPQRSTU
18 point (g:\ttfl_m\m0001322.ttf)

ԱՊԳՂՏԷԾԿՀՀԻՁ ՌԼՄՆՈՖՒՐՍ
18 point (g:\ttfl_m\m0001323.ttf)

ABCDEFGHIJKLMNOPQRSTUVWXY
18 point (g:\ttfl_m\m0001324.ttf)

ABCDEFGHIJKLMNOPQRSTUVWXYZABCDEFGHIJKLMNOPQRSTUVWXYZ
18 point (g:\ttfl_m\m0001307.ttf)

ABCDEFGHIJKLMNOPQRSTUVWXYZABDEFHIJKLMNPQRS
18 point (g:\ttfl_m\m0001325.ttf)

ABCDEFGHIJKLMNOPQRSTUVWXYZAB DEF HIJKLMN
18 point (g:\ttfl_m\m0001326.ttf)

ABCDEFGHIJKLMNOPQRSTUV
18 point (g:\ttfl_m\m0001328.ttf)

ABCDEFGHIJKLMNOPQRSTU
18 point (g:\ttfl_m\m0001329.ttf)

ABCDEFGHIJKLMNOPQRSTUV
18 point (g:\ttfl_m\m0001330.ttf)

ABCDEFGHIJKLMNOPQRSTU
18 point (g:\ttfl_m\m0001331.ttf)

ABCDEFGHIJKLMNO
18 point (g:\ttfl_m\m0001332.ttf)

ABCDEFGHIJKLMNO
18 point (g:\ttfl_m\m0001333.ttf)

ABCDEFGHIJKL
18 point (g:\ttfl_m\m0001334.ttf)

ABCDEFGHIJKLMNOPQRSTUVWX
18 point (g:\ttfl_m\m0001335.ttf)

ABCDEFGHIJKLMNOPQR
18 point (g:\ttfl_m\m0001338.ttf)

ABCDEFGHIJKL
18 point (g:\ttfl_m\m0001339.ttf)

ABCDEFGHIJKLMNOPQRSTUVWXYZabcdefg
18 point (g:\ttfl_m\m0001342.ttf)

ABCDEFGHIJKLMNOPQRSTUV
18 point (g:\ttfl_m\m0001343.ttf)

ABCDEFGHIJKLMNOPQRS
18 point (g:\ttfl_m\m0001344.ttf)

ABCDEFGHIJKLMNOPQRSTUV
18 point (g:\ttfl_m\m0001345.ttf)

ABCDEFGHIJKLMNOPQRSTUV
18 point (g:\ttfl_m\m0001346.ttf)

ABCDEFGHIJKLMNOPQR
18 point (g:\ttfl_m\m0001347.ttf)

ABCDEFGHIJKLMNOPQRSTUV
18 point (g:\ttfl_m\m0001348.ttf)

ABCDEFGHIJKLMNOPQRSTUV
18 point (g:\ttfl_m\m0001349.ttf)

ABCDEFGHIJKLMNOPQRSTUV
18 point (g:\ttfl_m\m0001350.ttf)

ABCDEFGHIJKLMNO
18 point (g:\ttfl_m\m0001351.ttf)

ABCDEFGHIJKLMNOPQ
18 point (g:\ttfl_m\m0001352.ttf)

ABCDEFGHIJKLMNOPQRSTUV
18 point (g:\ttfl_m\m0001353.ttf)

ABCDEFGHIJKLMNOPQRSTUV
18 point (g:\ttfl_m\m0001360.ttf)

ABCDEFGHIJKLMNOPQ
18 point (g:\ttfl_m\m0001361.ttf)

ABCDEFGHIJKLMNOPQRSTU
18 point (g:\ttfl_m\m0001362.ttf)

ABCDEFGHIJKLMNOP
18 point (g:\ttfl_m\m0001363.ttf)

ABCDEFGHIJKLMNOPQR
18 point (g:\ttfl_m\m0001365.ttf)

ABCDEFGHIJKLMNO
18 point (g:\ttfl_m\m0001366.ttf)

ABCDEFGHIJKLMNOPQRSTUVWXYZabcdefghijklmn
18 point (g:\ttfl_m\m0001367.ttf)

ABCDEFGHIJKLMNODQ
18 point (g:\ttfl_m\m0001368.ttf)

ABCDEFGHIJKLMNOPQR
18 point (g:\ttfl_m\m0001369.ttf)

ABCDEFGHIJKLMNOPQRSTUV
18 point (g:\ttfl_m\m0001370.ttf)

ABCDEFGHIJKLMNOPQRS
18 point (g:\ttfl_m\m0001372.ttf)

ABCDEFGHIJKLMNOPQRS
18 point (g:\ttfl_m\m0001373.ttf)

ABCDEFGHIJKLMNO
18 point (g:\ttfl_m\m0001374.ttf)

ABCDEFGHIJKLMNOPQRSTUVW
18 point (g:\ttfl_m\m0001376.ttf)

ABCDEFGHIJKLMNOPQRSTUVWX
18 point (g:\ttfl_m\m0001375.ttf)

ABCDEFGHIJKLMNOPQRSTU
18 point (g:\ttfl_m\m0001377.ttf)

ABCDEFGHIJKLMNOPQRST
18 point (g:\ttfl_m\m0001378.ttf)

ABCDEFGHIJKLMNOPQRSTUVWXYZ
18 point (g:\ttfl_m\m0001379.ttf)

ABCDEFGHIJKL
18 point (g:\ttfl_m\0001168.ttf)

BCDEFGHIJKLMNOPQRS
18 point (g:\ttfl_m\0001276.ttf)

ABCDE7GHIJKLMNOPQRSTUUWXYZabcdefghijklmnopqrstuvwxyz
18 point (g:\ttfl_m\m0001304.ttf)

BCDEFGHIJKLMNOPQRSTUVWX
18 point (g:\ttfl_m\0001277.ttf)

BCDEFGHIJKLMNOPQRSTUVWX
18 point (g:\ttfl_m\0001279.ttf)

BCDEFGHIJKLMNOPQRS
(g:\ttfl_m\0001280.ttf)

cdefghijklmnopqrstuvwxyzabcdefghijklmnopqrstuvwxyz
(g:\ttfl_m\0001281.ttf)

BCDEFGHIJKLMNOPQRSTUVWXYZabcdefghijklmnopq
18 point (g:\ttfl_m\m0001301.ttf)

ABCDEFGHIJKLMNOPQRSTUVWX
18 point (g:\ttfl_m\0001174.ttf)

BCDEFGHIJKLMNOPQRSTUVWX
18 point (g:\ttfl_m\m0001310.ttf)

ABCDEFGHIJKLMNOPQRSTU
18 point (g:\ttfl_m\m0001381.ttf)

ABCDEFGHIJKLMN
18 point (g:\ttfl_m\m0001380.ttf)

ABCDEFGHIJKLMNOPQRSTUVWXY
18 point (g:\ttfl_m\m0001382.ttf)

ABCDEFGHIJKLMNOPQ
18 point (g:\ttfl_m\m0001383.ttf)

BCDEFGHIJKLMNOPQRSTUVWXYZab
18 point (g:\ttfl_m\m0001384.ttf)

BCDEFGHIJKLMNOPQRSTUVWXYZabcde
18 point (g:\ttfl_m\m0001385.ttf)

BCDEFGHIJKLMNOPQRSTUVWX
18 point (g:\ttfl_m\m0001388.ttf)

BCDEFGHIJKLMNOPQRSTUV
18 point (g:\ttfl_m\m0001390.ttf)

BCDEFGHIJKLMNOPQRSTU
18 point (g:\ttfl_m\m0001391.ttf)

BCDEFGHIJKLMNOPQRSTUV
18 point (g:\ttfl_m\m0001392.ttf)

ABCDEFGHIJKLMNOPQ
18 point (g:\ttfl_m\m0001394.ttf)

ABCDEFGHIJKLMNOPQRSTUVWXYZabcdefg
18 point (g:\ttfl_m\m0001395.ttf)

ABCDEFGHIJKLMNOPQRSTU
18 point (g:\ttfl_m\m0001396.ttf)

ABCDEFGHIJKLMNOPQRST
18 point (g:\ttfl_m\m0001397.ttf)

ABCDEFGHIJKLMNOPQRSTUVWX
18 point (g:\ttfl_m\m0001398.ttf)

ABCDEFGHIJKLMNOPQRSTUVWX
18 point (g:\ttfl_m\m0001402.ttf)

ABCDEFGHIJKLMNOPQRSTUVWX
18 point (g:\ttfl_m\m0001400.ttf)

ABCDEFGHIJKLMNOPQRSTUVW
18 point (g:\ttfl_m\m0001399.ttf)

ABCDEFGHIJKLMNOPQRSTUVW
18 point (g:\ttfl_m\m0001401.ttf)

ABCDEFGHI JKLMNOPQRSTUVWXYZabc
18 point (g:\ttfl_m\m0001403.ttf)

18 point (g:\ttfl_m\m0001404.ttf)

ABCDEFGHIJKLMNOPQRSTUVWXYZABCDEFGHIJKLMNOP
18 point (g:\ttfl_m\m0001406.ttf)

ABCDEFGHIJKLMNOPQRSTUVWXY
18 point (g:\ttfl_m\m0001407.ttf)

ABCDEFGHIJKLMNOPQRST
18 point (g:\ttfl_m\m0001408.ttf)

ABCDEFGHIJKLMNOPQRS
18 point (g:\ttfl_m\m0001409.ttf)

ABCDEFGHIJKLMNOPQRST
18 point (g:\ttfl_m\m0001410.ttf)

ABCDEFGHIJKLMNOPQRSTU
18 point (g:\ttfl_m\m0001411.ttf)

ABCDEFGHIJKLMNOPQRSTUVWX
18 point (g:\ttfl_m\m0001414.ttf)

ABCDEFGHIJKLMNOPQRSTUVW
18 point (g:\ttfl_m\m0001415.ttf)

ABCDEFGHIJKLMNOPQRSTUVWXYZabcdefghijklmnopq
18 point (g:\ttfl_m\m0001417.ttf)

ABCDEFGHIJKLMNOPQRSTUVWXY
18 point (g:\ttfl_m\m0001393.ttf)

18 point (g:\ttfl_m\m0001405.ttf)

ABCDEFGHIJKLMNOPQRSTU
18 point (g:\ttfn_o\n0001427.ttf)

ABCDEFGHIJKLMNOPQRSTUVWXYZA
18 point (g:\ttfn_o\n0001418.ttf)

ABCDEFGHIJKLMNOP
18 point (g:\ttfn_o\n0001422.ttf)

ABCDEFGHIJKLMNOP
18 point (g:\ttfn_o\n0001421.ttf)

ABCDEFGHIJKLMNOPQRSTUVW
18 point (g:\ttfn_o\n0001420.ttf)

ABCDEFGHIJKLMNOPQRSTUVW
18 point (g:\ttfn_o\n0001423.ttf)

ABCDEFGHIJKLMNOPQRS
18 point (g:\ttfn_o\n0001424.ttf)

ABCDEFGHIJKLMNOPQRSTUVW
18 point (g:\ttfn_o\n0001425.ttf)

ABCDEFGHIJKLMNOPQRSTU
18 point (g:\ttfn_o\n0001426.ttf)

ABCDEFGHIJKLMNOPQRSTU
18 point (g:\ttfn_o\n0001428.ttf)

ABCDEFGHIJKLMNOPQRSTUVWX
18 point (g:\ttfn_o\n0001429.ttf)

ABCDEFGHIJKLMNOPQRSTU
18 point (g:\ttfn_o\n0001431.ttf)

ABCDEFGHIJKLMNOPQ
18 point (g:\ttfn_o\n0001432.ttf)

ABCDEFGHIJKLMNOPQRSTUVWX
18 point (g:\ttfn_o\n0001433.ttf)

ABCDEFGHIJKLMNOPQRSTUVWX
18 point (g:\ttfn_o\n0001434.ttf)

ABCDEFGHIJKLMNOPQRSTUVW
18 point (g:\ttfn_o\n0001435.ttf)

ABCDEFGHIJKLMNOP
18 point (g:\ttfn_o\n0001436.ttf)

ABCDEFGHIJKLMNOPQRS
18 point (g:\ttfn_o\n0001437.ttf)

ABCDEFGHIJKLMNOPQRSTUVWXY
18 point (g:\ttfn_o\n0001438.ttf)

ABCDEFGHIJKLMNOPQRS
18 point (g:\ttfn_o\n0001439.ttf)

ABCDEFGHIJKLMNO
18 point (g:\ttfn_o\n0001440.ttf)

ABCDEFGHIJKLMNOPQRST
18 point (g:\ttfn_o\n0001441.ttf)

ABCDEFGHIJKLMNOPQRST
18 point (g:\ttfn_o\n0001442.ttf)

ABCDEFGHIJKLMNOPQRS
18 point (g:\ttfn_o\n0001443.ttf)

ABCDEFGHIJKLMNOPQRSTUV
18 point (g:\ttfn_o\n0001444.ttf)

ABCDEFGHIJKLMNOPQRSTUVWX
18 point (g:\ttfn_o\n0001445.ttf)

ABCDEFGHIJKLMNOPQRST
18 point (g:\ttfn_o\n0001446.ttf)

ABCDEFGHIJKLMNOPQRSTUV
18 point (g:\ttfn_o\n0001447.ttf)

ABCDEFGHIJKLMNOPQRSTUV
18 point (g:\ttfn_o\n0001448.ttf)

ABCDEFGHIJKLMNOPQRSTU
18 point (g:\ttfn_o\n0001450.ttf)

ABCDEFGHIJKLMNOPQRSTU
18 point (g:\ttfn_o\n0001451.ttf)

ABCDEFGHIJKLMNOPQRS
18 point (g:\ttfn_o\n0001453.ttf)

ABCDEFGHIJKLMNOPQRSTUVWX
18 point (g:\ttfn_o\n0001454.ttf)

ABCDEFGHIJKLMNOPQRST
18 point (g:\ttfn_o\n0001455.ttf)

ABCDEFGHIJKLMNO
18 point (g:\ttfn_o\n0001457.ttf)

ABCDEFGHIJKLMNOPQR
18 point (g:\ttfn_o\n0001458.ttf)

ABCDEFGHIJKLMNOPQRSTUVW
18 point (g:\ttfn_o\n0001459.ttf)

ABCDEFGHIJKLMNOPQRS
18 point (g:\ttfn_o\n0001461.ttf)

ABCDEFGHIJKLMNO
18 point (g:\ttfn_o\n0001460.ttf)

ABCDEFGHIJKLMNOPQRS
18 point (g:\ttfn_o\n0001462.ttf)

ABCDEFGHIJKLM
18 point (g:\ttfn_o\n0001463.ttf)

ABCDEFGHIJKLMNOPQRST
18 point (g:\ttfn_o\n0001464.ttf)

BCDEFGHIJKLMNOPQRST
18 point (g:\ttfn_o\n0001465.ttf)

BCDEFGHIJKLMNOPQRSTUVWXYZa
18 point (g:\ttfn_o\n0001466.ttf)

ABCDEFGHIJKLM
18 point (g:\ttfn_o\n0001467.ttf)

ABCDEFGHIJKLMNOP
18 point (g:\ttfn_o\n0001468.ttf)

BCDEFGHIJKLMNOPQRSTUV
18 point (g:\ttfn_o\n0001473.ttf)

BCDEFGHIJKLMNOPQRSTUVWXYZabcd
18 point (g:\ttfn_o\n0001475.ttf)

BCDEFGHIJKLMNOPQRSTUVWXYZab
18 point (g:\ttfn_o\n0001474.ttf)

BCDEFGHIJKLMNOPQRSTUVWXY
18 point (g:\ttfn_o\n0001477.ttf)

BCDEFGHIJKLMNOPQRSTUVWXY
18 point (g:\ttfn_o\n0001482.ttf)

BCDEFGHIJKLMNOPQRSTUVWX
18 point (g:\ttfn_o\n0001478.ttf)

BCDEFGHIJKLMNOPQRSTUVWXYZabcdefghijk
18 point (g:\ttfn_o\n0001479.ttf)

ABCDEFGHIJKLMNOP
18 point (g:\ttfn_o\n0001480.ttf)

BCDEFGHIJKLMNOPQRSTUVWXY
18 point (g:\ttfn_o\n0001481.ttf)

ABCDEFGHIJKLMNOPQRST
18 point (g:\ttfn_o\n0001483.ttf)

BCDEFGHIJKLMNOPQRSTUVWXYZabcdefghij
18 point (g:\ttfn_o\n0001484.ttf)

BCDEFGHIJKLMNOPQRSTUVWXYZa
18 point (g:\ttfn_o\n0001491.ttf)

BCDEFGHIJKLMNOPQRSTUVWXY
18 point (g:\ttfn_o\n0001486.ttf)

BCDEFGHIJKLMNOPQRSTUVWXYZabcdefghijklmn
18 point (g:\ttfn_o\n0001487.ttf)

BCDEFGHIJKLMNOPQRSTUVWXYZabcdefghijklmn
18 point (g:\ttfn_o\n0001488.ttf)

ABCDEFGHIJKLMNOPQ
18 point (g:\ttfn_o\n0001489.ttf)

BCDEFGHIJKLMNOPQRSTUVWXYZa
18 point (g:\ttfn_o\n0001490.ttf)

ABCDEFGHIJKLMNOPQRSTUVWXYZa
18 point (g:\ttfn_o\n0001485.ttf)

ABCDEFGHIJKLMNOPQRSTUVWXYZa
18 point (g:\ttfn_o\n0001492.ttf)

ABCDEFGHIJKLMNOPQRST
18 point (g:\ttfn_o\n0001493.ttf)

ABCDEFGHIJKLMNOPQRSTUVWXYZabcde
18 point (g:\ttfn_o\n0001494.ttf)

ABCDEFGHIJKLMNOPQRSTUVWXYZabcde
18 point (g:\ttfn_o\n0001498.ttf)

ABCDEFGHIJKLMNOPQRSTUVWXYZab
18 point (g:\ttfn_o\n0001495.ttf)

ABCDEFGHIJKLMNOPQRSTU
18 point (g:\ttfn_o\n0001496.ttf)

ABCDEFGHIJKLMNOPQRSTUVWXYZabcde
18 point (g:\ttfn_o\n0001497.ttf)

ABCDEFGHIJKLMNOPQRSTUVWX
18 point (g:\ttfn_o\n0001499.ttf)

ABCDEFGHIJKLMNOPQRST
18 point (g:\ttfn_o\n0001501.ttf)

ABCDEFGHIJKLMNOP2RSTUVWXYabc
18 point (g:\ttfn_o\n0001502.ttf)

ABCDEFGHIJKLMNOP2RSTUVWXYabcdefghij
18 point (g:\ttfn_o\n0001503.ttf)

ABCDEFGHIJKLMNOPQ
18 point (g:\ttfn_o\n0001504.ttf)

ABCDEFGHIJKLMNOPQRSTUVWXY
18 point (g:\ttfn_o\n0001505.ttf)

ABCDEFGHIJKLMNOPQRSTUV
18 point (g:\ttfn_o\n0001507.ttf)

ABCDEFGHIJKLMNOPQRSTUV
18 point (g:\ttfn_o\n0001506.ttf)

ABCDEFG
18 point (g:\ttfn_o\o0001510.ttf)

ABCDEFGHIJKLMNOPQRST
(g:\ttfn_o\o0001511.ttf)

ABCDEFGHIJKLMNOPQRSTUV
18 point (g:\ttfn_o\o0001515.ttf)

ABCDEFGHIJKLMNOPQRSTUV
18 point (g:\ttfn_o\o0001514.ttf)

ABCDEFGHIJKLMNOPQRSTU
18 point (g:\ttfn_o\o0001512.ttf)

ABCDEFGHIJKLMNOPQRSTUV
18 point   (g:\ttfn_o\o0001516.ttf)

ABCDEFGHIJKLMNOPQRS.
18 point   (g:\ttfn_o\o0001518.ttf)

ABCDEFGHIJKLMNOPQRS
18 point   (g:\ttfn_o\o0001519.ttf)

ABCDEFGHIJKLMNOPQRS
18 point   (g:\ttfn_o\o0001521.ttf)

ABCDEFGHIJKLM
18 point   (g:\ttfn_o\o0001520.ttf)

ABCDEFGHIJKLMNO
18 point   (g:\ttfn_o\o0001522.ttf)

ABCDEFGHIJKLMN
18 point   (g:\ttfn_o\o0001523.ttf)

ABCDEFGHIJKLMNOPQRSTUVWXYZabcdefghijklmnopqrstuv
18 point   (g:\ttfn_o\o0001524.ttf)

ABCDEFGHIJKLMNOPQRSTUVWXYZabcd
18 point   (g:\ttfn_o\o0001525.ttf)

ABCDEFGHIJKLMNOPQRSTUVWXYZabcdefghijklmnopqrstuvwxyz
18 point   (g:\ttfn_o\o0001526.ttf)

ABCDEFGHIJKLMNOPQRSTUVWXYZabcdefghijklmnopqrstuvwxyz
18 point   (g:\ttfn_o\o0001527.ttf)

ABCDEFGHIJKLMNOPQRSTUVWXYZabcdefghijklmn
18 point   (g:\ttfn_o\o0001528.ttf)

ABCDEFGHIJKLMNOPQRSTUVWXY
18 point   (g:\ttfn_o\o0001529.ttf)

ABCDEFGHIJKLMNOPQRSTUVWXY
18 point   (g:\ttfn_o\o0001530.ttf)

ABCDEFGHIJKLMNOPQ
18 point   (g:\ttfn_o\o0001531.ttf)

ABCDEFGHIJKLMNOPQRSTUVWXYZah
18 point   (g:\ttfn_o\o0001532.ttf)

ABCDEFGHIJKLMNOPQRSTUVWXYZah
18 point   (g:\ttfn_o\o0001536.ttf)

ABCDEFGHIJKLMNOPQRSTUVWXYZabcdefghijkl
18 point   (g:\ttfn_o\o0001533.ttf)

ABCDEFGHIJKLMNOPQRS
18 point   (g:\ttfn_o\o0001534.ttf)

ABCDEFGHIJKLMNOPQRSTUVWXYZah
18 point   (g:\ttfn_o\o0001535.ttf)

ABCDEFGHIJKLMNOPQRSTUVW
18 point   (g:\ttfn_o\o0001537.ttf)

ABCDEFGHIJKLMNOPQRSTUV
18 point   (g:\ttfn_o\o0001540.ttf)

ABCDEFGHIJKLMNOPQRSTUVW
18 point   (g:\ttfn_o\o0001539.ttf)

ABCDEFGHIJKLMNO
18 point   (g:\ttfn_o\o0001546.ttf)

ABCDEFGHIJKLMNOPQRSTUV
18 point   (g:\ttfn_o\o0001541.ttf)

ABCDEFGHIJKLMN
18 point   (g:\ttfn_o\o0001542.ttf)

ABCDEFGHIJKLMNOPQRSTUVWXY
18 point   (g:\ttfn_o\o0001543.ttf)

ABCDEFGHIJKLMNOPQRSTUVWXYZabcdef
(g:\ttfn_o\o0001544.ttf)

ABCDEFGHIJKLMNOPQRJ
18 point   (g:\ttfn_o\o0001547.ttf)

ABCDEFGHIJKLMNOPQRSTUVWXY
18 point   (g:\ttfn_o\o0001548.ttf)

ABCDEFGHIJKLMNOPQ
18 point   (g:\ttfn_o\o0001549.ttf)

ABCDEFGHIJKLMNOPQRSTU
18 point   (g:\ttfn_o\o0001550.ttf)

ABCDEFGHIJKLMNOPQRSTUV
18 point   (g:\ttfn_o\o0001552.ttf)

ABCDEFGHIJKLMNOPQRSTUVWXYZabcdef
18 point   (g:\ttfn_o\o0001553.ttf)

ABCDEFGHIJKLMNOPQRSTUVWXYZabcdef
18 point   (g:\ttfn_o\o0001551.ttf)

ABCDEFGHIJKLMNOPQRSTUVWXYZabcdef
18 point   (g:\ttfn_o\o0001554.ttf)

ABCDEFGHIJKLMNOPQRSTUVWXYZabcdef
18 point   (g:\ttfn_o\o0001555.ttf)

ABCDEFGHIJKLMNOPQRSTUVWXYZabcdef
18 point   (g:\ttfn_o\o0001558.ttf)

ABCDEFGHIJKLMNOPQRSTUV
18 point   (g:\ttfn_o\o0001556.ttf)

ABCDEFGHIJKLMNOPQRSTUVWXYZabcdef
18 point   (g:\ttfn_o\o0001557.ttf)

ABCDEFGHIJKLMNOPQRSTUVWXYZabcdefghijklm
18 point   (g:\ttfn_o\o0001559.ttf)

ABCDEFGHIJKLMNOPQRSTUVWXY
18 point   (g:\ttfn_o\o0001560.ttf)

ABCDEFGHIJKLMNOPQRSTUVWXYZabcdefg
18 point (g:\ttfn_o\o0001561.ttf)

ABCDEFGHIJKLMNOPQRSTUVWXYZabcdefg
18 point (g:\ttfn_o\o0001564.ttf)

ABCDEFGHIJKLMNOPQRSTUVWXYZabcdefghijklmnopqrst
18 point (g:\ttfn_o\o0001562.ttf)

ABCDEFGHIJKLMNOPQRSTUV
18 point (g:\ttfn_o\o0001563.ttf)

ABCDEFGHIJKLMNOPQRSTUVWXYZabcdefghijklmn
18 point (g:\ttfn_o\o0001565.ttf)

ABCDEFGHIJKLMNOPQRSTUV
18 point (g:\ttfn_o\o0001568.ttf)

ABCDEFGHIJKLMNO
18 point (g:\ttfn_o\o0001569.ttf)

ABCDEFGHIJKLMNOPQRSTUVWXYZ
18 point (g:\ttfn_o\o0001570.ttf)

ABCDEFGHIJKLMNOPQR
18 point (g:\ttfn_o\o0001571.ttf)

ABCDEFGHIJKLMNOPQR
18 point (g:\ttfn_o\o0001572.ttf)

ABCDEFGHIJKLMNOPQR
18 point (g:\ttfn_o\o0001573.ttf)

ABCDEFGHIJKLMNOPQRSTUVWXYZabc
18 point (g:\ttfn_o\o0001580.ttf)

ABCDEFGHIJKLMNOPQRSTUVWXYZabc
18 point (g:\ttfn_o\o0001584.ttf)

ABCDEFGHIJKLMNOPQRSTUVWXYZa
18 point (g:\ttfn_o\o0001581.ttf)

ABCDEFGHIJKLMNOPQRSTUVWXYZabcdefghijklm
18 point (g:\ttfn_o\o0001582.ttf)

ABCDEFGHIJKLMNOPQRST
18 point (g:\ttfn_o\o0001583.ttf)

ABCDEFGHIJKLMNOPQRSTUVW
18 point (g:\ttfn_o\o0001585.ttf)

ABCDEFGHIJKLMNOPQRSTUVW
18 point (g:\ttfn_o\o0001586.ttf)

ABCDEFGHIJKLMNOPQ
18 point (g:\ttfn_o\o0001587.ttf)

ABCDEFGHIJKLMNOPQRSTUVW
18 point (g:\ttfn_o\o0001588.ttf)

ABCDEFGHIJKLMNOPQRSTUVWXYZ
18 point (g:\ttfn_o\n0001469.ttf)

ABCDEFGHIJKLMNOPQRSTUVWXYZ
18 point (g:\ttfn_o\n0001472.ttf)

ABCDEFGHIJKLMNOPQRSTUVWXYZabcdefghijkl
18 point (g:\ttfn_o\n0001470.ttf)

ABCDEFGHIJKLMNOPO
18 point (g:\ttfn_o\n0001471.ttf)

ABCDEFGHIJKLMNOPQR
18 point (g:\ttfn_o\o0001574.ttf)

ABCDEFGHIJKLMNOPQR
18 point (g:\ttfn_o\o0001578.ttf)

ABCDEFGHIJKLMNOPQ
18 point (g:\ttfn_o\o0001575.ttf)

ABCDEFGHIJKLMNOPQRSTUVWX
18 point (g:\ttfn_o\o0001576.ttf)

ABCDEFGHIJKL
18 point (g:\ttfn_o\o0001577.ttf)

ABCDEFGHIJKLMN
18 point (g:\ttfn_o\o0001579.ttf)

ABCDEFGHIJKLMNOPQR
18 point (g:\ttfp_q\p0001592.ttf)

ABCDEFGHIJKLMNOPQRSTUVW
18 point (g:\ttfp_q\p0001590.ttf)

ABCDEFGHIJKL
18 point (g:\ttfp_q\p0001591.ttf)

ABCDEFGHIJKLMNOPQR
18 point (g:\ttfp_q\p0001593.ttf)

ABCDEFGHIJKLMNOPQR
18 point (g:\ttfp_q\p0001589.ttf)

ABCDEFGHIJKLMNOPQRSTU
18 point (g:\ttfp_q\p0001594.ttf)

ABCDEFGHIJKLMN
18 point (g:\ttfp_q\p0001595.ttf)

ABCDEFGHIJKLMNOPQRSTU
(g:\ttfp_q\p0001596.ttf)

ABCDEFGHIJKLMNOPQRSTU
18 point (g:\ttfp_q\p0001600.ttf)

ABCDEFGHIJKLMNOPQRS
18 point (g:\ttfp_q\p0001597.ttf)

ABCDEFGHIJKLMNOPQRSTUVWXYZAB
18 point (g:\ttfp_q\p0001598.ttf)

ABCDEFGHIJKLM
18 point (g:\ttfp_q\p0001599.ttf)

ABCDEFGHIJKLMNOPQRSTU
(g:\ttfp_q\p0001601.ttf)

ABCDEFGHIJKLMNOP
(g:\ttfp_q\p0001602.ttf)

ABCDEFGHIJKLMNOPQRSTU
18 point (g:\ttfp_q\p0001603.ttf)

ABCDEFGHIJKLMNOPQRSTUV
18 point (g:\ttfp_q\p0001604.ttf)

ABCDEFGHIJKLMNOPQRST
18 point (g:\ttfp_q\p0001605.ttf)

ABCDEFGHIJKLMNOPQRSTUV
18 point (g:\ttfp_q\p0001608.ttf)

ABCDEFGHIJKLMNOPQRSTUV
18 point (g:\ttfp_q\p0001610.ttf)

ABCDEFGHIJKLMNOPQRST
18 point (g:\ttfp_q\p0001611.ttf)

ABCDEFGHIJKLMNOPQRSTU
18 point (g:\ttfp_q\p0001612.ttf)

ABCDEFGHIJKLMNOPQ
18 point (g:\ttfp_q\p0001613.ttf)

ABCDEFGHIJKLMNOPQRSTUV
(g:\ttfp_q\p0001614.ttf)

ABCDEFGHIJKLMNOPQRSTUVWXYZabcde
18 point (g:\ttfp_q\p0001615.ttf)

ABCDEFGHIJKLMNOPQR
18 point (g:\ttfp_q\p0001616.ttf)

ABCDEFGHIJKLMNOPQRSTU
18 point (g:\ttfp_q\p0001617.ttf)

ABCDEFGHIJKLMNOPQRSTUVWXYZabc
18 point (g:\ttfp_q\p0001618.ttf)

ABCDEFGHIJKLMN
18 point (g:\ttfp_q\p0001619.ttf)

ABCDEFGHIJKLMNOPQRSTUVWXY
18 point (g:\ttfp_q\p0001620.ttf)

ABCDEFGHIJKLMNOPQRSTUVWXYZab
18 point (g:\ttfp_q\p0001621.ttf)

ABCDEFGHIJKLMNOPQRSTUVWXYZabcdefghijklmnop
18 point (g:\ttfp_q\p0001622.ttf)

ABCDEFGHIJKLMNOPQRSTUV
18 point (g:\ttfp_q\p0001623.ttf)

ABCDEFGHIJKLMNOPQR
(g:\ttfp_q\p0001624.ttf)

ABCDEFGHIJKLMNOPQRSTUVWX
18 point (g:\ttfp_q\p0001626.ttf)

ABCDEFGHIJKLMNOPQRSTUV
18 point (g:\ttfp_q\p0001627.ttf)

ABCDEFGHIJKLMNOPQRST
18 point (g:\ttfp_q\p0001628.ttf)

ABCDEFGHIJKLMNOPQRST
18 point (g:\ttfp_q\p0001632.ttf)

ABCDEFGHIJKLMNOPQRS
18 point (g:\ttfp_q\p0001629.ttf)

ABCDEFGHIJKLMNOPQRSTUVWXYZ
18 point (g:\ttfp_q\p0001630.ttf)

ABCDEFGHIJKLMN
18 point (g:\ttfp_q\p0001631.ttf)

ABCDEFGHIJKLMNOP
18 point (g:\ttfp_q\p0001633.ttf)

ABCDEFGHIJKLMNOPQRST
18 point (g:\ttfp_q\p0001634.ttf)

ABCDEFGHIJKLMNOPQRSTUVWX
18 point (g:\ttfp_q\p0001635.ttf)

ABCDEFGHIJKLMNOPQRSTUVWX
18 point (g:\ttfp_q\p0001636.ttf)

BCDEFGHIJKLMNOPQRSTUVWXYZabcdefghijklmnopqrstuvwxyz
18 point (g:\ttfp_q\p0001637.ttf)

ABCDEFGHIJKLMNOPQRSTUV
18 point (g:\ttfp_q\p0001638.ttf)

ABCDEFGHIJKLMNOPQRSTUVWXYZab
18 point (g:\ttfp_q\p0001639.ttf)

ABCDEFGHIJKLMNOPQRSTUVWXYZabcdefghijklmnopqrst
18 point (g:\ttfp_q\p0001640.ttf)

ABCDEFGHIJKLMNOPQR
18 point (g:\ttfp_q\p0001641.ttf)

ABCDEFGHIJKLMNOPQRSTUV
18 point (g:\ttfp_q\p0001642.ttf)

ABCDEFGHIJKLMNOPQRSTUV
(g:\ttfp_q\p0001644.ttf)

ABCDEFGHIJKLMNOPQRSTUV
18 point (g:\ttfp_q\p0001646.ttf)

ABCDEFGHIJKLMNO
18 point (g:\ttfp_q\p0001645.ttf)

ABCDEFGHIJKLMNOPQ
18 point (g:\ttfp_q\p0001647.ttf)

ABCDEFGHIJKLMNOPQR
18 point (g:\ttfp_q\p0001648.ttf)

ABCDEFGHIJKLMNOPQ
18 point (g:\ttfp_q\p0001649.ttf)

ABCDEFGHIJKL
(g:\ttfp_q\p0001650.ttf)

ABCDEFGHIJKLMN
18 point (g:\ttfp_q\p0001651.ttf)

ABCDEFGHIJKLMNOPQR
18 point (g:\ttfp_q\p0001652.ttf)

ABCDEFGHIJKLMNOPQRSTUV
18 point (g:\ttfp_q\p0001654.ttf)

(g:\ttfp_q\p0001656.ttf)

ABCDEFGHIJKLMNOPQRSTU
18 point (g:\ttfp_q\p0001657.ttf)

ABCDEFGHIJKLMNOPQRS
18 point (g:\ttfp_q\p0001659.ttf)

ABCDEFGHIJKLMNOPQRSTU
18 point (g:\ttfp_q\p0001660.ttf)

ABCDEFGHIJKLMNOPQRSTUVWXYZab
18 point (g:\ttfp_q\p0001661.ttf)

ABCDEFGHIJKLMNOPQRSTUVW
18 point (g:\ttfp_q\p0001662.ttf)

ABCDEFGHIJKLMNOPQRSTUVW
18 point (g:\ttfp_q\p0001664.ttf)

ABCDEFGHIJKLMNO
18 point (g:\ttfp_q\p0001663.ttf)

ABCDEFGHIJKLMNOPQR
18 point (g:\ttfp_q\p0001665.ttf)

ABCDEFGHIJKLMNOPQRSTUVWXYZ
18 point (g:\ttfp_q\p0001666.ttf)

ABCDEFGHIJKLMNOPQRSTUVWXYZabcdefghijklm
18 point (g:\ttfp_q\p0001667.ttf)

ABCDEFGHIJKLMNOPQRSTUVWXYZa
(g:\ttfp_q\p0001671.ttf)

ABCDEFGHIJKLMNOPQRSTUVWXYZa
18 point (g:\ttfp_q\p0001669.ttf)

ABCDEFGHIJKLMNOPQRSTUVWXY
18 point (g:\ttfp_q\p0001670.ttf)

ABCDEFGHIJKLMNOPQRSTUVWXYZa
18 point (g:\ttfp_q\p0001672.ttf)

ABCDEFGHIJKLMNOPQRSTUVWXYZa
(g:\ttfp_q\p0001673.ttf)

ABCDEFGHIJKLMNOPQRSTUV
18 point (g:\ttfp_q\p0001674.ttf)

ABCDEFGHIJKLMNOPQRST
18 point (g:\ttfp_q\p0001675.ttf)

ABCDEFGHIJKLMNOPQRST
18 point (g:\ttfp_q\p0001676.ttf)

ABCDEFGHIJKLMNOPQRSTUVWXY
18 point (g:\ttfp_q\p0001677.ttf)

ABCDEFGHIJKLMNOPQRSTUVWXY
18 point (g:\ttfp_q\p0001681.ttf)

ABCDEFGHIJKLMNOPQRSTUVW
18 point (g:\ttfp_q\p0001678.ttf)

ABCDEFGHIJKLMNOPQRSTUVWXYZabcdefghijkl
18 point (g:\ttfp_q\p0001679.ttf)

ABCDEFGHIJKLMNOPQ
18 point (g:\ttfp_q\p0001680.ttf)

ABCDEFGHIJKLMNOPQRSTUVWXYZab
18 point (g:\ttfp_q\p0001682.ttf)

ABCDEFGHIJKLMNOPQRS
18 point (g:\ttfp_q\p0001683.ttf)

ABCDEFGHIJKLMNOPQRSTUVW
(g:\ttfp_q\p0001685.ttf)

ABCDEFGHIJKLMNOPQRSTUVW
18 point (g:\ttfp_q\p0001684.ttf)

ABCDEFGHIJKLMNOPQRSTUVWX
18 point (g:\ttfp_q\p0001687.ttf)

ABCDEFGHIJKLMNOPQRSTUVWX
18 point (g:\ttfp_q\p0001689.ttf)

ABCDEFGHIJKLMNOPQR
18 point (g:\ttfp_q\p0001690.ttf)

ABCDEFGHIJKLMNOPQR
18 point (g:\ttfp_q\p0001693.ttf)

ABCDEFGHIJKLMNOPQRSTUVW
18 point (g:\ttfp_q\p0001691.ttf)

ABCDEFGHIJKL
18 point (g:\ttfp_q\p0001692.ttf)

ABCDEFGHIJKLMN
18 point (g:\ttfp_q\p0001694.ttf)

ABCDEFGHIJKLMNOPQRSTUVW
18 point (g:\ttfp_q\p0001695.ttf)

ABCDEFGHIJKLM
18 point (g:\ttfp_q\p0001697.ttf)

ABCDEFGHIJKLMNOPQRST
(g:\ttfp_q\p0001696.ttf)

ABCDEFGHIJKLMNOPQRSTUV
18 point (g:\ttfp_q\p0001698.ttf)

ABCDEFGHIJKLMNOPQRSTUV
18 point (g:\ttfp_q\p0001701.ttf)

ABCDEFGHIJKLMNOPQRSTUVWXYZa
18 point (g:\ttfp_q\p0001699.ttf)

ABCDEFGHIJKLMNO
18 point (g:\ttfp_q\p0001700.ttf)

ABCDEFGHIJKLMNOPQRSTUVWXY
18 point (g:\ttfp_q\p0001702.ttf)

ABCDEFGHIJKLMNOPQR
18 point (g:\ttfp_q\p0001703.ttf)

ABCDEFGHIJKLMNOPQRSTUVWXYZabcdefghijklmnop
18 point (g:\ttfp_q\p0001704.ttf)

ABCDEFGHIJKLMNOPQRSTUV
18 point (g:\ttfp_q\p0001706.ttf)

ABCDEFGHIJKLMNOPQRSTUVWXY
18 point (g:\ttfp_q\p0001707.ttf)

ABCDEFGHIJKLMNOPQRSTUV
18 point (g:\ttfp_q\p0001709.ttf)

ABCDEFGHIJKLMNOPQRSTUV
18 point (g:\ttfp_q\p0001710.ttf)

ABCDEFGHIJKLMNOPQRSTUV
18 point (g:\ttfp_q\p0001711.ttf)

ABCDEFGHIJKLMNOPQR
18 point (g:\ttfp_q\p0001714.ttf)

ABCDEFGHIJKLMNOPQRSTUVWX
18 point (g:\ttfp_q\p0001715.ttf)

ABCDEFGHIJ
18 point (g:\ttfp_q\p0001716.ttf)

ABCDEFGHIJ
18 point (g:\ttfp_q\p0001717.ttf)

ABCDEFGHIJKLMN
18 point (g:\ttfp_q\p0001719.ttf)

ABCDEFG
18 point (g:\ttfp_q\p0001720.ttf)

ABCDEFGHIJKLMNOPQRST
18 point (g:\ttfp_q\p0001718.ttf)

ABCDEFGHIJKL
18 point (g:\ttfp_q\p0001721.ttf)

ABCDEFGH
18 point (g:\ttfp_q\p0001722.ttf)

ABCDEFGHIJKLMNOPQRSTUV
18 point (g:\ttfp_q\p0001724.ttf)

ABCDEFGHIJKLMNOPQRSTUVW
18 point (g:\ttfp_q\p0001725.ttf)

ABCDEFGHIJKLMNOPQRSTU
18 point (g:\ttfp_q\p0001726.ttf)

ABCDEFGHIJKLMNOPQRSTU
18 point (g:\ttfp_q\p0001728.ttf)

ABCDEFGHIJKLMN
18 point (g:\ttfp_q\p0001727.ttf)

ABCDEFGHIJKLMNOPQRSTUVW
18 point (g:\ttfp_q\p0001729.ttf)

ABCDEFGHIJKLMNOPQRSTU
18 point (g:\ttfp_q\p0001730.ttf)

ABCDEFGHIJKLMNOPQRSTUVWXYZabcdefghij
18 point   (g:\ttfp_q\p0001732.ttf)

ABCDEFGHIJKLMNOPQRSTUVWXYZabcdefghij
18 point   (g:\ttfp_q\p0001734.ttf)

ABCDEFGHIJKLMNOPQRSTUV
18 point   (g:\ttfp_q\p0001733.ttf)

ABCDEFGHIJKLMNOPQRSTUVWXYZabcdefghij
18 point   (g:\ttfp_q\p0001735.ttf)

ABCDEFGHIJJKLMNOPQRS
18 point   (g:\ttfp_q\p0001736.ttf)

ABCDEFGHIJJKLMNOPQRS
18 point   (g:\ttfp_q\p0001739.ttf)

ABCDEFGHIJJKLMNOPQRSTUVWX
18 point   (g:\ttfp_q\p0001737.ttf)

ABCDEFGHIJJKL
18 point   (g:\ttfp_q\p0001738.ttf)

ABCDEFGHIJJKLMNO
18 point   (g:\ttfp_q\p0001740.ttf)

ABCDEFGHIJKLMNOPQRSTUVWXYZ
18 point   (g:\ttfp_q\p0001741.ttf)

ABCDEFGHIJJKLMNOPQRS
18 point   (g:\ttfp_q\p0001742.ttf)

ABCDEFGHIJKLMNOPQRSTUVWX
18 point   (g:\ttfp_q\p0001745.ttf)

ABCDEFGHIJKLMNOPQRSTUV
18 point   (g:\ttfp_q\p0001743.ttf)

ABCDEFGHIJKLMNOPQRSTUV
18 point   (g:\ttfp_q\p0001744.ttf)

ABCDI I GHI IJKI MNO
18 point   (g:\ttfp_q\p0001747.ttf)

ABCD G JI OPQPS U
18 point   (g:\ttfp_q\p0001746.ttf)

ABCDI I GHI IJKI MNOPQR
18 point   (g:\ttfp_q\p0001749.ttf)

ABCDEFGHIJKLMNOPQRSTUV
18 point   (g:\ttfp_q\p0001750.ttf)

ABCDEFGHIJKLMNOPQRSTUV
18 point   (g:\ttfp_q\p0001753.ttf)

ABCDEFGHIJKLMNOPQRSTU
18 point   (g:\ttfp_q\p0001751.ttf)

ABCDEFGHIJKLMNO
18 point   (g:\ttfp_q\p0001752.ttf)

ABCDEFGHIJKLMNOPQ
18 point   (g:\ttfp_q\p0001754.ttf)

ABCDEFGHIJKLMNOPQRSTUV
18 point   (g:\ttfp_q\p0001755.ttf)

ABCDEFGHIJKLMNOPQRSTU
18 point   (g:\ttfp_q\p0001756.ttf)

ABCDEFGHIJKLMNO
18 point   (g:\ttfp_q\p0001757.ttf)

ABCDEFGHIJKLMNOPQRSTUVWXYZa
18 point   (g:\ttfp_q\p0001758.ttf)

ABCDEFGHIJKLMNOPQRSTUVWXYZa
18 point   (g:\ttfp_q\p0001759.ttf)

ABCDEFGHIJKLMNOPQRSTUVWXYP
18 point   (g:\ttfp_q\p0001760.ttf)

ABCDEFGHIJKLMNOPQRSTUVWXYZabcdefghij
18 point   (g:\ttfp_q\p0001761.ttf)

ABCDEFGHIJKLMNOPQR
18 point   (g:\ttfp_q\p0001762.ttf)

ABCDEFGHIJKLMNOPQRSTUVWXYZabcdefg
18 point   (g:\ttfp_q\p0001763.ttf)

ABCDEFGHIJKLMNOPQRSTUV
18 point   (g:\ttfp_q\p0001764.ttf)

ABCDEFGHIJKLMNOPQRSTUVWXYZABCDEFGHI
18 point   (g:\ttfp_q\q0001765.ttf)

ABCDEFGHIJKLMNOPQRSTUVWX
18 point   (g:\ttfp_q\q0001768.ttf)

ABCDEFGHIJKLMNOPQRSTUVWX
18 point   (g:\ttfp_q\q0001766.ttf)

ABCDEFGHIJKLMNOPQRSTUV
18 point   (g:\ttfp_q\q0001769.ttf)

ABCDEFGHIJKLMNOPQRSTUV
18 point   (g:\ttfp_q\q0001767.ttf)

ABCDEFGHIJKLMNOPQRSTUVWXYZ
18 point   (g:\ttfp_q\q0001771.ttf)

ABCDEFGHIJKLMNOPQRSTUVWX
18 point   (g:\ttfp_q\q0001772.ttf)

ABCDEFGHIJKLMNOPQRSTUVW
18 point   (g:\ttfp_q\q0001773.ttf)

ABCDEFGHIJKLMNOPQRSTUVWXYZabcdefghijklmnop
18 point   (g:\ttfp_q\p0001705.ttf)

abcdefghijklmnopqrstuvwxyzabcdefghijklmnopqrstuvwxy
18 point (g:\ttfr_r\r0001777.ttf)

abcdefghijklmnopqrstuvwxyzabcdefghijklmnopqrs
18 point (g:\ttfr_r\r0001775.ttf)

abcdefghijklmnopqrstuvwxyzabcdefgh
18 point (g:\ttfr_r\r0001776.ttf)

abcdefghijklmnopqrstuvwxyzabcdefghijklmnopqrstuvwxy
18 point (g:\ttfr_r\r0001774.ttf)

abcdefghijklmnopqrstuvwxyzabcdefghij
18 point (g:\ttfr_r\r0001778.ttf)

ABCDEFGHIJKLMNOPQRSTU
18 point (g:\ttfr_r\r0001779.ttf)

ABCDEFGHIJKLMNOPQRST
18 point (g:\ttfr_r\r0001781.ttf)

ABCDEFGHIJKLMNOPQRSTUVWXYZabcde
18 point (g:\ttfr_r\r0001782.ttf)

ABCDEFGHIJKLMN
18 point (g:\ttfr_r\r0001783.ttf)

ABCDEFGHIJKLMN
18 point (g:\ttfr_r\r0001784.ttf)

ABCDEFGHIJKLMNOPQRSTU
18 point (g:\ttfr_r\r0001785.ttf)

ABCDEFGHIJKLMNOPQ
18 point (g:\ttfr_r\r0001786.ttf)

ABCDEFGHIJKLMNOPQRSTU
18 point (g:\ttfr_r\r0001787.ttf)

ABCDEFGHIJKLMNOPQRSTUV
18 point (g:\ttfr_r\r0001789.ttf)

ABCDEFGHIJKLMN-OPQRSTUV
3 point (g:\ttfr_r\r0001790.ttf)

ABCDEFGHIJKLMNOPQRSTUV
18 point (g:\ttfr_r\r0001793.ttf)

ABCDEFGHIJKLMNOPQRSTUVWXYZab
18 point (g:\ttfr_r\r0001791.ttf)

ABCDEFGHIJKLMN
18 point (g:\ttfr_r\r0001792.ttf)

ABCDEFGHIJKLMN-OPQ
18 point (g:\ttfr_r\r0001794.ttf)

ABCDEFGHIJKLMN-OPQRSTUV
18 point (g:\ttfr_r\r0001795.ttf)

ABCDEFGHIJKLMNOPQRSTUVWXYZa
18 point (g:\ttfr_r\r0001796.ttf)

ABCDEFGHIJKLMNOPQRSTUVWXYZa
18 point (g:\ttfr_r\r0001800.ttf)

ABCDEFGHIJKLMNOPQRSTUVWX
18 point (g:\ttfr_r\r0001797.ttf)

ABCDEFGHIJKLMNOPQRSTUVWXYZabcdefghijklmno
18 point (g:\ttfr_r\r0001798.ttf)

ABCDEFGHIJKLMNOPQR
18 point (g:\ttfr_r\r0001799.ttf)

ABCDEFGHIJKLMNOPQRSTUV
18 point (g:\ttfr_r\r0001801.ttf)

ABCDEFGHIJKLMNOPQRSTUV
18 point (g:\ttfr_r\r0001802.ttf)

ABCDEFGHIJKLMNOPQR
18 point (g:\ttfr_r\r0001803.ttf)

ABCDEFGHIJKLMNOPQRSTUVWXYZ
18 point (g:\ttfr_r\r0001809.ttf)

ABCDEFGHIJKLMNOPQRSTUVWXYZabcdefghij
18 point (g:\ttfr_r\r0001810.ttf)

ABCDEFGHIJKLMNOPQ
18 point (g:\ttfr_r\r0001811.ttf)

ABCDEFGHIJKLMNOPQRSTUVWXYZ
18 point (g:\ttfr_r\r0001813.ttf)

ABCDEFGHIJKLMNOPQRSTU
18 point (g:\ttfr_r\r0001816.ttf)

ABCDEFGHIJKLMNOPQRST
18 point (g:\ttfr_r\r0001814.ttf)

ABCDEFGHIJKLMNOPQRSTU
18 point (g:\ttfr_r\r0001815.ttf)

ABCDEFGHIJKLMNOPQRSTU
18 point (g:\ttfr_r\r0001819.ttf)

ABCDEFGHIJKLMNOPQRST
18 point (g:\ttfr_r\r0001817.ttf)

ABCDEFGHIJKLMN
18 point (g:\ttfr_r\r0001818.ttf)

ABCDEFGHIJKLMNOPQ
18 point (g:\ttfr_r\r0001820.ttf)

ABCDEFGHIJKLMNOPQRSTU
18 point (g:\ttfr_r\r0001821.ttf)

ABCDEFGHIJKLMNOPQ
18 point (g:\ttfr_r\r0001822.ttf)

ABCDEFGHIJKLMNOPQRSTUVWXY
18 point (g:\ttfr_r\r0001823.ttf)

BCDEFGHIJKLMNOPQRSTUVWXYZabcde
18 point (g:\ttfr_r\r0001824.ttf)

ABCDEFGHIJKLMNOPQRSTUVWXYZABCDEFGHIJ
18 point (g:\ttfr_r\r0001825.ttf)

ABCDEFGHIJKLMNOPQRSTUVWXYZABCDEFGHIJ
18 point (g:\ttfr_r\r0001829.ttf)

ABCDEFGHIJKLMNOPQRSTUVWXYZABCDEF
18 point (g:\ttfr_r\r0001826.ttf)

ABCDEFGHIJKLMNOPQRSTUVWXYZABCDEFGHIJKLMNOPQR
18 point (g:\ttfr_r\r0001827.ttf)

ABCDEFGHIJKLMNOPQRSTUVW
18 point (g:\ttfr_r\r0001828.ttf)

ABCDEFGHIJKLMNOPQRSTUVWXYZAB
18 point (g:\ttfr_r\r0001830.ttf)

BCDEFGHIJKLMNOPQRSTUVWXYZABCDEFGHIJKLMNOPQRSTUVWXYZ
(g:\ttfr_r\r0001831.ttf)

ABCDEFGHIJKLMNOPQRSTUVWXYZab
18 point (g:\ttfr_r\r0001836.ttf)

ABCDEFGHIJKLMNOPQRSTUVWXYZab
18 point (g:\ttfr_r\r0001839.ttf)

ABCDEFGHIJKLMNOPQRSTUVWXYZabcdefghijklmno
18 point (g:\ttfr_r\r0001837.ttf)

ABCDEFGHIJKLMNOPQRS
18 point (g:\ttfr_r\r0001838.ttf)

ABCDEFGHIJKLMNOPQRSTUV
18 point (g:\ttfr_r\r0001840.ttf)

ABCDEFGHIJKLMNOPQRSTUVWX
18 point (g:\ttfr_r\r0001841.ttf)

ABCDEFGHIJKLMNOPQRSTUV
18 point (g:\ttfr_r\r0001843.ttf)

ABCDEFGHIJKLMNOPQRSTUV
18 point (g:\ttfr_r\r0001844.ttf)

ABCDEFGHIJKLMNOPQRSTUV
18 point (g:\ttfr_r\r0001842.ttf)

ABCDEFGHIJKLMNOPQRSTUV
18 point (g:\ttfr_r\r0001845.ttf)

ABCDEFGHIJKLMNOPQRSTUVWXYZa
18 point (g:\ttfr_r\r0001846.ttf)

ABCDEFGHIJKLMN
18 point (g:\ttfr_r\r0001847.ttf)

ABCDEFGHIJKLMNOPQRSTUVWXY
18 point (g:\ttfr_r\r0001848.ttf)

ABCDEFGHIJKLMNOPQ
18 point (g:\ttfr_r\r0001849.ttf)

ABCDEFGHIJKLMNOPQRSTUVWX
18 point (g:\ttfr_r\r0001850.ttf)

ABCDEFGHIJKLMNOPQRSTU
18 point (g:\ttfr_r\r0001851.ttf)

ABCDEFGHIJKLMNOPQRSTUVW
18 point (g:\ttfr_r\r0001852.ttf)

ABCDEFGHIJKLMNOPQRSTUVW
18 point (g:\ttfr_r\r0001855.ttf)

ABCDEFGHIJKLMNOPQRSTUVWXYZabcdef
18 point (g:\ttfr_r\r0001856.ttf)

ABCDEFGHIJKLMNOP
18 point (g:\ttfr_r\r0001857.ttf)

ABCDEFGHIJKLMNOPQ
18 point (g:\ttfr_r\r0001858.ttf)

ABCDEFGHIJKLMNOPQRS
18 point (g:\ttfr_r\r0001859.ttf)

ABCDEFGHIJKLMNOPQRS
18 point (g:\ttfr_r\r0001860.ttf)

ABCDEFGHIJKLMNOPQRSTUVWXYZABCDEFGHIJKLMNOPQRSTUVWXYZ
18 point (g:\ttfr_r\r0001863.ttf)

ABCDEFGHIJKLMNOPQRSTUVWXYZABCDEFGHIJKLMNOPQRSTUVWXYZ
18 point (g:\ttfr_r\r0001862.ttf)

ABCDEFGHIJKLMNOPQRSTUVWXYZABCDEFGHIJKLMNOPQRSTUVWXYZ
18 point (g:\ttfr_r\r0001861.ttf)

ABCDEFGHIJKLMNOPQRSTUVWXYZABCDEFGHIJKLMNOPQRSTUVWXYZ
18 point (g:\ttfr_r\r0001864.ttf)

ABCDEFGHIJKLMNOPQRSTUVWXYZABCDEFG
18 point (g:\ttfr_r\r0001867.ttf)

ABCDEFGHIJKLMNOPQRSTUV
18 point (g:\ttfr_r\r0001866.ttf)

ABCDEFGHIJKLMNOPQRSTUVWXYZABCDEFG
18 point (g:\ttfr_r\r0001865.ttf)

ABCDEFGHIJKLMNOPQRSTUVWXYZABCDEFGHIJKLM
18 point (g:\ttfr_r\r0001868.ttf)

ABCDEFGHIJKLMNOPQRS
18 point (g:\ttfr_r\r0001869.ttf)

A B C D E F G H I J K L
18 point (g:\ttfr_r\r0001833.ttf)

A B C D E F G H I
18 point (g:\ttfr_r\r0001834.ttf)

A B C D E F G H I J K
18 point   (g:\ttfr_r\r0001835.ttf)

ABCDEFGHIJKLMNOPQRSTUVWXYZabcdefg
18 point   (g:\ttfr_r\r0001870.ttf)

ABCDEFGHIJKLMNO
18 point   (g:\ttfr_r\r0001871.ttf)

ABCDEFGHIJKLMNOPQRSTUVWXYZa
18 point   (g:\ttfr_r\r0001872.ttf)

ABCDEFGHIJKLMNOPQRS
18 point   (g:\ttfr_r\r0001873.ttf)

ABCDEFGHIJKLMNOPQRSTUVW
18 point   (g:\ttfr_r\r0001874.ttf)

CDEFGHIJKLMNOPQRSTUUWXYZab
24 point (g:\ttfs_s\s0001918.ttf)

BCDEFGHIJKLMNOPQRSTU
24 point (g:\ttfs_s\s0001919.ttf)

BCDEFGHIJKLMNOP
24 point (g:\ttfs_s\s0001996.ttf)

BCDEFGHIJKLMNOP
24 point (g:\ttfs_s\s0001997.ttf)

BCDEFGHIJKLMNO
24 point (g:\ttfs_s\s0001998.ttf)

BCDEFGHIJKLMNOPQR
24 point (g:\ttfs_s\s0001999.ttf)

BCDEFGHIJKLMNOPQR
24 point (g:\ttfs_s\s0001877.ttf)

BCDEFGHIJKLMNOPQRST
24 point (g:\ttfs_s\s0001878.ttf)

BCDEFGHIJKLMNOP
24 point (g:\ttfs_s\s0001879.ttf)

BCDEFGHIJKLMNOP
24 point (g:\ttfs_s\s0001880.ttf)

BCDEFGHIJKLMNOPQRS
24 point (g:\ttfs_s\s0001875.ttf)

BCDEFGHIJKLMNOPQRSTUVW
24 point (g:\ttfs_s\s0001882.ttf)

BCDEFGHIJKLMNOP
24 point (g:\ttfs_s\s0001883.ttf)

ABCDEFGHIJ
24 point (g:\ttfs_s\s0001884.ttf)

ABCDEFGHIJKL
(g:\ttfs_s\s0001885.ttf)

BCDEFGHIJKLMN
24 point (g:\ttfs_s\s0001886.ttf)

ABCDEFGHIJ
24 point (g:\ttfs_s\s0001887.ttf)

BCDEFGHIJKLMNOPQRS
24 point (g:\ttfs_s\s0001889.ttf)

ABCDEFGHIJKLMNOPQRS
24 point (g:\ttfs_s\s0001888.ttf)

ABCDEFGHIJKLMNOPQRSTUV
24 point (g:\ttfs_s\s0001890.ttf)

ABCDEFGHIJKLMNO
24 point (g:\ttfs_s\s0001891.ttf)

ABCDEFGHIJKLMNOPQR
24 point (g:\ttfs_s\s0001893.ttf)

ABCDEFGHIJKLMNOPQRSTUV
24 point (g:\ttfs_s\s0001894.ttf)

ABCDEFGHIJKLMNO
(g:\ttfs_s\s0001895.ttf)

ABCDEFGHIJKLMN
24 point (g:\ttfs_s\s0001896.ttf)

ABCDEFGHIJKLMNO
24 point (g:\ttfs_s\s0001897.ttf)

ABCDEFGHIJKLMNOPQRSTUV
24 point (g:\ttfs_s\s0001898.ttf)

ABCDEFGHIJKLMNOP
24 point (g:\ttfs_s\s0001899.ttf)

ABCDEFGHIJKLMNOPQRSTUVWX
24 point (g:\ttfs_s\s0001900.ttf)

ABCDEFGHIJKLMNOPQRSTUVWX
24 point (g:\ttfs_s\s0001901.ttf)

ABCDEFGHIJKLMNOP
(g:\ttfs_s\s0001902.ttf)

ABCDEFGHIJKLMNOP
24 point (g:\ttfs_s\s0001903.ttf)

ABCDEFGHIJKLMNOPQR
24 point (g:\ttfs_s\s0001904.ttf)

ABCDEFGHIJKLMNOPQRS
24 point (g:\ttfs_s\s0001905.ttf)

ABCDEFGHIJKLMNO
24 point (g:\ttfs_s\s0001906.ttf)

ABCDEFGHIJKLMNOPQRSTUV
24 point (g:\ttfs_s\s0001907.ttf)

ABCDEFGHIJKLMNO
24 point (g:\ttfs_s\s0001908.ttf)

ABCDEFGHIJKLMNOPQR
24 point (g:\ttfs_s\s0001909.ttf)

ABCDEFGHIJKLM
24 point (g:\ttfs_s\s0001910.ttf)

ABCDEFGHIJKLMNO
24 point (g:\ttfs_s\s0001911.ttf)

ABCDEFGHIJKLMNOPQRSTUVWXYZ
24 point (g:\ttfs_s\s0001912.ttf)

ABCDEFGHIJKLMNOPQRSTUV
24 point (g:\ttfs_s\s0001913.ttf)

ABCDEFGHIJKLMNOPQ
24 point (g:\ttfs_s\s0001914.ttf)

ABCDEFGHIJKLM
24 point (g:\ttfs_s\s0001915.ttf)

ABCDEFGHIJKLM
24 point (g:\ttfs_s\s0001916.ttf)

ABCDEFGHIJKLMN
24 point (g:\ttfs_s\s0001917.ttf)

ABCDEFGHIJKLMNOP
24 point (g:\ttfs_s\s0001920.ttf)

ABCDEFGHIJKLMNOP
24 point (g:\ttfs_s\s0001921.ttf)

ABCDEFGHIJKLM
24 point (g:\ttfs_s\s0001922.ttf)

ABCDEFGHIJKLMNOP
24 point (g:\ttfs_s\s0001924.ttf)

ABCDEFGHIJKLMNOPQRSTU
24 point (g:\ttfs_s\s0001925.ttf)

ABCDEFGHIJK
24 point (g:\ttfs_s\s0001926.ttf)

ABCDEFGHIJKLM
24 point (g:\ttfs_s\s0001927.ttf)

ABCDEFGHIJKLMNOPQRST
24 point (g:\ttfs_s\s0001928.ttf)

PGCcOfgA\{N-eEkSJ&
24 point (g:\ttfs_s\s0001929.ttf)

ABCDEFGHIJKLMNO
24 point (g:\ttfs_s\s0001931.ttf)

ABCDEFGHIJ
24 point (g:\ttfs_s\s0001932.ttf)

ABCDEFGHIJKL
24 point (g:\ttfs_s\s0001933.ttf)

ABCDEFGHIJKLMNOP
24 point (g:\ttfs_s\s0001934.ttf)

ABCDEFGWISKLMN
24 point (g:\ttfs_s\s0001935.ttf)

ABCDEFGHIJKLM
24 point (g:\ttfs_s\s0001936.ttf)

ABCDEFGHIJKLMNOP
24 point (g:\ttfs_s\s0001937.ttf)

ABCDEFGHIJKLMNOPQRST
24 point (g:\ttfs_s\s0001939.ttf)

ABCDEFGHIJKL
24 point (g:\ttfs_s\s0001940.ttf)

ABCDEFGHIJK
24 point (g:\ttfs_s\s0001941.ttf)

ABCDEFGHIJKLM
24 point (g:\ttfs_s\s0001942.ttf)

ABCDEFGH
24 point (g:\ttfs_s\s0001943.ttf)

ABCDEFGHIJKL
24 point (g:\ttfs_s\s0001944.ttf)

ABCDEFGHIJK
24 point (g:\ttfs_s\s0001945.ttf)

ABCDEFGHIJKLMNOPQRSTUVWX
24 point (g:\ttfs_s\s0001946.ttf)

ABCDEFGHIJKLMN
24 point (g:\ttfs_s\s0001948.ttf)

ABCDEFGHIJKLMNOPQRSTUVWXYZab
24 point (g:\ttfs_s\s0001950.ttf)

BCDEFGHIJKLMNO
24 point (g:\ttfs_s\s0001951.ttf)

BCDEFGHIJKLM
24 point (g:\ttfs_s\s0001953.ttf)

BCDEFGHIJKLMNOPQR
24 point (g:\ttfs_s\s0001954.ttf)

BCDEFGHIJKLMNOP
24 point (g:\ttfs_s\s0001955.ttf)

ʒçðɛɤɢʰʳɥʜʒɱɲŋøθæɾʃθʋʊ
24 point (g:\ttfs_s\s0001957.ttf)

BCDEFGHIJ
24 point (g:\ttfs_s\s0001958.ttf)

BCDEFGHIJKL
24 point (g:\ttfs_s\s0001959.ttf)

BCDEFGHIJKLMNOPQRSTUV
24 point (g:\ttfs_s\s0001960.ttf)

ʒçðɛɤɢʰɪʲʜʒɱɲŋøøæʁ
24 point (g:\ttfs_s\s0001961.ttf)

ʒçðɛɤɢʰɪʲʜʒɱɲŋøøæʁʃθ
24 point (g:\ttfs_s\s0001962.ttf)

BCDEFGHIJ
24 point (g:\ttfs_s\s0001964.ttf)

BCDEFGHIJKLMNOP
24 point (g:\ttfs_s\s0001966.ttf)

BCDEFGHIJKLMNOPQRST
24 point (g:\ttfs_s\s0001967.ttf)

BCDEFGHIJKLMNOPQRSTUV
24 point (g:\ttfs_s\s0001968.ttf)

VBCDEFGHIJKLM
24 point (g:\ttfs_s\s0001969.ttf)

BCDEFGHIJKLMNOPQ
24 point (g:\ttfs_s\s0001970.ttf)

VBCDEFGHIJK
24 point (g:\ttfs_s\s0001971.ttf)

BCDEFGHIJKLMNOPQRST
24 point (g:\ttfs_s\s0001973.ttf)

ABCDEFGHIJKLM
24 point (g:\ttfs_s\s0001974.ttf)

ABCDEFGHIJKLM
24 point (g:\ttfs_s\s0001975.ttf)

ABCDEFGHIJKLMNOP
24 point (g:\ttfs_s\s0001976.ttf)

ABCDEFGHIJ
24 point (g:\ttfs_s\s0001977.ttf)

ABCDEFGHIJKLMNOPQR
24 point (g:\ttfs_s\s0001979.ttf)

ABCDEFGHIJKLMNOPQRST
24 point (g:\ttfs_s\s0001980.ttf)

ABCDEFGHIJKLMNOP
24 point (g:\ttfs_s\s0001984.ttf)

ABCDEFGHIJKLMNOP
24 point (g:\ttfs_s\s0001982.ttf)

ABCDEFGHIJKLMNO
24 point (g:\ttfs_s\s0001981.ttf)

ABCDEFGHIJKLMNO
24 point (g:\ttfs_s\s0001983.ttf)

ABCDEFGHIJKL
24 point (g:\ttfs_s\s0001985.ttf)

ABCDEFGHIJKLM
24 point (g:\ttfs_s\s0001986.ttf)

ABCDEFGHIJKLM
24 point (g:\ttfs_s\s0001989.ttf)

ABCDEFGHIJKLMNOPQRS
24 point (g:\ttfs_s\s0001992.ttf)

ABCDEFGHIJKLMNOPQRSTU
24 point (g:\ttfs_s\s0001993.ttf)

ABCDEFGHIJKLMNOPQRST
24 point (g:\ttfs_s\s0001994.ttf)

ABCDEFGHIJKLMNOPQRST
24 point (g:\ttfs_s\s0001995.ttf)

ABCDEFGHIJKLMNOP
24 point (g:\ttfs_s\s0002000.ttf)

ABCDEFGHIJKLM
24 point (g:\ttfs_s\s0002004.ttf)

ABCDEFGHIJKLM
24 point (g:\ttfs_s\s0002001.ttf)

ABCDEFGHIJKLM
24 point (g:\ttfs_s\s0002002.ttf)

ABCDEFGHIJKLMNOPQRST
24 point (g:\ttfs_s\s0002005.ttf)

ABCDEFGHIJKLMNOPQR
24 point (g:\ttfs_s\s0002006.ttf)

ABCDEFGHIJKLMNOP
24 point (g:\ttfs_s\s0002007.ttf)

ABCDEFGHIJKLMN
24 point (g:\ttfs_s\s0002008.ttf)

ABCDEFGHIJKLMNO
24 point (g:\ttfs_s\s0002009.ttf)

ABCDEFGHIJKLMNOP
24 point (g:\ttfs_s\s0002010.ttf)

ABCDEFGHIJKL
24 point (g:\ttfs_s\s0002011.ttf)

ABCDEFGHIJKLMNOP
24 point (g:\ttfs_s\s0002012.ttf)

ABCDEFGHIJKLMNO
24 point (g:\ttfs_s\s0002013.ttf)

ABCDEFGHIJKLMNOPQRSTUV
24 point (g:\ttfs_s\s0002014.ttf)

ABCDEFGHIJKLMN
24 point (g:\ttfs_s\s0002015.ttf)

ABCDEFGHIJKLMNOP
24 point (g:\ttfs_s\s0002016.ttf)

ABCDEFGHIJKLMNOPQR
24 point (g:\ttfs_s\s0002017.ttf)

ABCDEFGHIJKLM
24 point (g:\ttfs_s\s0002018.ttf)

ABCDEFGHIJKLMNOPQ
24 point (g:\ttfs_s\s0002019.ttf)

ABCDEFGHIJKLMNOPQR
24 point (g:\ttfs_s\s0002020.ttf)

ABCDEFGHIJKLMNOPQRS
24 point (g:\ttfs_s\s0002021.ttf)

ABCDEFGHIJKLMNOP
24 point (g:\ttfs_s\s0002022.ttf)

ABCDEFGHIJKLMNOP
24 point (g:\ttfs_s\s0002023.ttf)

ABCDEFGHIJKLMNOPQ
24 point (g:\ttfs_s\s0002025.ttf)

ABCDEFGHIJKLMNOPQRS
24 point (g:\ttfs_s\s0002024.ttf)

ABCDEFGHIJKLMNOPQR
24 point (g:\ttfs_s\s0002026.ttf)

ABCDEFGHIJKLMNOPQR
24 point (g:\ttfs_s\s0002027.ttf)

ABCDEFGHIJKL
24 point (g:\ttfs_s\s0002029.ttf)

ABCDEFGHI
24 point (g:\ttfs_s\s0002028.ttf)

ABCDEFGHIJKL
24 point (g:\ttfs_s\s0002030.ttf)

ABCDEFGHIJKLMNOPQRST
24 point (g:\ttfs_s\s0002031.ttf)

ABCDEFGHIJKLMNOPQRS
24 point (g:\ttfs_s\s0002032.ttf)

ABCDEFGHIJKLMNO
24 point (g:\ttfs_s\s0002033.ttf)

ABCDEFGHIJKLMNOPQR
24 point (g:\ttfs_s\s0002034.ttf)

ABCDEFGHIJKLMNOPQR
24 point (g:\ttfs_s\s0002035.ttf)

ABCDEFGHIJKLMNOPQR
24 point (g:\ttfs_s\s0002036.ttf)

ABCDEFGHIJKLMNOPQ
24 point (g:\ttfs_s\s0002037.ttf)

ABCDEFGHIJKLMNOPQ
24 point (g:\ttfs_s\s0002038.ttf)

ABCDEFGHIJKLMNOPQRST
24 point (g:\ttfs_s\s0002039.ttf)

BCDEFGHIJKLMNOPQRSTU
24 point (g:\ttfs_s\s0002040.ttf)

BCDEFGHIJKLMNOPQ
24 point (g:\ttfs_s\s0002041.ttf)

BXΔEΦΓHIϑKΛMNOΠ
24 point (g:\ttfs_s\s0002042.ttf)

ABCDEFGHIJKLMNOPQ
24 point (g:\ttft_f\0002085.ttf)

ABCDEFGHIJKLMNOPQ
24 point (g:\ttft_f\0002078.ttf)

ABCDEFGHIJKLMNOPQRSTU
24 point (g:\ttft_f\0002079.ttf)

ABCDEFGHIJK
24 point (g:\ttft_f\0002080.ttf)

ABCDEFGHIJKLM
24 point (g:\ttft_f\0002081.ttf)

ABCDEFGHIJKLMNOPQ
24 point (g:\ttft_f\0002116.ttf)

ABCDEFGHIJKLMNOPQRSTUVWXYZabcd
24 point (g:\ttft_f\0002141.ttf)

ABCDEFGH
24 point (g:\ttft_f\0002142.ttf)

ABCDEFGH
24 point (g:\ttft_f\0002143.ttf)

ABCDEFGH
24 point (g:\ttft_f\0002144.ttf)

ABCDEFGH
24 point (g:\ttft_f\0002145.ttf)

ABCDEFGH
24 point (g:\ttft_f\0002146.ttf)

ABCDEFGHIJKLMNOPQRSTUVW+Y
24 point (g:\ttft_f\0002043.ttf)

ABCDEFGHIJKLMNOPQRSTUVW+Y
24 point (g:\ttft_f\0002044.ttf)

ABCDEFGHIJKLMNOPQRSTUVW+YZabcdefghijkl
24 point (g:\ttft_f\0002046.ttf)

ABCDEFGHIJKLMNOP
24 point (g:\ttft_f\0002047.ttf)

ABCDEFGHIJKLMNOPQRS
24 point (g:\ttft_f\0002048.ttf)

ABCDEFGHIJKLMNO
(g:\ttft_f\0002049.ttf)

ABčðɛrghijkłunɔⱷⱷɷršθʊʊ
24 point (g:\ttft_f\0002050.ttf)

ABčðɛrghijkłunɔⱷⱷɷršθʊʊ
24 point (g:\ttft_f\0002051.ttf)

ABčðɛrghijkłunɔⱷⱷɷrš
24 point (g:\ttft_f\0002052.ttf)

ABčðɛrghijkłunɔⱷⱷɷršθʊʊmχγžabc
24 point (g:\ttft_f\0002053.ttf)

ABčðɛrghijkłunɔ
24 point (g:\ttft_f\0002054.ttf)

ABčðɛrghijkłunɔⱷ
24 point (g:\ttft_f\0002055.ttf)

ABCDEFGHIJKLMNOPQRSTU
24 point (g:\ttft_f\0002061.ttf)

ABCDEFGHIJKLMNOPQRST
24 point (g:\ttft_f\0002057.ttf)

ABCDEFGHIJKLMNOPQRSTUVWXYZ
24 point (g:\ttft_f\0002058.ttf)

ABCDEFGHIJKLMNOPQRSTUVW
24 point (g:\ttft_f\0002062.ttf)

ABCDEFGHIJKLMNOPQRS
24 point (g:\ttft_f\0002064.ttf)

ABCDEFGHIJKLMNOPQRS
24 point (g:\ttft_f\0002067.ttf)

ABCDEFGHIJKLMNOPQRSTUVWX
24 point (g:\ttft_f\0002065.ttf)

ABCDEFGHIJKLM
24 point (g:\ttft_f\0002066.ttf)

ABCDEFGHIJKLMNO
24 point (g:\ttft_f\0002068.ttf)

ABCDEFGHIJKLMNOPQRSTU
24 point (g:\ttft_f\0002069.ttf)

ABCDEFGHIJKLMNOPQRSTUVWX
24 point (g:\ttft_f\0002070.ttf)

ABCDEFGHIJK
24 point (g:\ttft_f\0002071.ttf)

ABCDEFGHIJKLM
24 point (g:\ttft_t\0002072.ttf)

BCDEFGHIJKLMNOPQ
24 point (g:\ttft_t\0002073.ttf)

BCDEFGHIJKLMNOPQRSTUV
24 point (g:\ttft_t\0002074.ttf)

ABCDEFGHIJK
24 point (g:\ttft_t\0002075.ttf)

ABCDEFGHIJKLM
24 point (g:\ttft_t\0002076.ttf)

ЯOИMLKJIHGFEDCB
24 point (g:\ttft_t\0002077.ttf)

BCDEFGHIJKLMNO
24 point (g:\ttft_t\0002083.ttf)

BCDEFGHIJKLM
24 point (g:\ttft_t\0002084.ttf)

BCDEFGHIJKLMNOPQRSTU
24 point (g:\ttft_t\0002087.ttf)

ABCDEFG
24 point (g:\ttft_t\0002088.ttf)

BCDEFGHIJKLMN
24 point (g:\ttft_t\0002091.ttf)

BCDEFGHIJKLMNOPQRS
24 point (g:\ttft_t\0002092.ttf)

ABCDEFGHIJKL
24 point (g:\ttft_t\0002093.ttf)

BCDEFGHIJKLMN
24 point (g:\ttft_t\0002094.ttf)

ABCDEFGHI
24 point (g:\ttft_t\0002095.ttf)

BCDEFGHIJKLMNOP
24 point (g:\ttft_t\0002096.ttf)

BCDEFGHIJKLMNOPQRSTUV
24 point (g:\ttft_t\0002097.ttf)

ABCDEFGHIJKLM
24 point (g:\ttft_t\0002098.ttf)

ABCDEFGHIJKLM
24 point (g:\ttft_t\0002099.ttf)

ABCDEFGHI
24 point (g:\ttft_t\0002100.ttf)

ABCDEFGHIJKLM
24 point (g:\ttft_t\0002090.ttf)

ABCDEFGHIJKLMNOP
24 point (g:\ttft_t\0002101.ttf)

ABCDEFGHIJKLMNO
24 point (g:\ttft_t\0002102.ttf)

ABCDEFGHIJ
24 point (g:\ttft_t\0002103.ttf)

ABCDEFGHIJKLMNO
24 point (g:\ttft_t\0002089.ttf)

ABCDEFGHIJKLMNOPQ
24 point (g:\ttft_t\0002104.ttf)

ABCDEFGHIJKL
24 point (g:\ttft_t\0002105.ttf)

ABCDEFGHIJKLMNOPQR
24 point (g:\ttft_t\0002106.ttf)

ABCDEFGHIJKLMNOPQ
24 point (g:\ttft_t\0002107.ttf)

ABCDEFGHIJKLMNOPQ
24 point (g:\ttft_t\0002108.ttf)

ABCDEFGHIJKLMNOPQ
24 point (g:\ttft_t\0002111.ttf)

ABCDEFGHIJKLMNOP
24 point (g:\ttft_t\0002112.ttf)

ABCDEFGHIJKLMNOP
24 point (g:\ttft_t\0002113.ttf)

ABCDEFGHIJKLMNOPQ
24 point (g:\ttft_t\0002114.ttf)

ABCDEFGHIJKLMNOPQ
24 point (g:\ttft_t\0002115.ttf)

ABCDEFGHIJKLMN
24 point (g:\ttft_t\0002117.ttf)

ABCDEFGHIJKLMN
24 point (g:\ttft_f\0002118.ttf)

ABCDEFGHIJKL
24 point (g:\ttft_f\0002119.ttf)

ABCDEFGHIJKLMN
24 point (g:\ttft_f\0002120.ttf)

ABCDEFGHIJKLM
24 point (g:\ttft_f\0002122.ttf)

ABCDEFGHIJKLM
24 point (g:\ttft_f\0002123.ttf)

ABCDEFGHIJKLM
24 point (g:\ttft_f\0002121.ttf)

ABCDEFGHIJKLMNOPQ
24 point (g:\ttft_f\0002124.ttf)

ABCDEFGHIJKLMNO
24 point (g:\ttft_f\0002125.ttf)

ABCDEFGHIJKLMNOPQRSTUVWXYZAB
24 point (g:\ttft_f\0002135.ttf)

ABCDEFGHIJKLMNOPQRSTUV
24 point (g:\ttft_f\0002136.ttf)

ABCDEFGHIJKLMNOPQRSTU
24 point (g:\ttft_f\0002137.ttf)

ABCDEFGHIJKLMNOPQRSTU
24 point (g:\ttft_f\0002139.ttf)

ABCDEFGHIJKLMNOPQRSTU
24 point (g:\ttft_f\0002138.ttf)

ABCDEFGHIJKLMNOPQRSTU
24 point (g:\ttft_f\0002140.ttf)

ABCDEFGHIJKLMN
24 point (g:\ttft_f\0002147.ttf)

ABCDEFGHIJKLMNOPQRST
24 point (g:\ttft_f\0002148.ttf)

ABCDEFGHIJ
24 point (g:\ttft_f\0002149.ttf)

ABCDEFGHIJKLMN
24 point (g:\ttft_f\0002150.ttf)

ABCDEFGHIJ
24 point (g:\ttft_f\0002153.ttf)

ABCDEFGHIJKLMNO
24 point (g:\ttft_f\0002151.ttf)

ABCDEFGHIJKLMNO
24 point (g:\ttft_f\0002152.ttf)

24 point (g:\ttft_f\0002154.ttf)

ABCDEFGHIJKLMNOPQRS
24 point (g:\ttft_f\0002155.ttf)

ABCDEFGHIJKLMNOPQRS
24 point (g:\ttft_f\0002156.ttf)

ABCDEFGHIJKLMNO
24 point (g:\ttft_f\0002157.ttf)

ABCDEFGHIJKLMNOPQRS
24 point (g:\ttft_f\0002158.ttf)

FONTS FROM AREA \TTFU_V

ΙbCdEFGHI JH 24 point (g:\ttfu_v\u0002170.ttf)	ABCDEFGHIJKLMNOPQR 24 point (g:\ttfu_v\u0002177.ttf)
ΙbCdEFGHI JH 24 point (g:\ttfu_v\u0002174.ttf)	ABCDEFGHIJKLMNOP 24 point (g:\ttfu_v\u0002178.ttf)
bCdEFGHI JHLMΠ 24 point (g:\ttfu_v\u0002171.ttf)	ABCDEFGHIJKLMNOPqRSTUV 24 point (g:\ttfu_v\u0002179.ttf)
ЭbCdEFG 24 point (g:\ttfu_v\u0002172.ttf)	ABCDEFGHIJKLMNOPqRSTUV 24 point (g:\ttfu_v\u0002183.ttf)
IbCdEFGHI JH 24 point (g:\ttfu_v\u0002173.ttf)	ABCDEFGHIJKLMNOPqRST 24 point (g:\ttfu_v\u0002180.ttf)
ЭbCdEFGH 24 point (g:\ttfu_v\u0002175.ttf)	ABCDEFGHIJKLMNOPqRSTUVWXYZaBC 24 point (g:\ttfu_v\u0002181.ttf)
BCDEFGHIJKLMNOPQRST 24 point (g:\ttfu_v\u0002216.ttf)	ABCDEFGHIJKLMN 24 point (g:\ttfu_v\u0002182.ttf)
BCDEFGHIJKLMNOPQ 24 point (g:\ttfu_v\u0002217.ttf)	ABCDEFGHIJKLMNOPq 24 point (g:\ttfu_v\u0002184.ttf)
BCDEFGHIJKLMNO 24 point (g:\ttfu_v\u0002160.ttf)	ABCDEFGHIJKLMNO 24 point (g:\ttfu_v\u0002186.ttf)
BCDEFGHIJKLMNOPQ 24 point (g:\ttfu_v\u0002163.ttf)	ABCDEFGHIJKLMNO 24 point (g:\ttfu_v\u0002187.ttf)
BCDEFGHIJKLMNOPQ 24 point (g:\ttfu_v\u0002164.ttf)	ABCDEFGHIJKLMNOP 24 point (g:\ttfu_v\u0002188.ttf)
BCDEFGHIJKLMNOP 24 point (g:\ttfu_v\u0002161.ttf)	ABCDEFGHIJKLM 24 point (g:\ttfu_v\u0002189.ttf)
BCDEFGHIJKLMNOP 24 point (g:\ttfu_v\u0002162.ttf)	ABCDEFGHIJKLM 24 point (g:\ttfu_v\u0002190.ttf)
BCDEFGHIJKLMNO 24 point (g:\ttfu_v\u0002165.ttf)	ABCDEFGHIJKLM 24 point (g:\ttfu_v\u0002191.ttf)
BCDEFGHIJKLMNOPQRST 24 point (g:\ttfu_v\u0002166.ttf)	ABCDEFGHIJKLM 24 point (g:\ttfu_v\u0002192.ttf)
ABCDEFGHIJ 24 point (g:\ttfu_v\u0002167.ttf)	ABCDEFGHIJKL 24 point (g:\ttfu_v\u0002193.ttf)
BCDEFGHIJKLMNOPQR 24 point (g:\ttfu_v\u0002168.ttf)	ABCDEFGHIJKL 24 point (g:\ttfu_v\u0002194.ttf)
BCDEFGHIJKL 24 point (g:\ttfu_v\u0002169.ttf)	ABCDEFGHIJKLMNOPQ 24 point (g:\ttfu_v\u0002195.ttf)

ABCDEFGHIJKLMNOP
24 point   (g:\ttfu_v\u0002196.ttf)

ABCDEFGHIJKLMNOPQ
24 point   (g:\ttfu_v\u0002197.ttf)

ABCDEFGHIJKLMNOPQR
24 point   (g:\ttfu_v\u0002198.ttf)

ABCDEFGHIJKLMNOPQ
24 point   (g:\ttfu_v\u0002199.ttf)

ABCDEFGHIJKLMN
24 point   (g:\ttfu_v\u0002200.ttf)

ABCDEFGHIJKLMNOP
24 point   (g:\ttfu_v\u0002201.ttf)

ABCDEFGHIJKLMNOPQRSTUV
24 point   (g:\ttfu_v\u0002202.ttf)

ABCDEFGHIJKLMNOPQRSTUVWXYZabcdefghi
24 point   (g:\ttfu_v\u0002203.ttf)

ABCDEFGHIJKLMNOPQRSTU
24 point   (g:\ttfu_v\u0002205.ttf)

ABCDEFGHIJKLMNOPQRSTUVWX
24 point   (g:\ttfu_v\u0002206.ttf)

ABCDEFGHIJKLMNOPQRST
24 point   (g:\ttfu_v\u0002207.ttf)

ABCDEFGHIJKLMNOPQ
24 point   (g:\ttfu_v\u0002208.ttf)

ABCDEFGHIJKLMNOPQRST
24 point   (g:\ttfu_v\u0002213.ttf)

ABCDEFGHIJKLMNOPQRS
24 point   (g:\ttfu_v\u0002210.ttf)

ABCDEFGHIJKLMNOPQRSTUVWXYZ
24 point   (g:\ttfu_v\u0002211.ttf)

ABCDEFGHIJKLMN
24 point   (g:\ttfu_v\u0002212.ttf)

ABCDEFGHIJKLMNOPQRST
24 point   (g:\ttfu_v\u0002209.ttf)

ABCDEFGHIJKLMNOPQRSTUVW
24 point   (g:\ttfu_v\u0002214.ttf)

ABCDEFGHIJKLMNOP
24 point   (g:\ttfu_v\u0002215.ttf)

ABCDEFGHIJKLMNOPQ
24 point   (g:\ttfu_v\u0002218.ttf)

ABCDEFGHIJKLMNOPQR
24 point   (g:\ttfu_v\u0002219.ttf)

ABCDEFGHIJKLMNOPQR
24 point   (g:\ttfu_v\u0002223.ttf)

ABCDEFGHIJKLMNOPQRSTUU
24 point   (g:\ttfu_v\u0002220.ttf)

ABCDEFGHIJKL
24 point   (g:\ttfu_v\u0002221.ttf)

ABCDEFGHIJKLMNOPQR
24 point   (g:\ttfu_v\u0002222.ttf)

ABCDEFGHIJKLMN
24 point   (g:\ttfu_v\u0002224.ttf)

ABCDEFGHIJKLMN
24 point   (g:\ttfu_v\u0002225.ttf)

ABCDEFGHIJKLMN
24 point   (g:\ttfu_v\u0002228.ttf)

ABCDEFGHIJKLMNOPQRS
24 point   (g:\ttfu_v\u0002226.ttf)

ABCDEFGHIJ
24 point   (g:\ttfu_v\u0002227.ttf)

ABCDEFGHIJKLMN
24 point   (g:\ttfu_v\u0002229.ttf)

ABCDEFGHIJK
24 point   (g:\ttfu_v\u0002230.ttf)

ABCDEFGHIJKLMNOPQRS
24 point   (g:\ttfu_v\u0002231.ttf)

ABCDEFGHIJKLMNOPQRSTUVV
24 point   (g:\ttfu_v\u0002232.ttf)

ABCDEFGHIJKLMNOPQRSTUV
24 point   (g:\ttfu_v\u0002233.ttf)

ABCDEFGHIJKLM
24 point   (g:\ttfu_v\u0002234.ttf)

BCDEFGHIJKLMNO
24 point (g:\ttfu_v\u0002235.ttf)

BCDEFGHIJKLMNO
24 point (g:\ttfu_v\u0002236.ttf)

BCDEFGHIJKLMNOP
24 point (g:\ttfu_v\u0002237.ttf)

BCDEFGHIJKLMN
24 point (g:\ttfu_v\u0002238.ttf)

BCDEFGHIJKLMNOP
24 point (g:\ttfu_v\u0002239.ttf)

BCDEFGHIJKLMNOPQ
24 point (g:\ttfu_v\u0002240.ttf)

BCDEFghijklmnop
24 point (g:\ttfu_v\u0002241.ttf)

BCDEFGHIJKLMNOPQRSTU
24 point (g:\ttfu_v\u0002244.ttf)

BCDEFGHIJKLMNOPQRS
24 point (g:\ttfu_v\u0002245.ttf)

CDEFGHIJKLMNOPQRSTUVWX
24 point (g:\ttfu_v\u0002246.ttf)

BCDEFGHIJKLM
24 point (g:\ttfu_v\u0002247.ttf)

BCDEFGHIJKLMNO
24 point (g:\ttfu_v\u0002248.ttf)

BCDEFGHIJKLMNOPQRST
24 point (g:\ttfu_v\u0002249.ttf)

BCDEFGHIJKLMNOPQRST
24 point (g:\ttfu_v\u0002251.ttf)

BCDEFGHIJKLM
24 point (g:\ttfu_v\u0002250.ttf)

BCDEFGHIJKLMNOPQRS
24 point (g:\ttfu_v\u0002254.ttf)

BCDEFGHIJKLMNOPQRST
24 point (g:\ttfu_v\u0002255.ttf)

BCDEFGHIJKLMNOP
24 point (g:\ttfu_v\u0002256.ttf)

ABCDEFGHIJKLMND
24 point (g:\ttfu_v\w0002257.ttf)

ABCDEFGHIJKLMND
24 point (g:\ttfu_v\w0002258.ttf)

ABCDEFGHIJ
24 point (g:\ttfu_v\w0002259.ttf)

ABCDEFGHIJKL
24 point (g:\ttfu_v\w0002260.ttf)

ABCDEFGHIJKLMNOPQRSTUVWXYZabcdefghijklmnopqrstuvwxyz
24 point (g:\ttfu_v\w0002261.ttf)

ABCDEFGHIJKLMNOPQRSTUVWXYZabcdefghij
24 point (g:\ttfu_v\w0002262.ttf)

ABCDEFGHIJKLMNOPQRSTUVWXYZabcdefghijklmnopqrs
24 point (g:\ttfu_v\w0002263.ttf)

ABCDEFGHIJKLMNOP
24 point (g:\ttfu_v\w0002264.ttf)

ABCDEFGHIJKLMNOPQRSTU
24 point (g:\ttfu_v\w0002267.ttf)

ABCDEFGHIJKLM
24 point (g:\ttfu_v\w0002268.ttf)

ABCDEFGHIJKLM
24 point (g:\ttfu_v\w0002270.ttf)

ABCDEFGHI
24 point (g:\ttfu_v\w0002269.ttf)

ABCDEFGHIJ
24 point (g:\ttfu_v\w0002271.ttf)

ABCDEF
24 point (g:\ttfu_v\w0002272.ttf)

ABCDEFGH
24 point (g:\ttfu_v\w0002273.ttf)

ABCDEFGHIJKLMNOPQRSTUVWX
24 point (g:\ttfu_v\w0002275.ttf)

ABCDEFGHIJKLMNOP
24 point (g:\ttfu_v\w0002276.ttf)

ABCDEFGHIJKLMNOPQR
24 point (g:\ttfu_v\w0002277.ttf)

ABCDEFGHIJ
24 point   (g:\ttfu_v\w0002278.ttf)

ABCDEFGHIJKLMNOPQRST
24 point   (g:\ttfu_v\w0002280.ttf)

ABCDEFGHIJKLMNOPQR
24 point   (g:\ttfu_v\w0002281.ttf)

ABCDEFGHIJKLM
24 point   (g:\ttfu_v\w0002282.ttf)

ABCDEFGHIJKLMNOPQRST
24 point   (g:\ttfu_v\w0002283.ttf)

ABCDEFGHIJKLMNOP
24 point   (g:\ttfu_v\w0002284.ttf)

BCDEFGHIJKL
24 point (g:\ttfw_z\w0002287.ttf)

BCDEFGHIJKLMNOPQ
24 point (g:\ttfw_z\w0002288.ttf)

CDEFGHIJKLMNOPQRSTUV
24 point (g:\ttfw_z\w0002289.ttf)

BCDEF6HJJKLMNOPQR
24 point (g:\ttfw_z\w0002290.ttf)

BCDEFGHIJKLMN
24 point (g:\ttfw_z\w0002291.ttf)

BCDEFGHIJKLMNOP
24 point (g:\ttfw_z\w0002292.ttf)

CDEFGHIJKLMNOPQRSTUV
24 point (g:\ttfw_z\w0002293.ttf)

BCDEFGHIJKLMNOPQRST
24 point (g:\ttfw_z\w0002294.ttf)

BCDEFGHIJKLMNOP
24 point (g:\ttfw_z\w0002295.ttf)

BCDEFGHIJKLM
24 point (g:\ttfw_z\w0002296.ttf)

BCDEFGHIJKLMNOPQR
24 point (g:\ttfw_z\w0002297.ttf)

BCDEFGHIJKLM
24 point (g:\ttfw_z\w0002298.ttf)

BCDEFGHIJKLMNOPQR
24 point (g:\ttfw_z\w0002299.ttf)

BCDEFGHIJKLMNO
24 point (g:\ttfw_z\w0002300.ttf)

BCDEFGHIJKLMNOPQRS
24 point (g:\ttfw_z\w0002301.ttf)

BCDEFGHIJKLMNOPQRS
24 point (g:\ttfw_z\w0002302.ttf)

BCDEFGHIJKLMNOPQRSTUV
24 point (g:\ttfw_z\w0002303.ttf)

BCDEFGHIJKLMNOP
24 point (g:\ttfw_z\w0002304.ttf)

ABCDEFGHIJKLMNOPQRSTUV
24 point (g:\ttfw_z\w0002305.ttf)

ABCDEFGHIJKLMNOP
24 point (g:\ttfw_z\w0002306.ttf)

ABCDEFGHIJKLMNOPQRS
24 point (g:\ttfw_z\w0002307.ttf)

ABCDEFGHIJKLMNOPQRS
24 point (g:\ttfw_z\w0002308.ttf)

ABCDEFGHIJKLMNOPQRSTUV
Extreme 24 point (g:\ttfw_z\w0002310.ttf)

ABCDEFGHIJKLMNOPQRSTUV
Wimpy Human 24 point (g:\ttfw_z\w0002309.ttf)

ABCDEFGHIJKLMNOPQRST
24 point (g:\ttfw_z\w0002311.ttf)

ABCDEFGHIJKLMNOPQRST
24 point (g:\ttfw_z\w0002316.ttf)

ABCDEFGHIJKLMNOPQRS
24 point (g:\ttfw_z\w0002313.ttf)

ABCDEFGHIJKLM
24 point (g:\ttfw_z\w0002314.ttf)

ABCDEFGHIJKLMNOPQRST
24 point (g:\ttfw_z\w0002315.ttf)

ABCDEFGHIJKLMNOPQRST
24 point (g:\ttfw_z\w0002312.ttf)

ABCDEFGHIJKLMNOP
24 point (g:\ttfw_z\w0002317.ttf)

ABCDEFGHIJKLMNOPQRSTUV
24 point (g:\ttfw_z\w0002318.ttf)

ABCDEFGHIJKLMNOPQRSTUV
24 point (g:\ttfw_z\w0002321.ttf)

ABCDEFGHIJKLMNOPQRSTU
24 point (g:\ttfw_z\w0002319.ttf)

ABCDEFGHIJKLMN
24 point (g:\ttfw_z\w0002320.ttf)

ABCDEFGHIJKLMNOPQR
24 point (g:\ttfw_z\w0002322.ttf)

ABCDEFGHIJKLMNOPQ
24 point (g:\ttfw_z\w0002323.ttf)

ABCDEFGHIJKL
24 point (g:\ttfw_z\w0002324.ttf)

ABCDEFGHIJKLMN
24 point (g:\ttfw_z\w0002325.ttf)

ABCDEFGHIJKLMNOPQRSTUVWX
24 point (g:\ttfw_z\w0002330.ttf)

ABCDEFGHIJKLMNOPQRSTUV
24 point (g:\ttfw_z\w0002327.ttf)

ABCDEFGHIJKLMNOPQRSTUVWXYZABCD
24 point (g:\ttfw_z\w0002328.ttf)

ABCDEFGHIJKLMNOPQ
24 point (g:\ttfw_z\w0002329.ttf)

ABCDEFGHIJKLMNOPQR
24 point (g:\ttfw_z\w0002331.ttf)

ABCDEFGHIJKLMNOPQRSTUVWX
24 point (g:\ttfw_z\w0002332.ttf)

ABCDEFGHIJKLMNO
24 point (g:\ttfw_z\w0002333.ttf)

ABCDEFGHIJKLMNO
24 point (g:\ttfw_z\w0002334.ttf)

ABCDEFGHIJKLMNOPQRST
24 point (g:\ttfw_z\w0002336.ttf)

ABCDEFGHIJ
24 point (g:\ttfw_z\w0002337.ttf)

ABCDEFGHIJKLMNOPQR
24 point (g:\ttfw_z\w0002338.ttf)

ABCDEFGHIJKL
24 point (g:\ttfw_z\w0002339.ttf)

ABCDEFGHIJKLMNOP
24 point (g:\ttfw_z\w0002341.ttf)

ABCDEFGHIJKLMNOPQ
24 point (g:\ttfw_z\w0002342.ttf)

ABCDEFGHIJKLMNOPQR
24 point (g:\ttfw_z\w0002343.ttf)

ABCDEFGHIJKLMNOPQ
24 point (g:\ttfw_z\y0002344.ttf)

ABCDEFGHIJKLMNO
24 point (g:\ttfw_z\y0002345.ttf)

ABCDEFGHIJKLMNOP
24 point (g:\ttfw_z\y0002348.ttf)

ABCDEFGHIJKLMNOP
24 point (g:\ttfw_z\y0002347.ttf)

ABCDEFGHIJKLMNO
24 point (g:\ttfw_z\y0002346.ttf)

ABCDEFGHIJKLMNO
24 point (g:\ttfw_z\y0002349.ttf)

ABCDEFGHIJKLMNOPQ
24 point (g:\ttfw_z\y0002350.ttf)

ABCDEFGHIJK
24 point (g:\ttfw_z\z0002355.ttf)

ABCDEFGHIJK
24 point (g:\ttfw_z\z0002352.ttf)

ABCDEFG
24 point (g:\ttfw_z\z0002353.ttf)

ABCDEFGHIJKL
24 point (g:\ttfw_z\z0002354.ttf)

ABCDEFGHIJKL
24 point (g:\ttfw_z\z0002351.ttf)

ABCDEFGHI
24 point (g:\ttfw_z\z0002356.ttf)

ABCDEFGHIJKL
24 point (g:\ttfw_z\z0002357.ttf)

ABCDEFGHIJKLMNOPQ
24 point (g:\ttfw_z\z0002359.ttf)

ABCDEFGHIJKL
24 point (g:\ttfw_z\z0002360.ttf)

ABCDEFGHIJKLMN
24 point (g:\ttfw_z\z0002362.ttf)

ABCDEFGHIJKLMNOPQRS
24 point (g:\ttfw_z\z0002363.ttf)

Page:

5000
Clip Art Images

Animals:\A0000001.PCX

Animals:\A0000002.PCX

Animals:\A0000003.PCX

Animals:\A0000004.PCX

Animals:\A0000005.PCX

Animals:\A0000006.PCX

Animals:\A0000007.PCX

Animals:\A0000008.PCX

Animals:\A0000009.PCX

Animals:\A0000010.PCX

Animals:\A0000011.PCX

Animals:\A0000012.PCX

Animals:\A0000013.PCX

Animals:\A0000014.PCX

Animals:\A0000015.PCX

Animals:\A0000016.PCX

Animals:\A0000019.PCX

Animals:\A0000020.PCX

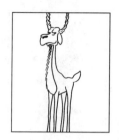

Animals:\A0000021.PCX

Animals:\A0000022.PCX

Animals:\A0000023.PCX

Animals:\A0000024.PCX

Animals:\A0000027.PCX

Animals:\A0000028.PCX

Animals:\A0000029.PCX

Animals:\A0000030.PCX

Animals:\A0000031.PCX

Animals:\A0000032.PCX

Animals:\A0000033.PCX

Animals:\A0000034.PCX

Animals:\A0000035.PCX

Animals:\A0000036.PCX

Animals:\A0000037.PCX

Animals:\A0000038.PCX

Animals:\A0000039.PCX

Animals:\A0000040.PCX

Animals:\A0000041.PCX

Animals:\A0000042.PCX

Animals:\A0000043.PCX

Animals:\A0000044.PCX

Animals:\A0000045.PCX

Animals:\A0000046.PCX

Animals:\A0000047.PCX

Animals:\A0000048.PCX

Animals:\A0000049.PCX

Animals:\A0000050.PCX

Animals:\A0000051.PCX

Animals:\A0000052.PCX

Animals:\A0000053.PCX

Animals:\A0000054.PCX

Animals:\A0000055.PCX

Animals:\A0000056.PCX

Animals:\A0000057.PCX

Animals:\A0000058.PCX

Animals:\A0000059.PCX

Animals:\A0000060.PCX

Animals:\A0000061.PCX

Animals:\A0000062.PCX

Animals:\A0000063.PCX

Animals:\A0000064.PCX

Animals:\A0000065.PCX

Animals:\A0000067.PCx

Animals:\A0000068.PCX

Animals:\A0000069.PCX

Animals:\A0000070.PCX

Animals:\A0000071.PCX

Animals:\A0000072.PCX

Animals:\A0000073.PCX

Animals:\A0000074.PCX

Animals:\A0000075.PCX

Animals:\A0000076.PCX

Animals:\A0000077.PCX

Animals:\A0000078.PCX

Animals:\A0000079.PCX

Animals:\A0000080.PCX

Animals:\A0000081.PCX

Animals:\A0000082.PCX

Animals:\A0000083.PCX

Animals:\A0000084.PCX

Animals:\A0000085.PCX

Animals:\A0000086.PCX

Animals:\A0000087.PCX

Animals:\A0000088.PCX

Animals:\A0000089.PCX

Animals:\A0000090.PCX

Animals:\A0000091.PCX

Animals:\A0000092.PCX

Animals:\A0000093.PCX

Animals:\A0000094.PCX

Animals:\A0000095.PCX

Animals:\A0000096.PCX

Animals:\A0000097.PCX

Animals:\A0000098.PCX

Animals:\A0000099.PCX

Animals:\A0000100.PCX

Animals:\A0000101.PCX

Animals:\A0000102.PCX

Animals:\A0000103.PCX

Animals:\A0000104.PCX

Animals:\A0000105.PCX

Animals:\A0000106.PCX

Animals:\A0000107.PCX

Animals:\A0000108.PCX

Animals:\A0000109.PCX

Animals:\A0000110.PCX

Animals:\A0000111.PCX

Animals:\A0000112.PCX

Animals:\A0000113.PCX

Animals:\A0000114.PCX

Animals:\A0000115.PCX

Animals:\A0000118.PCX

Animals:\A0000119.PCX

Animals:\A0000121.PCX

Animals:\A0000122.PCX

Animals:\A0000123.PCX

Animals:\A0000124.PCX

Animals:\A0000126.PCX

Animals:\A0000127.PCX

Animals:\A0000128.PCX

Animals:\A0000129.PCX

Animals:\A0000130.PCX

Animals:\A0000131.PCX

Animals:\A0000132.PCX

Animals:\A0000133.PCX

Animals:\A0000134.PCX

Animals:\A0000135.PCX

Animals:\A0000136.PCX

Animals:\A0000137.PCX

Animals:\A0000138.PCX

Animals:\A0000139.PCX

Animals:\A0000140.PCX

Animals:\A0000141.PCX

Animals:\A0000142.PCX

Animals:\A0000143.PCX

Animals:\A0000144.PCX

Animals:\A0000145.PCX

Animals:\A0000146.PCX

Animals:\A0000147.PCX

Animals:\A0000148.PCX

Animals:\A0000149.PCX

Animrept:\a0000150.pcx

Animrept:\a0000151.pcx

Animrept:\a0000152.pcx

Animrept:\a0000153.pcx

Animrept:\a0000154.pcx

Animrept:\a0000155.pcx

Animrept:\a0000156.pcx

Animrept:\a0000157.pcx

Animrept:\a0000158.pcx

Animrept:\a0000159.pcx

Animrept:\a0000160.pcx

Animrept:\a0000161.pcx

Animrept:\a0000162.pcx

Animrept:\a0000163.pcx

Animrept:\a0000164.pcx

Animrept:\a0000165.pcx

Animrept:\a0000166.pcx

Animrept:\a0000167.pcx

Animrept:\a0000168.pcx

Animrept:\a0000169.pcx

Animrept:\a0000170.pcx

Animrept:\a0000171.pcx

Animrept:\a0000172.pcx

Animrept:\a0000173.pcx

Animrept:\a0000174.pcx

Animrept:\a0000175.pcx

Animrept:\a0000176.pcx

Animrept:\a0000177.pcx

Animrept:\a0000178.pcx

Animrept:\a0000179.pcx

Animrept:\a0000180.pcx

Animrept:\a0000181.pcx

Animrept:\a0000182.pcx

Animrept:\a0000183.pcx

Animrept:\a0000184.pcx

Animrept:\a0000185.pcx

Animrept:\a0000186.pcx

Animrept:\a0000187.pcx

Animrept:\a0000188.pcx

Animrept:\a0000189.pcx

Animrept:\a0000190.pcx

Animrept:\a0000191.pcx

Animrept:\a0000192.pcx

Animrept:\a0000193.pcx

Animrept:\a0000194.pcx

Animrept:\a0000195.pcx

Animrept:\a0000196.pcx

Animrept:\a0000197.pcx

Animrept:\a0000198.pcx

Animrept:\a0000199.pcx

Animrept:\a0000200.pcx

Animrept:\a0000201.pcx

Animrept:\a0000202.pcx

Animrept:\a0000203.pcx

Animrept:\a0000204.pcx

Animrept:\a0000205.pcx

Animrept:\a0000206.pcx

Animrept:\a0000207.pcx

Animrept:\a0000208.pcx

Animrept:\a0000209.pcx

Animrept:\a0000210.pcx

Animrept:\a0000211.pcx

Animrept:\a0000212.pcx

Animrept:\a0000213.pcx

Animrept:\a0000214.pcx

Art:\a0000215.pcx

Art:\a0000216.pcx

Art:\a0000217.pcx

Art:\a0000218.pcx

Art:\a0000219.pcx

Art:\a0000220.pcx

Art:\a0000221.pcx

Art:\a0000222.pcx

Art:\a0000223.pcx

Art:\a0000224.pcx

Art:\a0000225.pcx

Art:\a0000226.pcx

Art:\a0000227.pcx

Art:\a0000228.pcx

Art:\a0000229.pcx

Art:\a0000230.pcx

Art:\a0000231.pcx

Art:\a0000232.pcx

Art:\a0000233.pcx

Art:\a0000234.pcx

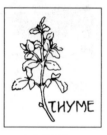

Art:\a0000235.pcx

Art:\a0000236.pcx

Art:\a0000237.pcx

Art:\a0000238.pcx

Art:\a0000239.pcx

Art:\a0000240.pcx

Art:\a0000241.pcx

Art:\a0000242.pcx

Art:\a0000243.pcx

Art:\a0000244.pcx

Art:\a0000245.pcx

Art:\a0000246.pcx

Art:\a0000247.pcx

Art:\a0000248.pcx

Art:\a0000249.pcx

Art:\a0000250.pcx

Art:\a0000251.pcx

Art:\a0000252.pcx

Art:\a0000253.pcx

Art:\a0000254.pcx

Art:\a0000255.pcx

Art:\a0000256.pcx

Art:\a0000257.pcx

Art:\a0000258.pcx

Art:\a0000259.pcx

Art:\a0000260.pcx

Art:\a0000261.pcx

Art:\a0000262.pcx

Art:\a0000263.pcx

Art:\a0000264.pcx

Art:\a0000265.pcx

Art:\a0000266.pcx

Art:\a0000267.pcx

Art:\a0000268.pcx

Art:\a0000269.pcx

Art:\a0000270.pcx

Art:\a0000271.pcx

Art:\a0000272.pcx

Art:\a0000273.pcx

Art:\a0000274.pcx

Art:\a0000275.pcx

Art:\a0000276.pcx

Art:\a0000277.pcx

Art:\a0000278.pcx

Art:\a0000279.pcx

Art:\a0000280.pcx

Art:\a0000281.pcx

Art:\a0000282.pcx

Art:\a0000283.pcx

Art:\a0000284.pcx

Art:\a0000285.pcx

Art:\a0000286.pcx

Art:\a0000287.pcx

Art:\a0000288.pcx

Art:\a0000289.pcx

Art:\a0000290.pcx

Art:\a0000291.pcx

Art:\a0000292.pcx

Art:\a0000293.pcx

Art:\a0000294.pcx

Art:\a0000295.pcx

Art:\a0000296.pcx

Art:\a0000297.pcx

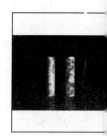

Art:\a0000298.pcx

Art:\a0000299.pcx

Art:\a0000301.pcx

Art:\a0000302.pcx

Art:\a0000303.pcx

Art:\a0000304.pcx

Art:\a0000305.pcx

Art:\a0000306.pcx

Art:\a0000307.pcx

Art:\a0000308.pcx

Art:\a0000309.pcx

Art:\a0000310.pcx

Art:\a0000311.pcx

Art:\a0000312.pcx

Art:\a0000314.pcx

Art:\a0000315.pcx

Art:\a0000316.pcx

Art:\a0000317.pcx

Art:\a0000318.pcx

Art:\a0000320.pcx

Astro:\a0000321.pcx

Astro:\a0000322.pcx

Astro:\a0000323.pcx

Astro:\a0000324.pcx

Astro:\a0000325.pcx

Astro:\a0000326.pcx

Astro:\a0000327.pcx

Astro:\a0000328.pcx

Astro:\a0000329.pcx

Astro:\a0000330.pcx

Astro:\a0000331.pcx

Astro:\a0000332.pcx

Astro:\a0000333.pcx

Astro:\a0000334.pcx

Astro:\a0000335.pcx

Astro:\a0000336.pcx

Astro:\a0000337.pcx

Astro:\a0000338.pcx

Astro:\a0000339.pcx

Astro:\a0000340.pcx

Astro:\a0000341.pcx

Astro:\a0000342.pcx

Astro:\a0000343.pcx

Astro:\a0000344.pcx

Astro:\a0000345.pcx

Astro:\a0000346.pcx

Astro:\a0000347.pcx

Astro:\a0000348.pcx

Astro:\a0000349.pcx

Astro:\a0000350.pcx

Astro:\a0000351.pcx

Astro:\a0000352.pcx

Astro:\a0000353.pcx

Astro:\a0000354.pcx

Astro:\a0000355.pcx

Astro:\a0000356.pcx

Birds:\b0000357.pcx

Birds:\b0000358.pcx

Birds:\b0000359.pcx

Birds:\b0000360.pcx

Birds:\b0000361.pcx

Birds:\b0000362.pcx

Birds:\b0000363.pcx

Birds:\b0000364.pcx

Birds:\b0000365.pcx

Birds:\b0000366.pcx

Birds:\b0000367.pcx

Birds:\b0000368.pcx

Birds:\b0000369.pcx

Birds:\b0000370.pcx

Birds:\b0000371.pcx

Birds:\b0000372.pcx

Birds:\b0000374.pcx

Birds:\b0000375.pcx

Birds:\b0000376.pcx

Birds:\b0000377.pcx

Birds:\b0000378.pcx

Birds:\b0000379.pcx

Birds:\b0000380.pcx

Birds:\b0000381.pcx

Birds:\b0000382.pcx

Birds:\b0000383.pcx

Birds:\b0000384.pcx

Birds:\b0000385.pcx

Birds:\b0000386.pcx

Birds:\b0000387.pcx

Birds:\b0000388.pcx

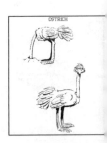

Birds:\b0000389.pcx

Birds:\b0000390.pcx

Birds:\b0000391.pcx

Birds:\b0000392.pcx

Birds:\b0000393.pcx

Birds:\b0000394.pcx

Birds:\b0000395.pcx

Birds:\b0000396.pcx

Birds:\b0000397.pcx

Birds:\b0000398.pcx

Birds:\b0000399.pcx

Birds:\b0000400.pcx

Birds:\b0000401.pcx

Birds:\b0000402.pcx

Birds:\b0000403.pcx

Birds:\b0000404.pcx

Birds:\b0000405.pcx

Birds:\b0000406.pcx

Birds:\b0000407.pcx

Birds:\b0000408.pcx

Birds:\b0000409.pcx

Birds:\b0000410.pcx

Birds:\b0000411.pcx

Birds:\b0000412.pcx

Birds:\b0000413.pcx

Birds:\b0000414.pcx

Birds:\b0000415.pcx

Bookplat:\b0000416.pcx

Bookplat:\b0000417.pcx

Bookplat:\b0000418.pcx

Bookplat:\b0000419.pcx

Bookplat:\b0000420.pcx

Bookplat:\b0000421.pcx

Bookplat:\b0000422.pcx

Bookplat:\b0000423.pcx

Bookplat:\b0000424.pcx

Bookplat:\b0000425.pcx

Bookplat:\b0000426.pcx

Bookplat:\b0000427.pcx

Bookplat:\b0000428.pcx

Bookplat:\b0000429.pcx

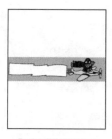

Borders:\b0000430.pcx

Borders:\b0000431.pcx

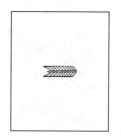

Borders:\b0000432.pcx

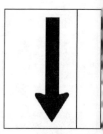

Borders:\b0000433.pcx

Borders:\b0000434.pcx

Borders:\b0000435.pcx

Borders:\b0000436.pcx

Borders:\b0000437.pcx

Borders:\b0000438.pcx

Borders:\b0000439.pcx

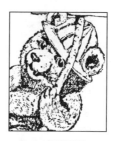

Borders:\b0000440.pcx

Borders:\b0000441.pcx

Borders:\b0000442.pcx

Borders:\b0000443.pcx

Borders:\b0000444.pcx

Borders:\b0000445.pcx

Borders:\b0000446.pcx

Borders:\b0000447.pcx

Borders:\b0000448.pcx

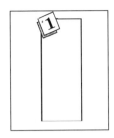

Borders:\b0000449.pcx

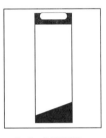

Borders:\b0000450.pcx

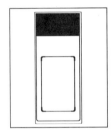

Borders:\b0000451.pcx

Borders:\b0000452.pcx

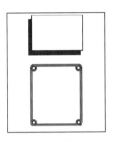

Borders:\b0000453.pcx

Borders:\b0000454.pcx

Borders:\b0000455.pcx

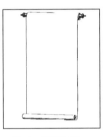

Borders:\b0000456.pcx

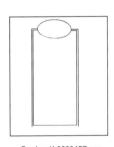

Borders:\b0000457.pcx

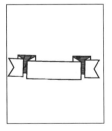

Borders:\b0000458.pcx

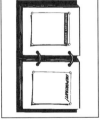

Borders:\b0000459.pcx

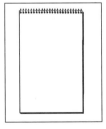

Borders:\b0000460.pcx

Borders:\b0000461.pcx

Borders:\b0000462.pcx

Borders:\b0000463.pcx

Borders:\b0000464.pcx

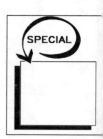

Borders:\b0000465.pcx

Borders:\b0000466.pcx

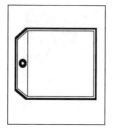

Borders:\b0000467.pcx

Borders:\b0000468.pcx

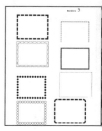

Borders:\b0000469.pcx

Borders:\b0000470.pcx

Borders:\b0000471.pcx

Borders:\b0000472.pcx

Borders:\b0000473.pcx

Borders:\b0000474.pcx

Borders:\b0000475.pcx

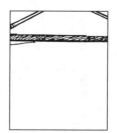

Borders:\b0000476.pcx

Borders:\b0000477.pcx

Borders:\b0000478.pcx

Borders:\b0000479.pcx

Borders:\b0000480.pcx

Borders:\b0000481.pcx

Borders:\b0000482.pcx

Borders:\b0000483.pcx

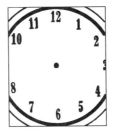

Borders:\b0000484.pcx

Borders:\b0000485.pcx

Borders:\b0000486.pcx

Borders:\b0000487.pcx

Borders:\b0000488.pcx

Borders:\b0000489.pcx

Borders:\b0000490.pcx

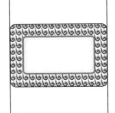

Borders:\b0000491.pcx

Borders:\b0000492.pcx

Borders:\b0000493.pcx

Borders:\b0000494.pcx

Borders:\b0000495.pcx

Borders:\b0000496.pcx

Borders:\b0000497.pcx

Borders:\b0000498.pcx

Borders:\b0000499.pcx

Borders:\b0000500.pcx

Borders:\b0000501.pcx

Borders:\b0000502.pcx

Borders:\b0000503.pcx

Borders:\b0000504.pcx

Borders:\b0000505.pcx

Borders:\b0000506.pcx

Borders:\b0000507.pcx

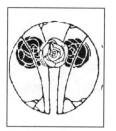

Borders:\b0000508.pcx

Borders:\b0000509.pcx

Borders:\b0000510.pcx

Borders:\b0000511.pcx

Borders:\b0000512.pcx

Borders:\b0000513.pcx

Borders:\b0000514.pcx

Borders:\b0000515.pcx

Borders:\b0000516.pcx

Borders:\b0000517.pcx

Borders:\b0000518.pcx

Borders:\b0000519.pcx

Borders:\b0000520.pcx

Borders:\b0000521.pcx

Borders:\b0000522.pcx

Borders:\b0000523.pcx

Borders:\b0000524.pcx

Borders:\b0000525.pcx

Borders:\b0000526.pcx

Borders:\b0000527.pcx

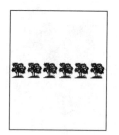

Borders:\b0000528.pcx

Borders:\b0000529.pcx

Borders:\b0000530.pcx

Borders:\b0000531.pcx

Borders:\b0000532.pcx

Borders:\b0000533.pcx

Borders:\b0000534.pcx

Borders:\b0000535.pcx

Borders:\b0000536.pcx

Borders:\b0000537.pcx

Borders:\b0000538.pcx

Borders:\b0000539.pcx

Borders:\b0000540.pcx

Borders:\b0000541.pcx

Borders:\b0000542.pcx

Borders:\b0000543.pcx

Borders:\b0000544.pcx

Borders:\b0000545.pcx

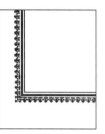

Borders:\b0000546.pcx

Borders:\b0000547.pcx

Borders:\b0000548.pcx

Borders:\b0000549.pcx

Borders:\b0000550.pcx

Borders:\b0000551.pcx

Borders:\b0000552.pcx

Borders:\b0000553.pcx

Borders:\b0000554.pcx

Borders:\b0000555.pcx

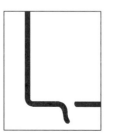

Borders:\b0000556.pcx

Borders:\b0000557.pcx

Borders:\b0000558.pcx

Borders:\b0000559.pcx

Borders:\b0000560.pcx

Borders:\b0000561.pcx

Borders:\b0000562.pcx

Borders:\b0000563.pcx

Borders:\b0000564.pcx

Borders:\b0000565.pcx

Borders:\b0000566.pcx

Borders:\b0000567.pcx

Borders:\b0000568.pcx

Borders:\b0000569.pcx

Borders:\b0000570.pcx

Borders:\b0000571.pcx

Borders:\b0000572.pcx

Borders:\b0000573.pcx

Borders:\b0000574.pcx

Borders:\b0000575.pcx

Borders:\b0000576.pcx

Borders:\b0000577.pcx

Borders:\b0000578.pcx

Borders:\b0000579.pcx

Borders:\b0000580.pcx

Borders:\b0000581.pcx

Borders:\b0000582.pcx

Borders:\b0000583.pcx

Borders:\b0000584.pcx

Borders:\b0000585.pcx

Borders:\b0000586.pcx

Borders:\b0000587.pcx

Borders:\b0000588.pcx

Borders:\b0000589.pcx

Borders:\b0000590.pcx

Borders:\b0000591.pcx

Borders:\b0000592.pcx

Borders:\b0000593.pcx

Borders:\b0000594.pcx

Borders:\b0000595.pcx

Borders:\b0000596.pcx

Borders:\b0000597.pcx

Borders:\b0000598.pcx

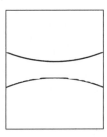

Borders:\b0000599.pcx

Borders:\b0000600.pcx

Borders:\b0000601.pcx

Borders:\b0000602.pcx

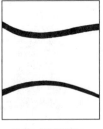

Borders:\b0000603.pcx

Borders:\b0000604.pcx

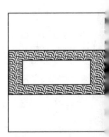

Borders:\b0000605.pcx

Borders:\b0000606.pcx

Borders:\b0000607.pcx

Borders:\b0000608.pcx

Borders:\b0000609.pcx

Borders:\b0000610.pcx

Borders:\b0000611.pcx

Borders:\b0000612.pcx

Borders:\b0000613.pcx

Borders:\b0000614.pcx

Borders:\b0000615.pcx

Borders:\b0000616.pcx

Borders:\b0000617.pcx

Borders:\b0000618.pcx

Borders:\b0000619.pcx

Borders:\b0000620.pcx

Borders:\b0000621.pcx

Building:\b0000622.pcx

Building:\b0000623.pcx

Building:\b0000624.pcx

Building:\b0000625.pcx

Building:\b0000626.pcx

Building:\b0000627.pcx

Building:\b0000628.pcx

Building:\b0000629.pcx

Building:\b0000630.pcx

Building:\b0000631.pcx

Building:\b0000632.pcx

Building:\b0000633.pcx

Building:\b0000634.pcx

Building:\b0000635.pcx

Building:\b0000636.pcx

Building:\b0000637.pcx

Building:\b0000638.pcx

Building:\b0000639.pcx

Building:\b0000640.pcx

Building:\b0000641.pcx

Building:\b0000642.pcx

Building:\b0000643.pcx

Building:\b0000644.pcx

Building:\b0000645.pcx

Building:\b0000646.pcx

Building:\b0000647.pcx

Building:\b0000648.pcx

Building:\b0000649.pcx

Building:\b0000650.pcx

Building:\b0000651.pcx

Building:\b0000652.pcx

Building:\b0000653.pcx

Building:\b0000654.pcx

Building:\b0000655.pcx

Building:\b0000656.pcx

Building:\b0000657.pcx

Building:\b0000658.pcx

Building:\b0000659.pcx

Building:\b0000660.pcx

Building:\b0000661.pcx

Building:\b0000662.pcx

Building:\b0000663.pcx

Building:\b0000664.pcx

Building:\b0000665.pcx

Building:\b0000666.pcx

Building:\b0000667.pcx

Building:\b0000668.pcx

Building:\b0000669.pcx

Busines1:\b0000670.pcx

Busines1:\b0000671.pcx

Busines1:\b0000672.pcx

Busines1:\b0000673.pcx

Busines1:\b0000674.pcx

Busines1:\b0000675.pcx

Busines1:\b0000676.pcx

Busines1:\b0000677.pcx

Busines1:\b0000678.pcx

Busines1:\b0000679.pcx

Busines1:\b0000680.pcx

Busines1:\b0000681.pcx

Busines1:\b0000682.pcx

Busines1:\b0000683.pcx

Busines1:\b0000684.pcx

Busines1:\b0000685.pcx

Busines1:\b0000686.pcx

Busines1:\b0000687.pcx

Busines1:\b0000688.pcx

Busines1:\b0000689.pcx

Busines1:\b0000690.pcx

Busines1:\b0000691.pcx

Busines1:\b0000692.pcx

Busines1:\b0000693.pcx

Busines1:\b0000694.pcx

Busines1:\b0000695.pcx

Busines1:\b0000696.pcx

Busines1:\b0000697.pcx

Busines1:\b0000698.pcx

Busines1:\b0000699.pcx

Busines1:\b0000700.pcx

Busines1:\b0000701.pcx

Busines1:\b0000702.pcx

Busines1:\b0000703.pcx

Busines1:\b0000704.pcx

Busines1:\b0000705.pcx

Busines1:\b0000706.pcx

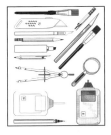

Busines1:\b0000707.pcx

Busines1:\b0000708.pcx

Busines1:\b0000709.pcx

Busines1:\b0000710.pcx

Busines1:\b0000711.pcx

Busines1:\b0000712.pcx

Busines1:\b0000713.pcx

Busines1:\b0000714.pcx

Busines1:\b0000715.pcx

Busines1:\b0000716.pcx

Busines1:\b0000717.pcx

Busines1:\b0000718.pcx

Busines1:\b0000719.pcx

Busines1:\b0000720.pcx

Busines1:\b0000721.pcx

Busines1:\b0000722.pcx

Busines1:\b0000723.pcx

Busines1:\b0000724.pcx

Busines1:\b0000725.pcx

Busines1:\b0000726.pcx

Busines1:\b0000727.pcx

Busines1:\b0000728.pcx

Busines1:\b0000729.pcx

Busines1:\b0000730.pcx

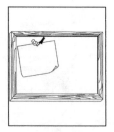

Busines1:\b0000731.pcx

Busines1:\b0000732.pcx

Busines1:\b0000733.pcx

Busines1:\b0000734.pcx

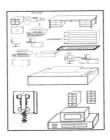

Busines1:\b0000735.pcx

Busines1:\b0000736.pcx

Busines1:\b0000737.pcx

Busines1:\b0000738.pcx

Busines1:\b0000739.pcx

Busines1:\b0000740.pcx

Busines1:\b0000741.pcx

Busines1:\b0000742.pcx

Busines1:\b0000743.pcx

Busines1:\b0000744.pcx

Busines1:\b0000745.pcx

Busines1:\b0000746.pcx

Busines1:\b0000747.pcx

Busines1:\b0000749.pcx

Busines1:\b0000750.pcx

Busines1:\b0000751.pcx

Busines1:\b0000752.pcx

Busines1:\b0000753.pcx

Busines1:\b0000754.pcx

Busines1:\b0000755.pcx

Busines1:\b0000756.pcx

Busines1:\b0000757.pcx

Busines1:\b0000758.pcx

Busines1:\b0000759.pcx

Busines1:\b0000760.pcx

Busines1:\b0000761.pcx

Busines1:\b0000762.pcx

Busines1:\b0000763.pcx

Busines1:\b0000764.pcx

Busines1:\b0000765.pcx

Busines1:\b0000766.pcx

Busines1:\b0000767.pcx

Busines1:\b0000768.pcx

Busines1:\b0000769.pcx

Busines1:\b0000770.pcx

Busines1:\b0000771.pcx

Busines1:\b0000772.pcx

Busines2:\b0000773.pcx

Busines2:\b0000774.pcx

Busines2:\b0000775.pcx

Busines2:\b0000776.pcx

Busines2:\b0000777.pcx

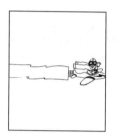

Busines2:\b0000778.pcx

Busines2:\b0000779.pcx

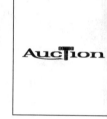

Busines2:\b0000780.pcx

Busines2:\b0000781.pcx

Busines2:\b0000782.pcx

Busines2:\b0000783.pcx

Busines2:\b0000784.pcx

Busines2:\b0000785.pcx

Busines2:\b0000786.pcx

Busines2:\b0000787.pcx

Busines2:\b0000788.pcx

Busines2:\b0000789.pcx

Busines2:\b0000790.pcx

Busines2:\b0000793.pcx

Busines2:\b0000794.pcx

Busines2:\b0000795.pcx

Busines2:\b0000796.pcx

Busines2:\b0000797.pcx

Busines2:\b0000798.pcx

Busines2:\b0000799.pcx

Busines2:\b0000800.pcx

Busines2:\b0000801.pcx

Busines2:\b0000802.pcx

Busines2:\b0000803.pcx

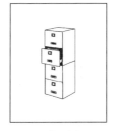

Busines2:\b0000804.pcx

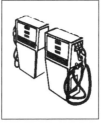

Busines2:\b0000805.pcx

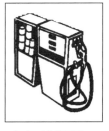

Busines2:\b0000806.pcx

Busines2:\b0000807.pcx

Busines2:\b0000808.pcx

Busines2:\b0000809.pcx

Busines2:\b0000810.pcx

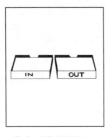

Busines2:\b0000811.pcx

Busines2:\b0000812.pcx

Busines2:\b0000813.pcx

Busines2:\b0000814.pcx

Busines2:\b0000815.pcx

Busines2:\b0000816.pcx

Busines2:\b0000817.pcx

Busines2:\b0000818.pcx

Busines2:\b0000819.pcx

Busines2:\b0000820.pcx

Busines2:\b0000821.pcx

Busines2:\b0000822.pcx

Busines2:\b0000823.pcx

Busines2:\b0000824.pcx

Busines2:\b0000825.pcx

Busines2:\b0000826.pcx

Busines2:\b0000827.pcx

Busines2:\b0000828.pcx

Busines2:\b0000829.pcx

Busines2:\b0000830.pcx

Busines2:\b0000831.pcx

Busines2:\b0000832.pcx

Busines2:\b0000833.pcx

Busines2:\b0000834.pcx

Busines2:\b0000835.pcx

Busines2:\b0000836.pcx

Busines2:\b0000837.pcx

Busines2:\b0000838.pcx

Busines2:\b0000839.pcx

Busines2:\b0000840.pcx

Busines2:\b0000841.pcx

Busines2:\b0000842.pcx

Busines2:\b0000843.pcx

Busines2:\b0000844.pcx

Busines2:\b0000845.pcx

Busines2:\b0000846.pcx

Busines2:\b0000847.pcx

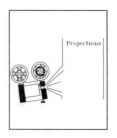

Busines2:\b0000848.pcx

Busines2:\b0000849.pcx

Busines2:\b0000850.pcx

Busines2:\b0000851.pcx

Busines2:\b0000852.pcx

Busines2:\b0000853.pcx

Busines2:\b0000854.pcx

Busines2:\b0000855.pcx

Busines2:\b0000856.pcx

Busines2:\b0000857.pcx

Busines2:\b0000858.pcx

Busines2:\b0000859.pcx

Busines2:\b0000860.pcx

Busines2:\b0000861.pcx

Busines2:\b0000862.pcx

Busines2:\b0000863.pcx

Busines2:\b0000864.pcx

Busines2:\b0000865.pcx

Busines2:\b0000866.pcx

Busines2:\b0000867.pcx

Busines2:\b0000868.pcx

Busines2:\b0000869.pcx

Busines2:\b0000870.pcx

Busines2:\b0000871.pcx

Busines2:\b0000872.pcx

Cart1:\c0000873.pcx

Cart1:\c0000874.pcx

Cart1:\c0000875.pcx

Cart1:\c0000876.pcx

Cart1:\c0000877.pcx

Cart1:\c0000878.pcx

Cart1:\c0000879.pcx

Cart1:\c0000880.pcx

Cart1:\c0000881.pcx

Cart1:\c0000882.pcx

Cart1:\c0000883.pcx

Cart1:\c0000884.pcx

Cart1:\c0000885.pcx

Cart1:\c0000886.pcx

Cart1:\c0000887.pcx

Cart1:\c0000888.pcx

Cart1:\c0000889.pcx

Cart1:\c0000890.pcx

Cart1:\c0000891.pcx

Cart1:\c0000892.pcx

Cart1:\c0000893.pcx

Cart1:\c0000894.pcx

Cart1:\c0000895.pcx

Cart1:\c0000896.pcx

Cart1:\c0000897.pcx

Cart1:\c0000898.pcx

Cart1:\c0000899.pcx

Cart1:\c0000900.pcx

Cart1:\c0000901.pcx

Cart1:\c0000902.pcx

Cart1:\c0000903.pcx

Cart1:\c0000904.pcx

Cart1:\c0000905.pcx

Cart1:\c0000906.pcx

Cart1:\c0000907.pcx

Cart1:\c0000908.pcx

Cart1:\c0000909.pcx

Cart1:\c0000910.pcx

Cart1:\c0000911.pcx

Cart1:\c0000912.pcx

Cart1:\c0000913.pcx

Cart1:\c0000914.pcx

Cart1:\c0000915.pcx

Cart1:\c0000916.pcx

Cart1:\c0000917.pcx

Cart1:\c0000918.pcx

Cart1:\c0000919.pcx

Cart1:\c0000920.pcx

Cart1:\c0000921.pcx

Cart1:\c0000922.pcx

Cart1:\c0000923.pcx

Cart1:\c0000924.pcx

Cart1:\c0000925.pcx

Cart1:\c0000926.pcx

Cart1:\c0000927.pcx

Cart1:\c0000928.pcx

Cart1:\c0000929.pcx

Cart1:\c0000930.pcx

Cart1:\c0000931.pcx

Cart1:\c0000933.pcx

Cart1:\c0000934.pcx

Cart1:\c0000935.pcx

Cart1:\c0000936.pcx

Cart1:\c0000937.pcx

Cart1:\c0000938.pcx

Cart1:\c0000939.pcx

Cart1:\c0000940.pcx

Cart1:\c0000941.pcx

Cart1:\c0000942.pcx

Cart1:\c0000943.pcx

Cart1:\c0000944.pcx

Cart1:\c0000945.pcx

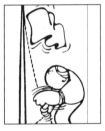

Cart1:\c0000946.pcx

Cart1:\c0000947.pcx

Cart1:\c0000948.pcx

Cart1:\c0000949.pcx

Cart1:\c0000950.pcx

Cart1:\c0000951.pcx

Cart1:\c0000952.pcx

Cart1:\c0000953.pcx

Cart1:\c0000954.pcx

Cart1:\c0000955.pcx

Cart1:\c0000956.pcx

Cart1:\c0000957.pcx

Cart1:\c0000958.pcx

Cart1:\c0000959.pcx

Cart1:\c0000960.pcx

Cart1:\c0000961.pcx

Cart1:\c0000962.pcx

Cart1:\c0000963.pcx

Cart1:\c0000964.pcx

Cart1:\c0000965.pcx

Cart1:\c0000966.pcx

Cart1:\c0000967.pcx

Cart1:\c0000968.pcx

Cart1:\c0000969.pcx

Cart1:\c0000970.pcx

Cart1:\c0000971.pcx

Cart1:\c0000972.pcx

Cart1:\c0000973.pcx

Cart1:\c0000974.pcx

Cart1:\c0000975.pcx

Cart1:\c0000976.pcx

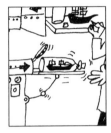

Cart1:\c0000978.pcx

Cart1:\c0000979.pcx

Cart1:\c0000980.pcx

Cart1:\c0000981.pcx

Cart1:\c0000982.pcx

Cart1:\c0000983.pcx

Cart1:\c0000992.pcx

Cart1:\c0000993.pcx

Cart1:\c0000994.pcx

Cart1:\c0000995.pcx

Cart1:\c0000996.pcx

Cart1:\c0000997.pcx

Cart1:\c0000998.pcx

Cart1:\c0000999.pcx

Cart1:\c0001000.pcx

Cart1:\c0001001.pcx

Cart1:\c0001002.pcx

Cart1:\c0001003.pcx

Cart1:\c0001004.pcx

Cart1:\c0001005.pcx

Cart1:\c0001006.pcx

Cart1:\c0001007.pcx

Cart1:\c0001008.pcx

Cart1:\c0001009.pcx

Cart1:\c0001010.pcx

Cart1:\c0001011.pcx

Cart1:\c0001012.pcx

Cart1:\c0001013.pcx

Cart1:\c0001014.pcx

Cart1:\c0001015.pcx

Cart1:\c0001016.pcx

Cart1:\c0001017.pcx

Cart1:\c0001018.pcx

Cart1:\c0001019.pcx

Cart1:\c0001020.pcx

Cart1:\c0001021.pcx

Cart1:\c0001022.pcx

Cart1:\c0001023.pcx

Cart1:\c0001024.pcx

Cart1:\c0001025.pcx

Cart1:\c0001026.pcx

Cart1:\c0001027.pcx

Cart1:\c0001028.pcx

Cart1:\c0001029.pcx

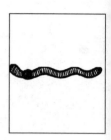

Cart1:\c0001030.pcx

Cart1:\c0001031.pcx

Cart1:\c0001032.pcx

Cart1:\c0001033.pcx

Cart2:\c0001034.pcx

Cart2:\c0001035.pcx

Cart2:\c0001036.pcx

Cart2:\c0001037.pcx

Cart2:\c0001038.pcx

Cart2:\c0001039.pcx

Cart2:\c0001040.pcx

Cart2:\c0001042.pcx

Cart2:\c0001043.pcx

Cart2:\c0001045.pcx

Cart2:\c0001046.pcx

Cart2:\c0001047.pcx

Cart2:\c0001048.pcx

Cart2:\c0001049.pcx

Cart2:\c0001050.pcx

Cart2:\c0001051.pcx

Cart2:\c0001054.pcx

Cart2:\c0001055.pcx

Cart2:\c0001056.pcx

Cart2:\c0001057.pcx

Cart2:\c0001058.pcx

Cart2:\c0001059.pcx

Cart2:\c0001060.pcx

Cart2:\c0001061.pcx

Cart2:\c0001062.pcx

Cart2:\c0001063.pcx

Cart2:\c0001064.pcx

Cart2:\c0001066.pcx

Cart2:\c0001067.pcx

Cart2:\c0001068.pcx

Cart2:\c0001069.pcx

Cart2:\c0001070.pcx

Cart2:\c0001071.pcx

Cart2:\c0001072.pcx

Cart2:\c0001073.pcx

Cart2:\c0001074.pcx

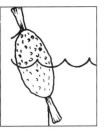

Cart2:\c0001075.pcx

Cart2:\c0001076.pcx

Cart2:\c0001077.pcx

Cart2:\c0001078.pcx

Cart2:\c0001079.pcx

Cart2:\c0001080.pcx

Cart2:\c0001081.pcx

Cart2:\c0001082.pcx

Cart2:\c0001083.pcx

Cart2:\c0001084.pcx

Cart2:\c0001085.pcx

Cart2:\c0001087.pcx

Cart2:\c0001089.pcx

Cart2:\c0001090.pcx

Cart2:\c0001091.pcx

Cart2:\c0001092.pcx

Cart2:\c0001093.pcx

Cart2:\c0001094.pcx

Cart2:\c0001095.pcx

Cart2:\c0001096.pcx

Cart2:\c0001097.pcx

Cart2:\c0001098.pcx

Cart2:\c0001099.pcx

Cart2:\c0001100.pcx

Cart2:\c0001101.pcx

Cart2:\c0001102.pcx

Cart2:\c0001103.pcx

Cart2:\c0001104.pcx

Cart2:\c0001105.pcx

Cart2:\c0001106.pcx

Cart2:\c0001107.pcx

Cart2:\c0001108.pcx

Cart2:\c0001109.pcx

Cart2:\c0001110.pcx

Cart2:\c0001111.pcx

Cart2:\c0001112.pcx

Cart2:\c0001113.pcx

Cart2:\c0001114.pcx

Cart2:\c0001115.pcx

Cart2:\c0001117.pcx

Cart2:\c0001118.pcx

Cart2:\c0001119.pcx

Cart2:\c0001120.pcx

Cart2:\c0001121.pcx

Cart2:\c0001122.pcx

Cart2:\c0001123.pcx

Cart2:\c0001124.pcx

Cart2:\c0001125.pcx

Cart2:\c0001126.pcx

Cart2:\c0001127.pcx

Cart2:\c0001128.pcx

Cart2:\c0001129.pcx

Cart2:\c0001130.pcx

Cart2:\c0001131.pcx

Cart2:\c0001132.pcx

Cart2:\c0001133.pcx

Cart2:\c0001134.pcx

Cart2:\c0001135.pcx

Cart2:\c0001136.pcx

Cart2:\c0001137.pcx

Cart2:\c0001138.pcx

Cart2:\c0001139.pcx

Cart2:\c0001140.pcx

Cart2:\c0001141.pcx

Cart2:\c0001142.pcx

Cart2:\c0001143.pcx

Cart2:\c0001144.pcx

Cart2:\c0001145.pcx

Cart2:\c0001146.pcx

Cart2:\c0001147.pcx

Cart2:\c0001148.pcx

Cart2:\c0001149.pcx

Cart2:\c0001150.pcx

Cart2:\c0001151.pcx

Cart2:\c0001152.pcx

Cart2:\c0001153.pcx

Cart2:\c0001154.pcx

Cart2:\c0001155.pcx

Cart2:\c0001156.pcx

Cart2:\c0001157.pcx

Cart2:\c0001158.pcx

Cart2:\c0001159.pcx

Cart2:\c0001160.pcx

Cart2:\c0001161.pcx

Cart2:\c0001162.pcx

Cart2:\c0001163.pcx

Cart2:\c0001164.pcx

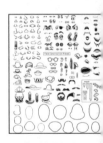

Cart2:\c0001165.pcx

Cart2:\c0001166.pcx

Cart2:\c0001167.pcx

Cart2:\c0001168.pcx

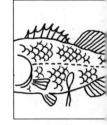

Cart2:\c0001169.pcx

Cart2:\c0001170.pcx

Cart2:\c0001171.pcx

Cart2:\c0001172.pcx

Cart2:\c0001173.pcx

Cart2:\c0001174.pcx

Cart2:\c0001175.pcx

Cart2:\c0001176.pcx

Cart2:\c0001177.pcx

Cart2:\c0001178.pcx

Cart2:\c0001179.pcx

Cart2:\c0001181.pcx

Cart2:\c0001182.pcx

Cart2:\c0001183.pcx

Cart2:\c0001184.pcx

Cart2:\c0001185.pcx

Cart2:\c0001186.pcx

Cart2:\c0001187.pcx

Cart2:\c0001188.pcx

Cart2:\c0001189.pcx

Cart2:\c0001190.pcx

Cart2:\c0001191.pcx

Cart2:\c0001193.pcx

Cart2:\c0001194.pcx

Cart2:\c0001196.pcx

Cart2:\c0001197.pcx

Cart2:\c0001198.pcx

Cart2:\c0001199.pcx

Cart2:\c0001200.pcx

Cart2:\c0001202.pcx

Cart2:\c0001203.pcx

Cart2:\c0001204.pcx

Cart2:\c0001205.pcx

Cats:\c0001218.pcx

Cats:\c0001219.pcx

Cats:\c0001220.pcx

Cats:\c0001221.pcx

Cats:\c0001222.pcx

Cats:\c0001223.pcx

Cats:\c0001224.pcx

Cats:\c0001225.pcx

Cats:\c0001226.pcx

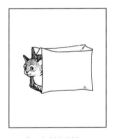

Cats:\c0001227.pcx

Cats:\c0001230.pcx

Cats:\c0001231.pcx

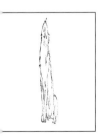

Cats:\c0001232.pcx

Cats:\c0001233.pcx

Cats:\c0001234.pcx

Cats:\c0001235.pcx

Cats:\c0001236.pcx

Cats:\c0001237.pcx

Cats:\c0001238.pcx

Cats:\c0001239.pcx

Cats:\c0001240.pcx

Cats:\c0001241.pcx

Cats:\c0001242.pcx

Cats:\c0001243.pcx

Cats:\c0001244.pcx

Cats:\c0001245.pcx

Cats:\c0001246.pcx

Cats:\c0001247.pcx

Cats:\c0001248.pcx

Cats:\c0001250.pcx

Cats:\c0001251.pcx

Cats:\c0001252.pcx

Cats:\c0001253.pcx

Cats:\c0001254.pcx

Cats:\c0001255.pcx

Cats:\c0001256.pcx

Cats:\c0001257.pcx

Cats:\c0001258.pcx

Cats:\c0001259.pcx

Cats:\c0001260.pcx

Cats:\c0001261.pcx

Cats:\c0001263.pcx

Cats:\c0001264.pcx

Cats:\c0001269.pcx

Cats:\c0001270.pcx

Cats:\c0001271.pcx

Cats:\c0001272.pcx

Cats:\c0001274.pcx

Cats:\c0001275.pcx

Cats:\c0001277.pcx

Cats:\c0001278.pcx

Cats:\c0001279.pcx

Cats:\c0001280.pcx

Cats:\c0001281.pcx

Cats:\c0001282.pcx

Cats:\c0001284.pcx

Cats:\c0001285.pcx

Cats:\c0001286.pcx

Cats:\c0001287.pcx

Cats:\c0001288.pcx

Cats:\c0001289.pcx

Cats:\c0001291.pcx

Cats:\c0001292.pcx

Cats:\c0001293.pcx

Cats:\c0001294.pcx

Cats:\c0001295.pcx

Cats:\c0001296.pcx

Cats:\c0001297.pcx

Cats:\c0001300.pcx

Cats:\c0001301.pcx

Cats:\c0001307.pcx

Cats:\c0001308.pcx

Cats:\c0001310.pcx

Cats:\c0001311.pcx

Cats:\c0001312.pcx

Cats:\c0001313.pcx

Cats:\c0001314.pcx

Computer:\c0001315.pcx

Computer:\c0001316.pcx

Computer:\c0001318.pcx

Computer:\c0001319.pc

Computer:\c0001321.pcx

Computer:\c0001322.pcx

Computer:\c0001323.pcx

Computer:\c0001324.pc

Computer:\c0001325.pcx

Computer:\c0001326.pcx

Computer:\c0001327.pcx

Computer:\c0001329.pc

Computer:\c0001330.pcx

Computer:\c0001331.pcx

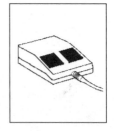

Computer:\c0001335.pcx

Computer:\c0001336.pc

Computer:\c0001337.pcx

Computer:\c0001338.pcx

Computer:\c0001339.pcx

Computer:\c0001340.pcx

Computer:\c0001343.pcx

Computer:\c0001344.pcx

Computer:\c0001346.pcx

Computer:\c0001347.pcx

Computer:\c0001348.pcx

Computer:\c0001349.pcx

Computer:\c0001350.pcx

Computer:\c0001351.pcx

Computer:\c0001352.pcx

Computer:\c0001353.pcx

Computer:\c0001354.pcx

Computer:\c0001355.pcx

Computer:\c0001356.pcx

Computer:\c0001357.pcx

Computer:\c0001359.pcx

Computer:\c0001363.pcx

Computer:\c0001364.pcx

Computer:\c0001365.pcx

Computer:\c0001366.pcx

Computer:\c0001367.pcx

Computer:\c0001368.pcx

Computer:\c0001369.pcx

Computer:\c0001370.pcx

Computer:\c0001371.pcx

Computer:\c0001372.pcx

Computer:\c0001373.pcx

Computer:\c0001374.pcx

Computer:\c0001375.pcx

Computer:\c0001376.pcx

Computer:\c0001377.pcx

Computer:\c0001378.pcx

Computer:\c0001379.pcx

Computer:\c0001380.pcx

Computer:\c0001381.pcx

Computer:\c0001382.pcx

Computer:\c0001383.pcx

Computer:\c0001384.pcx

Computer:\c0001386.pcx

Computer:\c0001387.pcx

Computer:\c0001388.pcx

Computer:\c0001389.pcx

Computer:\c0001391.pcx

Computer:\c0001392.pcx

Computer:\c0001395.pcx

Computer:\c0001396.pcx

Computer:\c0001397.pcx

Computer:\c0001399.pcx

Computer:\c0001400.pcx

Computer:\c0001403.pcx

Computer:\c0001404.pcx

Computer:\c0001405.pcx

Computer:\c0001406.pcx

Computer:\c0001408.pcx

Dogs:\d0001409.pcx

Dogs:\d0001410.pcx

Dogs:\d0001411.pcx

Dogs:\d0001412.pcx

Dogs:\d0001413.pcx

Dogs:\d0001414.pcx

Dogs:\d0001415.pcx

Dogs:\d0001416.pcx

Dogs:\d0001417.pcx

Dogs:\d0001418.pcx

Dogs:\d0001419.pcx

Dogs:\d0001420.pcx

Dogs:\d0001421.pcx

Dogs:\d0001422.pcx

Dogs:\d0001423.pcx

Dogs:\d0001424.pcx

Dogs:\d0001425.pcx

Dogs:\d0001426.pcx

Dogs:\d0001427.pcx

Dogs:\d0001428.pcx

Dogs:\d0001429.pcx

Dogs:\d0001430.pcx

Dogs:\d0001431.pcx

Dogs:\d0001432.pcx

Dogs:\d0001433.pcx

Dogs:\d0001434.pcx

Dogs:\d0001435.pcx

Dogs:\d0001436.pcx

Dogs:\d0001437.pcx

Dogs:\d0001438.pcx

Dogs:\d0001439.pcx

Dogs:\d0001440.pcx

Dogs:\d0001441.pcx

Dogs:\d0001442.pcx

Dogs:\d0001443.pcx

Dogs:\d0001444.pcx

Dogs:\d0001445.pcx

Dogs:\d0001446.pcx

Dogs:\d0001447.pcx

Dogs:\d0001448.pcx

Dogs:\d0001449.pcx

Dogs:\d0001450.pcx

Dogs:\d0001451.pcx

Dogs:\d0001452.pcx

Dogs:\d0001453.pcx

Dogs:\d0001455.pcx

Dogs:\d0001456.pcx

Dogs:\d0001457.pcx

Dogs:\d0001458.pcx

Dogs:\d0001459.pcx

Dogs:\d0001460.pcx

Dogs:\d0001461.pcx

Dogs:\d0001462.pcx

Dogs:\d0001463.pcx

Dogs:\d0001464.pcx

Dogs:\d0001465.pcx

Dogs:\d0001466.pcx

Dogs:\d0001467.pcx

Dogs:\d0001468.pcx

Dogs:\d0001469.pcx

Educatio:\e0001470.pcx

Educatio:\e0001471.pcx

Educatio:\e0001472.pcx

Educatio:\e0001473.pcx

Educatio:\e0001474.pcx

Educatio:\e0001475.pcx

Educatio:\e0001476.pcx

Educatio:\e0001477.pcx

Educatio:\e0001478.pcx

Educatio:\e0001479.pcx

Educatio:\e0001480.pcx

Educatio:\e0001481.pcx

Educatio:\e0001482.pcx

Educatio:\e0001483.pcx

Educatio:\e0001484.pcx

Educatio:\e0001485.pcx

Educatio:\e0001486.pcx

Educatio:\e0001487.pcx

Educatio:\e0001488.pcx

Educatio:\e0001489.pcx

Educatio:\e0001490.pcx

Educatio:\e0001491.pcx

Educatio:\e0001492.pcx

Educatio:\e0001493.pcx

Educatio:\e0001494.pcx

Educatio:\e0001495.pcx

Educatio:\e0001496.pcx

Educatio:\e0001498.pcx

Educatio:\e0001499.pcx

Educatio:\e0001500.pcx

Educatio:\e0001501.pcx

Educatio:\e0001502.pcx

Educatio:\e0001503.pcx

Educatio:\e0001504.pcx

Educatio:\e0001505.pcx

Educatio:\e0001506.pcx

Educatio:\e0001507.pcx

Educatio:\e0001508.pcx

Educatio:\e0001509.pcx

Educatio:\e0001511.pcx

Educatio:\e0001512.pcx

Educatio:\e0001513.pcx

Educatio:\e0001514.pcx

Educatio:\e0001515.pcx

Educatio:\e0001516.pcx

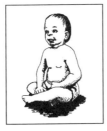

Educatio:\e0001517.pcx

Educatio:\e0001518.pcx

Educatio:\e0001519.pcx

Educatio:\e0001520.pcx

Educatio:\e0001521.pcx

Educatio:\e0001522.pcx

Educatio:\e0001523.pcx

Educatio:\e0001524.pcx

Educatio:\e0001525.pcx

Educatio:\e0001526.pcx

Educatio:\e0001527.pcx

Educatio:\e0001528.pcx

Educatio:\e0001529.pcx

Educatio:\e0001530.pcx

Educatio:\e0001531.pcx

Educatio:\e0001532.pcx

Educatio:\e0001533.pcx

Educatio:\e0001534.pcx

Educatio:\e0001535.pcx

Educatio:\e0001536.pcx

Educatio:\e0001537.pcx

Educatio:\e0001539.pcx

Educatio:\e0001544.pcx

Educatio:\e0001545.pcx

Educatio:\e0001546.pcx

Educatio:\e0001547.pcx

Educatio:\e0001548.pcx

Educatio:\e0001549.pcx

Educatio:\e0001550.pcx

Educatio:\e0001551.pcx

Educatio:\e0001552.pcx

Educatio:\e0001553.pcx

Educatio:\e0001554.pcx

Educatio:\e0001555.pcx

Educatio:\e0001556.pcx

Educatio:\e0001557.pcx

Educatio:\e0001558.pcx

Educatio:\e0001559.pcx

Educatio:\e0001560.pcx

Educatio:\e0001561.pcx

Educatio:\e0001562.pcx

Educatio:\e0001563.pcx

Educatio:\e0001564.pcx

Educatio:\e0001565.pcx

Educatio:\e0001566.pcx

Educatio:\e0001567.pcx

Educatio:\e0001568.pcx

Educatio:\e0001569.pcx

Educatio:\e0001570.pcx

Educatio:\e0001571.pcx

Educatio:\e0001572.pcx

Educatio:\e0001573.pcx

Educatio:\e0001574.pcx

Educatio:\e0001575.pcx

Educatio:\e0001576.pcx

Educatio:\e0001577.pcx

Ethnic:\e0001578.pcx

Ethnic:\e0001579.pcx

Ethnic:\e0001580.pcx

Ethnic:\e0001581.pcx

Ethnic:\e0001582.pcx

Ethnic:\e0001583.pcx

Ethnic:\e0001584.pcx

Ethnic:\e0001585.pcx

Ethnic:\e0001586.pcx

Ethnic:\e0001587.pcx

Ethnic:\e0001588.pcx

Ethnic:\e0001589.pcx

Ethnic:\e0001590.pcx

Ethnic:\e0001591.pcx

Ethnic:\e0001592.pcx

Ethnic:\e0001593.pcx

Ethnic:\e0001594.pcx

Ethnic:\e0001595.pcx

Ethnic:\e0001596.pcx

Ethnic:\e0001597.pcx

Ethnic:\e0001598.pcx

Ethnic:\e0001599.pcx

Ethnic:\e0001600.pcx

Ethnic:\e0001601.pcx

Ethnic:\e0001602.pcx

Ethnic:\e0001603.pcx

Ethnic:\e0001604.pcx

Ethnic:\e0001605.pcx

Ethnic:\e0001606.pcx

Ethnic:\e0001607.pcx

Ethnic:\e0001608.pcx

Ethnic:\e0001609.pcx

Ethnic:\e0001610.pcx

Ethnic:\e0001611.pcx

Ethnic:\e0001612.pcx

Ethnic:\e0001613.pcx

Ethnic:\e0001614.pcx

Ethnic:\e0001615.pcx

Ethnic:\e0001616.pcx

Ethnic:\e0001617.pcx

Ethnic:\e0001618.pcx

Ethnic:\e0001619.pcx

Ethnic:\e0001620.pcx

Ethnic:\e0001622.pcx

Ethnic:\e0001623.pcx

Ethnic:\e0001624.pcx

Ethnic:\e0001625.pcx

Ethnic:\e0001626.pcx

Ethnic:\e0001627.pcx

Ethnic:\e0001629.pcx

Ethnic:\e0001630.pcx

Ethnic:\e0001631.pcx

Ethnic:\e0001632.pcx

Ethnic:\e0001633.pcx

Ethnic:\e0001634.pcx

Ethnic:\e0001635.pcx

Ethnic:\e0001636.pcx

Ethnic:\e0001637.pcx

Ethnic:\e0001638.pcx

Ethnic:\e0001639.pcx

Ethnic:\e0001640.pcx

Ethnic:\e0001641.pcx

Ethnic:\e0001642.pcx

Ethnic:\e0001643.pcx

Ethnic:\e0001644.pcx   Ethnic:\e0001645.pcx   Ethnic:\e0001647.pcx

Fantasy:\f0001649.pcx

Fantasy:\f0001650.pcx

Fantasy:\f0001651.pcx

Fantasy:\f0001652.pcx

Fantasy:\f0001653.pcx

Fantasy:\f0001654.pcx

Fantasy:\f0001655.pcx

Fantasy:\f0001658.pcx

Fantasy:\f0001659.pcx

Fantasy:\f0001660.pcx

Fantasy:\f0001662.pcx

Fantasy:\f0001663.pcx

Fantasy:\f0001664.pcx

Fantasy:\f0001665.pcx

Fantasy:\f0001667.pcx

Fantasy:\f0001669.pcx

Fantasy:\f0001670.pcx

Fantasy:\f0001672.pcx

Fantasy:\f0001673.pcx

Fantasy:\f0001674.pcx

Fantasy:\f0001675.pcx

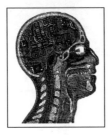

Fantasy:\f0001676.pcx

Fantasy:\f0001677.pcx

Fantasy:\f0001678.pcx

Fantasy:\f0001679.pcx

Fantasy:\f0001680.pcx

Fantasy:\f0001681.pcx

Fantasy:\f0001682.pcx

Fantasy:\f0001683.pcx

Fantasy:\f0001684.pcx

Fantasy:\f0001690.pcx

Fantasy:\f0001691.pcx

Fantasy:\f0001692.pcx

Fantasy:\f0001693.pcx

Fantasy:\f0001694.pcx

Fantasy:\f0001695.pcx

Fantasy:\f0001696.pcx

Fantasy:\f0001697.pcx

Fantasy:\f0001698.pcx

Fantasy:\f0001699.pcx

Fantasy:\f0001700.pcx

Fantasy:\f0001701.pcx

Fantasy:\f0001702.pcx

Fantasy:\f0001703.pcx

Fantasy:\f0001704.pcx

Fantasy:\f0001706.pcx

Fantasy:\f0001707.pcx

Fantasy:\f0001708.pcx

Fantasy:\f0001709.pcx

Fantasy:\f0001710.pcx

Fantasy:\f0001711.pcx

Fantasy:\f0001712.pcx

Fantasy:\f0001713.pcx

Fantasy:\f0001714.pcx

Fantasy:\f0001715.pcx

Fantasy:\f0001716.pcx

Fantasy:\f0001717.pcx

Fantasy:\f0001718.pcx

Fantasy:\f0001719.pcx

Fantasy:\f0001720.pcx

Fantasy:\f0001721.pcx

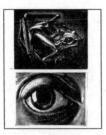

Fantasy:\f0001722.pcx

Fantasy:\f0001723.pcx

Fantasy:\f0001725.pcx

Fantasy:\f0001726.pcx

Fantasy:\f0001727.pcx

Fantasy:\f0001728.pcx

Fantasy:\f0001729.pcx

Fantasy:\f0001730.pcx

Fantasy:\f0001731.pcx

Fantasy:\f0001732.pcx

Fantasy:\f0001733.pcx

Fantasy:\f0001734.pcx

Fantasy:\f0001735.pcx

Fantasy:\f0001736.pcx

Fantasy:\f0001737.pcx

Fantasy:\f0001738.pcx

Fantasy:\f0001740.pcx

Fantasy:\f0001741.pcx

Fantasy:\f0001743.pcx

Fantasy:\f0001744.pcx

Fantasy:\f0001745.pcx

Fantasy:\f0001746.pcx

Fantasy:\f0001747.pcx

Fantasy:\f0001748.pcx

Fantasy:\f0001749.pcx

Fantasy:\f0001750.pcx

Fantasy:\f0001751.pcx

Fantasy:\f0001752.pcx

Fantasy:\f0001753.pcx

Fantasy:\f0001754.pcx

Fantasy:\f0001755.pcx

Fantasy:\f0001756.pcx

Fantasy:\f0001757.pcx

Fantasy:\f0001758.pcx

Fantasy:\f0001759.pcx

Fantasy:\f0001760.pcx

Fantasy:\f0001761.pcx

Fantasy:\f0001762.pcx

Fantasy:\f0001763.pcx

Fantasy:\f0001764.pcx

Fantasy:\f0001765.pcx

Fantasy:\f0001766.pcx

Fantasy:\f0001767.pcx

Fantasy:\f0001769.pcx

Fantasy:\f0001771.pcx

Fantasy:\f0001772.pcx

Fantasy:\f0001773.pcx

Fantasy:\f0001774.pcx

Fantasy:\f0001775.pcx

Fantasy:\f0001776.pcx

Fantasy:\f0001777.pcx

Fantasy:\f0001779.pcx

Fantasy:\f0001780.pcx

Fantasy:\f0001781.pcx

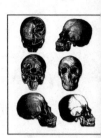

Fantasy:\f0001782.pcx

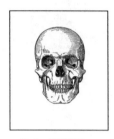

Fantasy:\f0001783.pcx

Fantasy:\f0001784.pcx

Fantasy:\f0001785.pcx

Fantasy:\f0001786.pcx

Fantasy:\f0001787.pcx

Fantasy:\f0001788.pcx

Fantasy:\f0001789.pcx

Fantasy:\f0001790.pcx

Fantasy:\f0001791.pcx

Fantasy:\f0001792.pcx

Fantasy:\f0001793.pcx

Fantasy:\f0001794.pcx

Fantasy:\f0001795.pcx

Fantasy:\f0001797.pcx

Fantasy:\f0001798.pcx

Fantasy:\f0001800.pcx

Fantasy:\f0001801.pcx

Festiv:\f0001802.pcx

Festiv:\f0001803.pcx

Festiv:\f0001804.pcx

Festiv:\f0001805.pcx

Festiv:\f0001806.pcx

Festiv:\f0001807.pcx

Festiv:\f0001808.pcx

Festiv:\f0001809.pcx

Festiv:\f0001810.pcx

Festiv:\f0001811.pcx

Festiv:\f0001812.pcx

Festiv:\f0001813.pcx

Festiv:\f0001814.pcx

Festiv:\f0001815.pcx

Festiv:\f0001816.pcx

Festiv:\f0001817.pcx

Festiv:\f0001818.pcx

Festiv:\f0001819.pcx

Festiv:\f0001820.pcx

Festiv:\f0001821.pcx

Festiv:\f0001822.pcx

Festiv:\f0001823.pcx

Festiv:\f0001824.pcx

Festiv:\f0001825.pcx

Festiv:\f0001826.pcx

Festiv:\f0001827.pcx

Festiv:\f0001828.pcx

Festiv:\f0001829.pcx

Festiv:\f0001830.pcx

Festiv:\f0001831.pcx

Festiv:\f0001832.pcx

Festiv:\f0001833.pcx

Festiv:\f0001834.pcx

Festiv:\f0001835.pcx

Festiv:\f0001836.pcx

Festiv:\f0001837.pcx

Festiv:\f0001838.pcx

Festiv:\f0001839.pcx

Festiv:\f0001840.pcx

Festiv:\f0001841.pcx

Festiv:\f0001842.pcx

Festiv:\f0001843.pcx

Festiv:\f0001844.pcx

Festiv:\f0001845.pcx

Festiv:\f0001846.pcx

Festiv:\f0001847.pcx

Festiv:\f0001848.pcx

Festiv:\f0001849.pcx

Festiv:\f0001850.pcx

Festiv:\f0001851.pcx

Festiv:\f0001852.pcx

Festiv:\f0001853.pcx

Festiv:\f0001854.pcx

Festiv:\f0001855.pcx

Festiv:\f0001856.pcx

Festiv:\f0001857.pcx

Festiv:\f0001858.pcx

Festiv:\f0001859.pcx

Festiv:\f0001860.pcx

Festiv:\f0001861.pcx

Festiv:\f0001862.pcx

Festiv:\f0001863.pcx

Festiv:\f0001864.pcx

Festiv:\f0001865.pcx

Festiv:\f0001866.pcx

Festiv:\f0001867.pcx

Festiv:\f0001868.pcx

Festiv:\f0001869.pcx

Festiv:\f0001870.pcx

Festiv:\f0001871.pcx

Festiv:\f0001872.pcx

Festiv:\f0001873.pcx

Festiv:\f0001874.pcx

Festiv:\f0001875.pcx

Festiv:\f0001876.pcx

Festiv:\f0001877.pcx

Festiv:\f0001878.pcx

Festiv:\f0001879.pcx

Festiv:\f0001880.pcx

Festiv:\f0001881.pcx

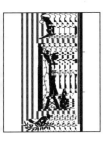

Festiv:\f0001882.pcx

Festiv:\f0001883.pcx

Festiv:\f0001884.pcx

Festiv:\f0001885.pcx

Festiv:\f0001886.pcx

Festiv:\f0001887.pcx

Festiv:\f0001888.pcx

Festiv:\f0001889.pcx

Festiv:\f0001890.pcx

Festiv:\f0001891.pcx

Festiv:\f0001892.pcx

Festiv:\f0001894.pcx

Festiv:\f0001895.pcx

Festiv:\f0001896.pcx

Festiv:\f0001897.pcx

Festiv:\f0001898.pcx

Festiv:\f0001899.pcx

Festiv:\f0001900.pcx

Festiv:\f0001901.pcx

Festiv:\f0001902.pcx

Festiv:\f0001903.pcx

Festiv:\f0001904.pcx

Festiv:\f0001905.pcx

Festiv:\f0001906.pcx

Festiv:\f0001907.pcx

Festiv:\f0001908.pcx

Festiv:\f0001909.pcx

Festiv:\f0001910.pcx

Festiv:\f0001911.pcx

Festiv:\f0001912.pcx

Festiv:\f0001913.pcx

Festiv:\f0001914.pcx

Festiv:\f0001915.pcx

Festiv:\f0001916.pcx

Festiv:\f0001917.pcx

Festiv:\f0001918.pcx

Festiv:\f0001919.pcx

Festiv:\f0001920.pcx

Festiv:\f0001921.pcx

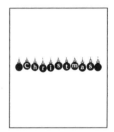

Festiv:\f0001922.pcx

Festiv:\f0001923.pcx

Festiv:\f0001924.pcx

Festiv:\f0001925.pcx

Festiv:\f0001926.pcx

Festiv:\f0001927.pcx

Festiv:\f0001928.pcx

Festiv:\f0001929.pcx

Festiv:\f0001930.pcx

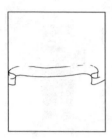

Festiv:\f0001931.pcx

Festiv:\f0001932.pcx

Festiv:\f0001934.pcx

Festiv:\f0001935.pcx

Festiv:\f0001936.pcx

Festiv:\f0001938.pcx

Festiv:\f0001941.pcx

Festiv:\f0001942.pcx

Festiv:\f0001943.pcx

Festiv:\f0001944.pcx

Festiv:\f0001945.pcx

Festiv:\f0001946.pcx

Festiv:\f0001947.pcx

Festiv:\f0001948.pcx

Festiv:\f0001949.pcx

Festiv:\f0001950.pcx

Festiv:\f0001951.pcx

Festiv:\f0001952.pcx

Festiv:\f0001953.pcx

Festiv:\f0001954.pcx

Festiv:\f0001955.pcx

Festiv:\f0001956.pcx

Festiv:\f0001957.pcx

Festiv:\f0001958.pcx

Festiv:\f0001959.pcx

Festiv:\f0001960.pcx

Festiv:\f0001961.pcx

Festiv:\f0001962.pcx

Festiv:\f0001963.pcx

Festiv:\f0001964.pcx

Festiv:\f0001965.pcx

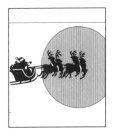

Festiv:\f0001966.pcx

Festiv:\f0001967.pcx

Festiv:\f0001968.pcx

Festiv:\f0001969.pcx

Festiv:\f0001970.pcx

Festiv:\f0001971.pcx

Festiv:\f0001972.pcx

Festiv:\f0001973.pcx

Festiv:\f0001974.pcx

Festiv:\f0001975.pcx

Festiv:\f0001976.pcx

Festiv:\f0001977.pcx

Festiv:\f0001978.pcx

Festiv:\f0001979.pcx

Festiv:\f0001980.pcx

Festiv:\f0001981.pcx

Festiv:\f0001982.pcx

Festiv:\f0001984.pcx

Festiv:\f0001985.pcx

Festiv:\f0001986.pcx

Festiv:\f0001987.pcx

Festiv:\f0001988.pcx

Festiv:\f0001989.pcx

Festiv:\f0001990.pcx

Festiv:\f0001991.pcx

Festiv:\f0001992.pcx

Festiv:\f0001993.pcx

Festiv:\f0001994.pcx

Festiv:\f0001995.pcx

Fish:\f0001996.pcx

Fish:\f0001997.pcx

Fish:\f0001998.pcx

Fish:\f0001999.pcx

Fish:\f0002000.pcx

Fish:\f0002001.pcx

Fish:\f0002002.pcx

Fish:\f0002003.pcx

Fish:\f0002004.pcx

Fish:\f0002005.pcx

Fish:\f0002006.pcx

Fish:\f0002007.pcx

Fish:\f0002008.pcx

Fish:\f0002009.pcx

Fish:\f0002010.pcx

Fish:\f0002011.pcx

Fish:\f0002012.pcx

Fish:\f0002013.pcx

Fish:\f0002014.pcx

Fish:\f0002015.pcx

Fish:\f0002016.pcx

Fish:\f0002017.pcx

Fish:\f0002018.pcx

Fish:\f0002019.pcx

Fish:\f0002020.pcx

Fish:\f0002021.pcx

Fish:\f0002022.pcx

Fish:\f0002023.pcx

Fish:\f0002024.pcx

Fish:\f0002025.pcx

Fish:\f0002026.pcx

Fish:\f0002027.pcx

Fish:\f0002028.pcx

Fish:\f0002029.pcx

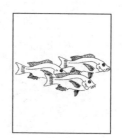

Fish:\f0002030.pcx

Fish:\f0002031.pcx

Fish:\f0002032.pcx

Fish:\f0002033.pcx

Fish:\f0002034.pcx

Fish:\f0002035.pcx

Fish:\f0002036.pcx

Fish:\f0002037.pcx

Fish:\f0002038.pcx

Fish:\f0002039.pcx

Fish:\f0002040.pcx

Fish:\f0002041.pcx

Fish:\f0002042.pcx

Fish:\f0002043.pcx

Fish:\f0002044.pcx

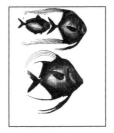

Fish:\f0002045.pcx

Fish:\f0002046.pcx

Fish:\f0002048.pcx

Fish:\f0002049.pcx

Fish:\f0002050.pcx

Fish:\f0002051.pcx

Fish:\f0002052.pcx

Fish:\f0002053.pcx

Fish:\f0002054.pcx

Fish:\f0002055.pcx

Fish:\f0002056.pcx

Fish:\f0002057.pcx

Fish:\f0002058.pcx

Fish:\f0002059.pcx

Fish:\f0002060.pcx

Fish:\f0002061.pcx

Fish:\f0002062.pcx

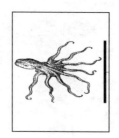

Fish:\f0002063.pcx

Fish:\f0002064.pcx

Fish:\f0002065.pcx

Fish:\f0002066.pcx

Fish:\f0002067.pcx

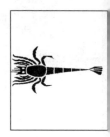

Fish:\f0002068.pcx

Fish:\f0002069.pcx

Fish:\f0002070.pcx

Fish:\f0002071.pcx

Fish:\f0002072.pcx

Fish:\f0002073.pcx

Fish:\f0002074.pcx

Fish:\f0002075.pcx

Fish:\f0002076.pcx

Fish:\f0002077.pcx

Fish:\f0002078.pcx

Fish:\f0002079.pcx

Fish:\f0002080.pcx

Fish:\f0002081.pcx

Fish:\f0002082.pcx

Fish:\f0002083.pcx

Fish:\f0002084.pcx

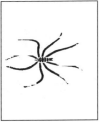

Fish:\f0002085.pcx

Fish:\f0002086.pcx

Fish:\f0002087.pcx

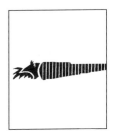

Fish:\f0002088.pcx

Fish:\f0002089.pcx

Fish:\f0002090.pcx

Fish:\f0002091.pcx

Fish:\f0002092.pcx

Fish:\f0002093.pcx

Fish:\f0002094.pcx

Fish:\f0002095.pcx

Fish:\f0002096.pcx

Fish:\f0002097.pcx

Fish:\f0002098.pcx

Fish:\f0002099.pcx

Fish:\f0002100.pcx

Fish:\f0002101.pcx

Fish:\f0002102.pcx

Fish:\f0002103.pcx

Fish:\f0002104.pcx

Fish:\f0002105.pcx

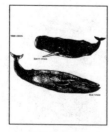

Fish:\f0002106.pcx

Fish:\f0002107.pcx

Fish:\f0002108.pcx

Fish:\f0002109.pcx

Fish:\f0002110.pcx

Fish:\f0002111.pcx

Fish:\f0002112.pcx

Fish:\f0002113.pcx

Fish:\f0002114.pcx

Fish:\f0002115.pcx

Fish:\f0002116.pcx

Fish:\f0002117.pcx

Flowers:\f0002118.pcx

Flowers:\f0002119.pcx

Flowers:\f0002120.pcx

Flowers:\f0002121.pcx

Flowers:\f0002122.pcx

Flowers:\f0002123.pcx

Flowers:\f0002124.pcx

Flowers:\f0002125.pcx

Flowers:\f0002126.pcx

Flowers:\f0002127.pcx

Flowers:\f0002128.pcx

Flowers:\f0002129.pcx

Flowers:\f0002130.pcx

Flowers:\f0002131.pcx

Flowers:\f0002132.pcx

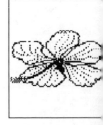

Flowers:\f0002133.pcx

Flowers:\f0002134.pcx

Flowers:\f0002135.pcx

Flowers:\f0002136.pcx

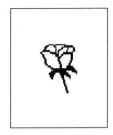

Flowers:\f0002137.pcx

Flowers:\f0002138.pcx

Flowers:\f0002139.pcx

Flowers:\f0002140.pcx

Flowers:\f0002141.pcx

Flowers:\f0002142.pcx

Flowers:\f0002143.pcx

Flowers:\f0002144.pcx

Flowers:\f0002145.pcx

Flowers:\f0002146.pcx

Flowers:\f0002147.pcx

Flowers:\f0002148.pcx

Flowers:\f0002149.pcx

Flowers:\f0002150.pcx

Flowers:\f0002151.pcx

Flowers:\f0002152.pcx

Flowers:\f0002153.pcx

Flowers:\f0002154.pcx

Flowers:\f0002155.pcx

Flowers:\f0002156.pcx

Flowers:\f0002157.pcx

Flowers:\f0002158.pcx

Flowers:\f0002159.pcx

Flowers:\f0002160.pcx

Flowers:\f0002161.pcx

Flowers:\f0002162.pcx

Flowers:\f0002163.pcx

Flowers:\f0002164.pcx

Flowers:\f0002165.pcx

Flowers:\f0002166.pcx

Flowers:\f0002167.pcx

Flowers:\f0002168.pcx

Flowers:\f0002169.pcx

Flowers:\f0002170.pcx

Flowers:\f0002171.pcx

Flowers:\f0002172.pcx

Flowers:\f0002173.pcx

Flowers:\f0002174.pcx

Flowers:\f0002175.pcx

Flowers:\f0002176.pcx

Food:\f0002177.pcx

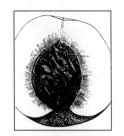

Food:\f0002178.pcx

Food:\f0002179.pcx

Food:\f0002180.pcx

Food:\f0002181.pcx

Food:\f0002182.pcx

Food:\f0002183.pcx

Food:\f0002184.pcx

Food:\f0002185.pcx

Food:\f0002186.pcx

Food:\f0002187.pcx

Food:\f0002188.pcx

Food:\f0002189.pcx

Food:\f0002190.pcx

Food:\f0002191.pcx

Food:\f0002192.pcx

Food:\f0002193.pcx

Food:\f0002194.pcx

Food:\f0002195.pcx

Food:\f0002196.pcx

Food:\f0002197.pcx

Food:\f0002198.pcx

Food:\f0002199.pcx

Food:\f0002200.pcx

Food:\f0002201.pcx

Food:\f0002202.pcx

Food:\f0002203.pcx

Food:\f0002204.pcx

Food:\f0002205.pcx

Food:\f0002206.pcx

Food:\f0002207.pcx

Food:\f0002208.pcx

Food:\f0002209.pcx

Food:\f0002210.pcx

Food:\f0002211.pcx

Food:\f0002212.pcx

Food:\f0002213.pcx

Food:\f0002214.pcx

Food:\f0002215.pcx

Food:\f0002216.pcx

Food:\f0002217.pcx

Food:\f0002218.pcx

Food:\f0002219.pcx

Food:\f0002220.pcx

Food:\f0002221.pcx

Food:\f0002222.pcx

Food:\f0002223.pcx

Food:\f0002224.pcx

Food:\f0002225.pcx

Food:\f0002226.pcx

Food:\f0002227.pcx

Food:\f0002228.pcx

Food:\f0002229.pcx

Food:\f0002230.pcx

Food:\f0002231.pcx

Food:\f0002232.pcx

Food:\f0002233.pcx

Food:\f0002234.pcx

Food:\f0002235.pcx

Food:\f0002236.pcx

Food:\f0002237.pcx

Food:\f0002238.pcx

Food:\f0002239.pcx

Food:\f0002240.pcx

Food:\f0002241.pcx

Food:\f0002242.pcx

Food:\f0002243.pcx

Food:\f0002244.pcx

Food:\f0002245.pcx

Food:\f0002246.pcx

Food:\f0002247.pcx

Food:\f0002248.pcx

Food:\f0002249.pcx

Food:\f0002250.pcx

Food:\f0002251.pcx

Food:\f0002252.pcx

Food:\f0002253.pcx

Food:\f0002254.pcx

Food:\f0002255.pcx

Food:\f0002256.pcx

Food:\f0002257.pcx

Food:\f0002258.pcx

Food:\f0002259.pcx

Food:\f0002260.pcx

Food:\f0002261.pcx

Food:\f0002262.pcx

Food:\f0002263.pcx

Food:\f0002264.pcx

Food:\f0002265.pcx

Food:\f0002266.pcx

Food:\f0002267.pcx

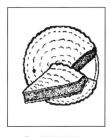

Food:\f0002268.pcx

Food:\f0002269.pcx

Food:\f0002270.pcx

Food:\f0002271.pcx

Food:\f0002272.pcx

Food:\f0002273.pcx

Food:\f0002274.pcx

Food:\f0002275.pcx

Food:\f0002276.pcx

Food:\f0002277.pcx

Food:\f0002278.pcx

Food:\f0002279.pcx

Food:\f0002280.pcx

Food:\f0002281.pcx

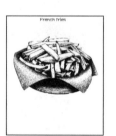

Food:\f0002282.pcx

Food:\f0002283.pcx

Food:\f0002284.pcx

Food:\f0002285.pcx

Food:\f0002286.pcx

Food:\f0002287.pcx

Food:\f0002288.pcx

Food:\f0002289.pcx

Food:\f0002290.pcx

Food:\f0002291.pcx

Food:\f0002292.pcx

Food:\f0002293.pcx

Food:\f0002294.pcx

Food:\f0002295.pcx

Food:\f0002296.pcx

Food:\f0002297.pcx

Food:\f0002298.pcx

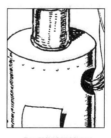

Food:\f0002299.pcx

Food:\f0002300.pcx

Food:\f0002301.pcx

Food:\f0002302.pcx

Food:\f0002303.pcx

Food:\f0002304.pcx

Food:\f0002305.pcx

Food:\f0002306.pcx

Food:\f0002307.pcx

Food:\f0002308.pcx

Food:\f0002309.pcx

Food:\f0002310.pcx

Food:\f0002311.pcx

Food:\f0002312.pcx

Food:\f0002313.pcx

Food:\f0002314.pcx

Food:\f0002315.pcx

Food:\f0002316.pcx

Food:\f0002317.pcx

Food:\f0002318.pcx

Food:\f0002319.pcx

Food:\f0002320.pcx

Food:\f0002321.pcx

Food:\f0002322.pcx

Food:\f0002323.pcx

Food:\f0002324.pcx

Food:\f0002325.pcx

Food:\f0002326.pcx

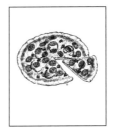

Food:\f0002327.pcx

Food:\f0002328.pcx

Food:\f0002329.pcx

Food:\f0002330.pcx

Food:\f0002331.pcx

Food:\f0002332.pcx

Food:\f0002333.pcx

Food:\f0002334.pcx

Food:\f0002335.pcx

Food:\f0002336.pcx

Food:\f0002337.pcx

Food:\f0002338.pcx

Food:\f0002339.pcx

Food:\f0002340.pcx

Food:\f0002341.pcx

Food:\f0002342.pcx

Food:\f0002343.pcx

Food:\f0002344.pcx

Food:\f0002345.pcx

Food:\f0002346.pcx

Food:\f0002347.pcx

Food:\f0002348.pcx

Food:\f0002349.pcx

Food:\f0002350.pcx

Food:\f0002351.pcx

Food:\f0002352.pcx

Food:\f0002353.pcx

Food:\f0002354.pcx

Food:\f0002355.pcx

Food:\f0002356.pcx

Food:\f0002357.pcx

Food:\f0002358.pcx

Food:\f0002359.pcx

Food:\f0002360.pcx

Food:\f0002361.pcx

Food:\f0002362.pcx

Food:\f0002363.pcx

Food:\f0002364.pcx

Food:\f0002365.pcx

Food:\f0002366.pcx

Food:\f0002367.pcx

Food:\f0002368.pcx

Food:\f0002369.pcx

Garden:\g0002370.pcx

Garden:\g0002371.pcx

Garden:\g0002372.pcx

Garden:\g0002373.pcx

Garden:\g0002374.pcx

Garden:\g0002375.pcx

Garden:\g0002376.pcx

Garden:\g0002377.pcx

Garden:\g0002378.pcx

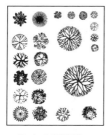

Garden:\g0002379.pcx

Garden:\g0002380.pcx

Garden:\g0002381.pcx

Garden:\g0002382.pcx

Garden:\g0002383.pcx

Garden:\g0002384.pcx

Garden:\g0002385.pcx

Garden:\g0002386.pcx

Garden:\g0002387.pcx

Garden:\g0002388.pcx

Garden:\g0002389.pcx

Garden:\g0002390.pcx

Garden:\g0002391.pcx

Garden:\g0002392.pcx

Garden:\g0002393.pcx

Garden:\g0002394.pcx

Garden:\g0002395.pcx

Garden:\g0002396.pcx

Garden:\g0002397.pcx

Garden:\g0002398.pcx

Garden:\g0002399.pcx

Garden:\g0002400.pcx

Garden:\g0002401.pcx

Garden:\g0002402.pcx

Garden:\g0002403.pcx

Garden:\g0002404.pcx

Garden:\g0002405.pcx

Garden:\g0002406.pcx

Garden:\g0002407.pcx

Garden:\g0002408.pcx

Garden:\g0002409.pcx

Garden:\g0002410.pcx

Garden:\g0002411.pcx

Garden:\g0002412.pcx

Garden:\g0002413.pcx

Garden:\g0002414.pcx

Garden:\g0002415.pcx

Garden:\g0002416.pcx

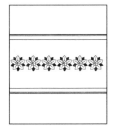

Garden:\g0002417.pcx

Garden:\g0002418.pcx

Garden:\g0002419.pcx

Garden:\g0002420.pcx

Garden:\g0002421.pcx

Garden:\g0002422.pcx

Garden:\g0002423.pcx

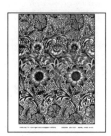

Garden:\g0002424.pcx

Garden:\g0002425.pcx

Garden:\g0002426.pcx

Garden:\g0002427.pcx

Garden:\g0002428.pcx

Garden:\g0002429.pcx

Garden:\g0002430.pcx

Garden:\g0002431.pcx

Garden:\g0002432.pcx

Garden:\g0002433.pcx

Garden:\g0002434.pcx

Garden:\g0002435.pcx

Garden:\g0002436.pcx

Garden:\g0002437.pcx

Garden:\g0002438.pcx

Garden:\g0002439.pcx

Garden:\g0002440.pcx

Garden:\g0002441.pcx

Garden:\g0002442.pcx

Garden:\g0002443.pcx

Garden:\g0002444.pcx

Garden:\g0002445.pcx

Garden:\g0002446.pcx

Garden:\g0002447.pcx

Garden:\g0002448.pcx

Garden:\g0002449.pcx

Garden:\g0002450.pcx

Garden:\g0002451.pcx

Garden:\g0002452.pcx

Garden:\g0002453.pcx

Garden:\g0002454.pcx

Garden:\g0002455.pcx

Garden:\g0002456.pcx

Garden:\g0002457.pcx

Garden:\g0002458.pcx

Garden:\g0002459.pcx

Garden:\g0002460.pcx

Garden:\g0002461.pcx

Garden:\g0002462.pcx

Garden:\g0002463.pcx

Garden:\g0002464.pcx

Garden:\g0002465.pcx

Garden:\g0002466.pcx

Garden:\g0002467.pcx

Garden:\g0002468.pcx

Garden:\g0002469.pcx

Garden:\g0002470.pcx

Garden:\g0002471.pcx

Garden:\g0002472.pcx

Garden:\g0002473.pcx

Garden:\g0002474.pcx

Garden:\g0002475.pcx

Garden:\g0002476.pcx

Garden:\g0002477.pcx

Garden:\g0002478.pcx

Garden:\g0002479.pcx

Garden:\g0002480.pcx

Garden:\g0002481.pcx

Garden:\g0002482.pcx

Garden:\g0002483.pcx

Garden:\g0002484.pcx

Garden:\g0002485.pcx

Garden:\g0002486.pcx

Garden:\g0002487.pcx

Garden:\g0002488.pcx

Garden:\g0002489.pcx

Garden:\g0002490.pcx

Garden:\g0002491.pcx

Garden:\g0002492.pcx

Garden:\g0002493.pcx

Garden:\g0002494.pcx

Garden:\g0002495.pcx

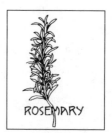

Garden:\g0002496.pcx

Garden:\g0002497.pcx

Garden:\g0002498.pcx

Garden:\g0002499.pcx

Garden:\g0002500.pcx

Garden:\g0002501.pcx

Garden:\g0002502.pcx

Garden:\g0002503.pcx

Garden:\g0002504.pcx

Garden:\g0002505.pcx

Garden:\g0002506.pcx

Garden:\g0002507.pcx

Garden:\g0002508.pcx

Garden:\g0002509.pcx

Garden:\g0002510.pcx

Garden:\g0002511.pcx

Garden:\g0002512.pcx

Garden:\g0002513.pcx

Garden:\g0002514.pcx

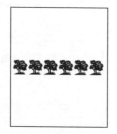

Garden:\g0002515.pcx

Garden:\g0002516.pcx

Garden:\g0002517.pcx

Garden:\g0002518.pcx

Garden:\g0002519.pcx

Garden:\g0002520.pcx

Graphic1:\g0002521.pcx

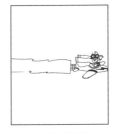

Graphic1:\g0002522.pcx

Graphic1:\g0002523.pcx

Graphic1:\g0002524.pcx

Graphic1:\g0002525.pcx

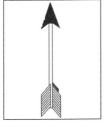

Graphic1:\g0002526.pcx

Graphic1:\g0002527.pcx

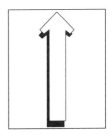

Graphic1:\g0002528.pcx

Graphic1:\g0002529.pcx

Graphic1:\g0002530.pcx

Graphic1:\g0002531.pcx

Graphic1:\g0002532.pcx

Graphic1:\g0002533.pcx

Graphic1:\g0002534.pcx

Graphic1:\g0002535.pcx

Graphic1:\g0002536.pcx

Graphic1:\g0002537.pcx

Graphic1:\g0002538.pcx

Graphic1:\g0002539.pcx

Graphic1:\g0002540.pcx

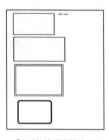

Graphic1:\g0002541.pcx

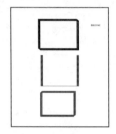

Graphic1:\g0002542.pcx

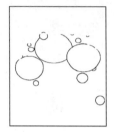

Graphic1:\g0002543.pcx

Graphic1:\g0002544.pcx

Graphic1:\g0002545.pcx

Graphic1:\g0002546.pcx

Graphic1:\g0002547.pcx

Graphic1:\g0002548.pcx

Graphic1:\g0002549.pcx

Graphic1:\g0002550.pcx

Graphic1:\g0002551.pcx

Graphic1:\g0002552.pcx

Graphic1:\g0002553.pcx

Graphic1:\g0002554.pcx

Graphic1:\g0002555.pcx

Graphic1:\g0002556.pcx

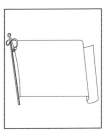

Graphic1:\g0002557.pcx

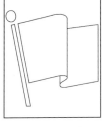

Graphic1:\g0002558.pcx

Graphic1:\g0002559.pcx

Graphic1:\g0002560.pcx

Graphic1:\g0002561.pcx

Graphic1:\g0002562.pcx

Graphic1:\g0002563.pcx

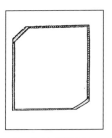

Graphic1:\g0002564.pcx

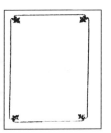

Graphic1:\g0002565.pcx

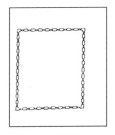

Graphic1:\g0002566.pcx

Graphic1:\g0002567.pcx

Graphic1:\g0002568.pcx

Graphic1:\g0002569.pcx

Graphic1:\g0002570.pcx

Graphic1:\g0002571.pcx

Graphic1:\g0002572.pcx

Graphic1:\g0002573.pcx

Graphic1:\g0002574.pcx

Graphic1:\g0002575.pcx

Graphic1:\g0002576.pcx

Graphic1:\g0002577.pcx

Graphic1:\g0002578.pcx

Graphic1:\g0002579.pcx

Graphic1:\g0002580.pcx

Graphic1:\g0002581.pcx

Graphic1:\g0002582.pcx

Graphic1:\g0002583.pcx

Graphic1:\g0002584.pcx

Graphic1:\g0002585.pcx

Graphic1:\g0002586.pcx

Graphic1:\g0002587.pcx

Graphic1:\g0002588.pcx

Graphic1:\g0002589.pcx

Graphic1:\g0002590.pcx

Graphic1:\g0002591.pcx

Graphic1:\g0002592.pcx

Graphic1:\g0002593.pcx

Graphic1:\g0002594.pcx

Graphic1:\g0002595.pcx

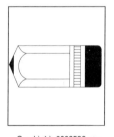

Graphic1:\g0002596.pcx

Graphic1:\g0002597.pcx

Graphic1:\g0002598.pcx

Graphic1:\g0002599.pcx

Graphic1:\g0002600.pcx

Graphic1:\g0002601.pcx

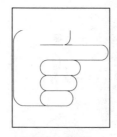

Graphic1:\g0002602.pcx

Graphic1:\g0002603.pcx

Graphic1:\g0002604.pcx

Graphic1:\g0002605.pcx

Graphic1:\g0002606.pcx

Graphic1:\g0002607.pcx

Graphic1:\g0002608.pcx

Graphic1:\g0002609.pcx

Graphic1:\g0002610.pcx

Graphic1:\g0002611.pcx

Graphic1:\g0002612.pcx

Graphic1:\g0002613.pcx

Graphic1:\g0002614.pcx

Graphic1:\g0002615.pcx

Graphic1:\g0002616.pcx

Graphic1:\g0002617.pcx

Graphic1:\g0002618.pcx

Graphic1:\g0002619.pcx

Graphic1:\g0002620.pcx

Graphic1:\g0002621.pcx

Graphic1:\g0002622.pcx

Graphic1:\g0002623.pcx

Graphic1:\g0002624.pcx

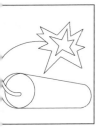

Graphic1:\g0002625.pcx

Graphic1:\g0002626.pcx

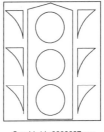

Graphic1:\g0002627.pcx

Graphic1:\g0002628.pcx

Graphic1:\g0002629.pcx

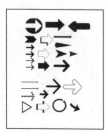

Graphic2:\g0002630.pcx

Graphic2:\g0002631.pcx

Graphic2:\g0002632.pcx

Graphic2:\g0002633.pc:

Graphic2:\g0002634.pcx

Graphic2:\g0002635.pcx

Graphic2:\g0002636.pcx

Graphic2:\g0002637.pc:

Graphic2:\g0002638.pcx

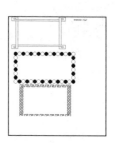

Graphic2:\g0002639.pcx

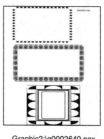

Graphic2:\g0002640.pcx

Graphic2:\g0002641.pc:

Graphic2:\g0002642.pcx

Graphic2:\g0002643.pcx

Graphic2:\g0002644.pcx

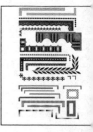

Graphic2:\g0002645.pc:

Graphic2:\g0002646.pcx

Graphic2:\g0002647.pcx

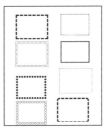

Graphic2:\g0002648.pcx

Graphic2:\g0002649.pcx

Graphic2:\g0002650.pcx

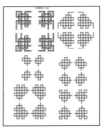

Graphic2:\g0002651.pcx

Graphic2:\g0002652.pcx

Graphic2:\g0002655.pcx

Graphic2:\g0002656.pcx

Graphic2:\g0002657.pcx

Graphic2:\g0002658.pcx

Graphic2:\g0002659.pcx

Graphic2:\g0002660.pcx

Graphic2:\g0002661.pcx

Graphic2:\g0002662.pcx

Graphic2:\g0002663.pcx

Graphic2:\g0002664.pcx

Graphic2:\g0002665.pcx

Graphic2:\g0002666.pcx

Graphic2:\g0002667.pcx

Graphic2:\g0002668.pcx

Graphic2:\g0002669.pcx

Graphic2:\g0002670.pcx

Graphic2:\g0002671.pc

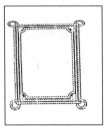

Graphic2:\g0002672.pcx

Graphic2:\g0002673.pcx

Graphic2:\g0002674.pcx

Graphic2:\g0002675.pc

Graphic2:\g0002676.pcx

Graphic2:\g0002677.pcx

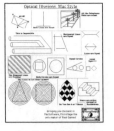

Graphic2:\g0002678.pcx

Graphic2:\g0002679.pc

Graphic2:\g0002680.pcx

Graphic2:\g0002681.pcx

Graphic2:\g0002682.pcx

Graphic2:\g0002683.pcx

Graphic2:\g0002684.pcx

Graphic2:\g0002685.pcx

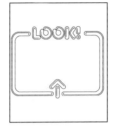

Graphic2:\g0002686.pcx

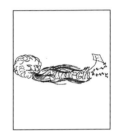

Graphic2:\g0002688.pcx

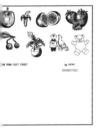

Graphic2:\g0002689.pcx

Graphic2:\g0002690.pcx

Graphic2:\g0002691.pcx

Graphic2:\g0002692.pcx

Graphic2:\g0002693.pcx

Graphic2:\g0002694.pcx

Graphic2:\g0002695.pcx

Graphic2:\g0002696.pcx

Graphic2:\g0002697.pcx

Graphic2:\g0002698.pcx

Graphic2:\g0002699.pcx

Graphic2:\g0002700.pc:

Graphic2:\g0002701.pcx

Graphic2:\g0002702.pcx

Graphic2:\g0002703.pcx

Graphic2:\g0002704.pc

Graphic2:\g0002705.pcx

Graphic2:\g0002706.pcx

Graphic2:\g0002707.pcx

Graphic2:\g0002708.pc

Graphic2:\g0002709.pcx

Graphic2:\g0002710.pcx

Graphic2:\g0002711.pcx

Graphic2:\g0002712.pc

Graphic2:\g0002713.pcx

Graphic2:\g0002714.pcx

Graphic2:\g0002715.pcx

Graphic2:\g0002716.pcx

Graphic2:\g0002717.pcx

Graphic2:\g0002718.pcx

Graphic2:\g0002719.pcx

Graphic2:\g0002720.pcx

Graphic2:\g0002721.pcx

Graphic2:\g0002722.pcx

Graphic2:\g0002723.pcx

Graphic2:\g0002724.pcx

Graphic2:\g0002725.pcx

Graphic2:\g0002726.pcx

Graphic2:\g0002727.pcx

Graphic2:\g0002728.pcx

Graphic2:\g0002729.pcx

Graphic2:\g0002730.pcx

Graphic2:\g0002731.pcx

Graphic2:\g0002732.pc

Graphic2:\g0002733.pcx

Graphic2:\g0002734.pcx

Graphic2:\g0002735.pcx

Graphic2:\g0002736.pc

Graphic2:\g0002737.pcx

Graphic2:\g0002738.pcx

Graphic2:\g0002739.pcx

Graphsce:\g0002740.pcx

Graphsce:\g0002741.pcx

Graphsce:\g0002742.pcx

Graphsce:\g0002743.pcx

Graphsce:\g0002744.pcx

Graphsce:\g0002745.pcx

Graphsce:\g0002746.pcx

Graphsce:\g0002747.pcx

Graphsce:\g0002748.pcx

Graphsce:\g0002749.pcx

Graphsce:\g0002750.pcx

Graphsce:\g0002751.pcx

Graphsce:\g0002752.pcx

Graphsce:\g0002753.pcx

Graphsce:\g0002754.pcx

Graphsce:\g0002755.pcx

Graphsce:\g0002756.pcx

Graphsce:\g0002757.pcx

Graphsce:\g0002758.pcx

Graphsce:\g0002759.pc

Graphsce:\g0002760.pcx

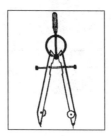

Graphsce:\g0002761.pcx

Graphsce:\g0002762.pcx

Graphsce:\g0002763.pc

Graphsce:\g0002764.pcx

Graphsce:\g0002765.pcx

Graphsce:\g0002766.pcx

Graphsce:\g0002767.pc

Graphsce:\g0002768.pcx

Graphsce:\g0002769.pcx

Graphsce:\g0002770.pcx

Graphsce:\g0002771.pc

Graphsce:\g0002772.pcx

Graphsce:\g0002773.pcx

Graphsce:\g0002774.pcx

Graphsce:\g0002775.pcx

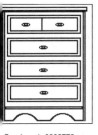

Graphsce:\g0002776.pcx

Graphsce:\g0002777.pcx

Graphsce:\g0002778.pcx

Graphsce:\g0002779.pcx

Graphsce:\g0002780.pcx

Graphsce:\g0002781.pcx

Graphsce:\g0002782.pcx

Graphsce:\g0002783.pcx

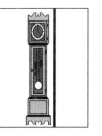

Graphsce:\g0002784.pcx

Graphsce:\g0002785.pcx

Graphsce:\g0002786.pcx

Graphsce:\g0002787.pcx

Graphsce:\g0002788.pcx

Graphsce:\g0002789.pcx

Graphsce:\g0002790.pcx

Graphsce:\g0002791.pc

Graphsce:\g0002792.pcx

Graphsce:\g0002793.pcx

Graphsce:\g0002794.pcx

Graphsce:\g0002795.pe

Graphsce:\g0002796.pcx

Graphsce:\g0002797.pcx

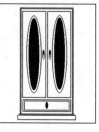

Graphsce:\g0002798.pcx

Graphsce:\g0002799.pc

Graphsce:\g0002800.pcx

Graphsce:\g0002801.pcx

Graphsce:\g0002802.pcx

Graphsce:\g0002803.pc

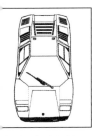

Graphsce:\g0002804.pcx

Graphsce:\g0002805.pcx

Graphsce:\g0002806.pcx

Graphsce:\g0002807.pcx

Graphsce:\g0002808.pcx

Graphsce:\g0002809.pcx

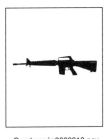

Graphsce:\g0002810.pcx

Graphsce:\g0002811.pcx

Graphsce:\g0002812.pcx

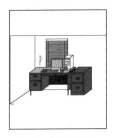

Graphsce:\g0002813.pcx

Graphsce:\g0002814.pcx

Graphsce:\g0002815.pcx

Graphsce:\g0002816.pcx

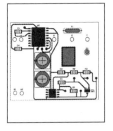

Graphsce:\g0002817.pcx

Graphsce:\g0002818.pcx

Graphsce:\g0002819.pcx

Graphsce:\g0002820.pcx

Graphsce:\g0002821.pcx

Graphsce:\g0002822.pcx

Gringrap:\g0002823.pcx

Gringrap:\g0002824.pcx

Gringrap:\g0002825.pcx

Gringrap:\g0002826.pcx

Gringrap:\g0002827.pcx

Gringrap:\g0002828.pcx

Gringrap:\g0002829.pcx

Gringrap:\g0002830.pcx

Gringrap:\g0002831.pcx

Gringrap:\g0002832.pcx

Gringrap:\g0002833.pcx

Gringrap:\g0002834.pcx

Gringrap:\g0002835.pcx

Gringrap:\g0002836.pcx

Gringrap:\g0002837.pcx

Gringrap:\g0002838.pcx

Gringrap:\g0002839.pcx

Gringrap:\g0002840.pcx

Gringrap:\g0002841.pcx

Gringrap:\g0002842.pcx

Gringrap:\g0002843.pcx

Gringrap:\g0002844.pcx

Gringrap:\g0002845.pcx

Gringrap:\g0002846.pcx

Gringrap:\g0002847.pcx

Gringrap:\g0002848.pcx

Gringrap:\g0002849.pcx

Gringrap:\g0002850.pcx

Gringrap:\g0002851.pcx

Gringrap:\g0002852.pcx

Gringrap:\g0002853.pcx

Gringrap:\g0002854.pcx

Gringrap:\g0002855.pcx

Gringrap:\g0002856.pcx

Gringrap:\g0002857.pcx

Gringrap:\g0002858.pcx

Gringrap:\g0002859.pcx

Gringrap:\g0002860.pcx

Gringrap:\g0002861.pcx

Gringrap:\g0002862.pcx

Gringrap:\g0002863.pcx

Gringrap:\g0002864.pcx

Gringrap:\g0002865.pcx

Gringrap:\g0002866.pcx

Gringrap:\g0002867.pcx

Gringrap:\g0002868.pcx

Gringrap:\g0002869.pcx

Gringrap:\g0002870.pcx

Gringrap:\g0002871.pcx

Gringrap:\g0002872.pcx

Gringrap:\g0002873.pcx

Gringrap:\g0002874.pcx

Gringrap:\g0002875.pcx

Gringrap:\g0002876.pcx

Gringrap:\g0002877.pcx

Gringrap:\g0002878.pc

Gringrap:\g0002879.pcx

Gringrap:\g0002880.pcx

Gringrap:\g0002881.pcx

Gringrap:\g0002882.pc

Gringrap:\g0002883.pcx

Gringrap:\g0002884.pcx

Gringrap:\g0002885.pcx

Gringrap:\g0002886.pc

Gringrap:\g0002887.pcx

Gringrap:\g0002888.pcx

Gringrap:\g0002889.pcx

Gringrap:\g0002890.pcx

Gringrap:\g0002891.pcx

Gringrap:\g0002892.pcx

Gringrap:\g0002893.pcx

Gringrap:\g0002894.pcx

Gringrap:\g0002895.pcx

Gringrap:\g0002896.pcx

Gringrap:\g0002897.pcx

Gringrap:\g0002898.pcx

Gringrap:\g0002899.pcx

Gringrap:\g0002900.pcx

Gringrap:\g0002901.pcx

Gringrap:\g0002902.pcx

Gringrap:\g0002903.pcx

Gringrap:\g0002904.pcx

Gringrap:\g0002905.pcx

Gringrap:\g0002906.pcx

Gringrap:\g0002907.pcx

Gringrap:\g0002908.pcx

Gringrap:\g0002909.pcx

Gringrap:\g0002910.pcx

Gringrap:\g0002911.pcx

Gringrap:\g0002912.pcx

Gringrap:\g0002913.pcx

Gringrap:\g0002914.pcx

Gringrap:\g0002915.pcx

Gringrap:\g0002916.pcx

Gringrap:\g0002917.pcx

Gringrap:\g0002918.pcx

Gringrap:\g0002919.pcx

Gringrap:\g0002920.pcx

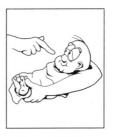

Gringrap:\g0002921.pcx

Gringrap:\g0002922.pcx

Ham:\h0002923.pcx

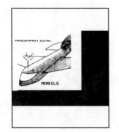

Ham:\h0002924.pcx

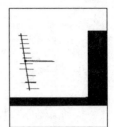

Ham:\h0002925.pcx

Ham:\h0002926.pcx

Ham:\h0002927.pcx

Ham:\h0002928.pcx

Ham:\h0002929.pcx

Ham:\h0002930.pcx

Ham:\h0002931.pcx

Ham:\h0002932.pcx

Ham:\h0002933.pcx

Ham:\h0002934.pcx

Ham:\h0002935.pcx

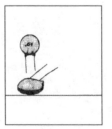

Ham:\h0002936.pcx

Ham:\h0002937.pcx

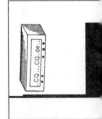

Ham:\h0002938.pcx

Ham:\h0002939.pcx

Ham:\h0002940.pcx

Ham:\h0002941.pcx

Ham:\h0002942.pcx

Ham:\h0002943.pcx

Ham:\h0002944.pcx

Ham:\h0002945.pcx

Ham:\h0002946.pcx

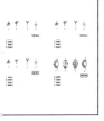

Ham:\h0002947.pcx

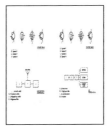

Ham:\h0002948.pcx

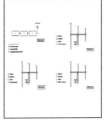

Ham:\h0002949.pcx

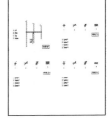

Ham:\h0002950.pcx

Ham:\h0002951.pcx

Ham:\h0002952.pcx

Ham:\h0002953.pcx

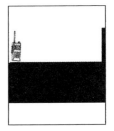

Ham:\h0002954.pcx

Ham:\h0002955.pcx

Ham:\h0002956.pcx

Ham:\h0002957.pcx

Ham:\h0002958.pcx

Ham:\h0002959.pcx

Ham:\h0002960.pcx

Ham:\h0002961.pcx

Ham:\h0002962.pcx

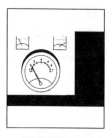

Ham:\h0002963.pcx

Ham:\h0002964.pcx

Ham:\h0002965.pcx

Ham:\h0002966.pcx

Ham:\h0002967.pcx

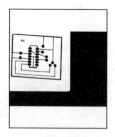

Ham:\h0002968.pcx

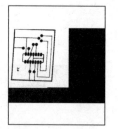

Ham:\h0002969.pcx

Ham:\h0002970.pcx

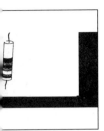

Ham:\h0002971.pcx

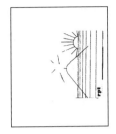

Ham:\h0002972.pcx

Ham:\h0002973.pcx

Ham:\h0002974.pcx

Ham:\h0002975.pcx

Ham:\h0002976.pcx

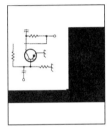

Ham:\h0002977.pcx

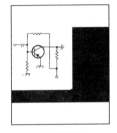

Ham:\h0002978.pcx

Ham:\h0002979.pcx

Ham:\h0002980.pcx

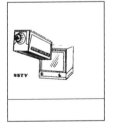

Ham:\h0002981.pcx

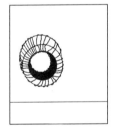

Ham:\h0002982.pcx

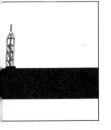

Ham:\h0002983.pcx

Ham:\h0002984.pcx

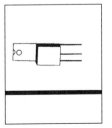

Ham:\h0002985.pcx

Ham:\h0002986.pcx

Ham:\h0002987.pcx

Ham:\h0002988.pcx

Ham:\h0002989.pcx

Ham:\h0002990.pcx

Hands:\h0002991.pcx

Hands:\h0002992.pcx

Hands:\h0002993.pcx

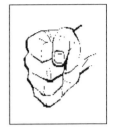

Hands:\h0002994.pcx

Hands:\h0002995.pcx

Hands:\h0002996.pcx

Hands:\h0002997.pcx

Hands:\h0002998.pcx

Hands:\h0002999.pcx

Hands:\h0003000.pcx

Hands:\h0003001.pcx

Hands:\h0003002.pcx

Hands:\h0003003.pcx

Hands:\h0003004.pcx

Hands:\h0003005.pcx

Hands:\h0003006.pcx

Hands:\h0003007.pcx

Hands:\h0003008.pcx

Hands:\h0003009.pcx

Hands:\h0003010.pcx

Hands:\h0003011.pcx

Hands:\h0003012.pcx

Hands:\h0003013.pcx

Hands:\h0003014.pcx

Hands:\h0003015.pcx

Hands:\h0003016.pcx

Hands:\h0003017.pcx

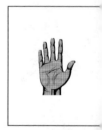

Hands:\h0003018.pcx

Hands:\h0003019.pcx

Hands:\h0003020.pcx

Hands:\h0003021.pcx

Hands:\h0003022.pcx

Hands:\h0003023.pcx

Hands:\h0003024.pcx

Hands:\h0003025.pcx

Hands:\h0003026.pcx

Hands:\h0003027.pcx

Hands:\h0003028.pcx

Hands:\h0003029.pcx

Hands:\h0003030.pcx

Hands:\h0003031.pcx

Hands:\h0003032.pcx

Hands:\h0003033.pcx

Hands:\h0003034.pcx

Hands:\h0003035.pcx

Hands:\h0003036.pcx

Hands:\h0003037.pcx

Hands:\h0003038.pcx

Hands:\h0003039.pcx

Hands:\h0003040.pcx

Hands:\h0003041.pcx

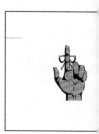

Hands:\h0003042.pcx

Hands:\h0003043.pcx

Hands:\h0003044.pcx

Hands:\h0003045.pcx

Hands:\h0003046.pcx

Hands:\h0003047.pcx

Hands:\h0003048.pcx

Hands:\h0003049.pcx

Hands:\h0003050.pcx

Hands:\h0003051.pcx

Hands:\h0003052.pcx

Hands:\h0003053.pcx

Hands:\h0003054.pcx

Hands:\h0003055.pcx

Hands:\h0003056.pcx

Hands:\h0003057.pcx

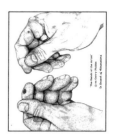

Hands:\h0003058.pcx

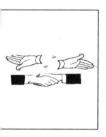

Hands:\h0003059.pcx

Hands:\h0003060.pcx

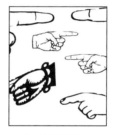

Hands:\h0003061.pcx

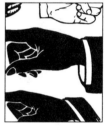

Hands:\h0003062.pcx

Hands:\h0003063.pcx

Hands:\h0003064.pcx

Hands:\h0003065.pcx

Holiday:\h0003122.pcx

Holiday:\h0003123.pcx

Holiday:\h0003124.pcx

Holiday:\h0003125.pcx

Holiday:\h0003126.pcx

Holiday:\h0003127.pcx

Holiday:\h0003128.pcx

Holiday:\h0003129.pcx

Holiday:\h0003130.pcx

Holiday:\h0003131.pcx

Holiday:\h0003132.pcx

Holiday:\h0003133.pcx

Holiday:\h0003134.pcx

Holiday:\h0003135.pcx

Holiday:\h0003136.pcx

Holiday:\h0003137.pcx

Holiday:\h0003138.pcx

Holiday:\h0003139.pcx

Holiday:\h0003140.pcx

Holiday:\h0003141.pcx

Holiday:\h0003142.pcx

Holiday:\h0003143.pcx

Holiday:\h0003144.pcx

Holiday:\h0003145.pcx

Holiday:\h0003146.pcx

Holiday:\h0003147.pcx

Holiday:\h0003148.pcx

Holiday:\h0003149.pcx

Holiday:\h0003150.pcx

Holiday:\h0003151.pcx

Holiday:\h0003152.pcx

Holiday:\h0003153.pcx

Holiday:\h0003154.pcx

Holiday:\h0003155.pcx

Holiday:\h0003156.pcx

Holiday:\h0003157.pcx

Holiday:\h0003158.pcx

Holiday:\h0003159.pcx

Holiday:\h0003160.pcx

Holiday:\h0003161.pcx

Holiday:\h0003162.pcx

Holiday:\h0003163.pcx

Holiday:\h0003164.pcx

Holiday:\h0003165.pcx

Holiday:\h0003166.pcx

Holiday:\h0003167.pcx

Holiday:\h0003168.pcx

Holiday:\h0003169.pcx

Holiday:\h0003170.pcx

Holiday:\h0003171.pcx

Holiday:\h0003172.pcx

Holiday:\h0003173.pcx

Holiday:\h0003174.pcx

Holiday:\h0003175.pcx

Holiday:\h0003176.pcx

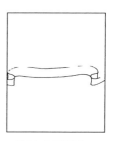

Holiday:\h0003177.pcx

Holiday:\h0003178.pcx

Holiday:\h0003179.pcx

Holiday:\h0003180.pcx

Holiday:\h0003181.pcx

Holiday:\h0003182.pcx

Holiday:\h0003183.pcx

Holiday:\h0003184.pcx

Home:\h0003185.pcx

Home:\h0003186.pcx

Home:\h0003187.pcx

Home:\h0003188.pcx

Home:\h0003189.pcx

Home:\h0003190.pcx

Home:\h0003191.pcx

Home:\h0003192.pcx

Home:\h0003193.pcx

Home:\h0003194.pcx

Home:\h0003195.pcx

Home:\h0003196.pcx

Home:\h0003197.pcx

Home:\h0003198.pcx

Home:\h0003199.pcx

Home:\h0003200.pcx

Home:\h0003201.pcx

Home:\h0003202.pcx

Home:\h0003203.pcx

Home:\h0003204.pcx

Home:\h0003205.pcx

Home:\h0003206.pcx

Home:\h0003207.pcx

Home:\h0003208.pcx

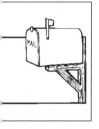

Home:\h0003209.pcx

Home:\h0003210.pcx

Home:\h0003211.pcx

Home:\h0003212.pcx

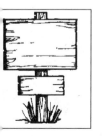

Home:\h0003213.pcx

Home:\h0003214.pcx

Home:\h0003215.pcx

Home:\h0003216.pcx

Home:\h0003217.pcx

Home:\h0003218.pcx

Home:\h0003219.pcx

Home:\h0003220.pcx

Home:\h0003221.pcx

Home:\h0003222.pcx

Home:\h0003223.pcx

Home:\h0003224.pcx

Home:\h0003225.pcx

Home:\h0003226.pcx

Home:\h0003227.pcx

Home:\h0003228.pcx

Home:\h0003229.pcx

Home:\h0003230.pcx

Home:\h0003231.pcx

Home:\h0003232.pcx

Home:\h0003233.pcx

Home:\h0003234.pcx

Home:\h0003235.pcx

Home:\h0003236.pcx

Home:\h0003237.pcx

Home:\h0003238.pcx

Home:\h0003239.pcx

Home:\h0003240.pcx

Home:\h0003241.pcx

Home:\h0003242.pcx

Home:\h0003243.pcx

Home:\h0003244.pcx

Home:\h0003245.pcx

Home:\h0003247.pcx

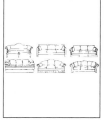

Home:\h0003249.pcx

Home:\h0003250.pcx

Home:\h0003251.pcx

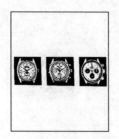

Home:\h0003252.pcx

Home:\h0003253.pcx

Hornback:\h0003254.pcx

Hornback:\h0003255.pcx

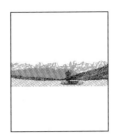

Hornback:\h0003256.pcx

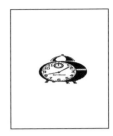

Hornback:\h0003257.pcx

Hornback:\h0003258.pcx

Hornback:\h0003259.pcx

Hornback:\h0003260.pcx

Hornback:\h0003261.pcx

Hornback:\h0003262.pcx

Hornback:\h0003263.pcx

Hornback:\h0003264.pcx

Hornback:\h0003265.pcx

Hornback:\h0003266.pcx

Hornback:\h0003267.pcx

Hornback:\h0003268.pcx

Hornback:\h0003269.pcx

Hornback:\h0003270.pcx

Hornback:\h0003271.pcx

Hornback:\h0003272.pcx

Hornback:\h0003273.pc

Hornback:\h0003274.pcx

Hornback:\h0003275.pcx

Hornback:\h0003276.pcx

Hornback:\h0003277.pc

Hornback:\h0003278.pcx

Hornback:\h0003279.pcx

Hornback:\h0003280.pcx

Hornback:\h0003281.pc

Hornback:\h0003282.pcx

Hornback:\h0003283.pcx

Hornback:\h0003284.pcx

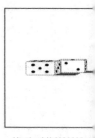

Hornback:\h0003285.pc

Hornback:\h0003286.pcx

Hornback:\h0003287.pcx

Hornback:\h0003288.pcx

Hornback:\h0003289.pcx

Hornback:\h0003290.pcx

Hornback:\h0003291.pcx

Hornback:\h0003292.pcx

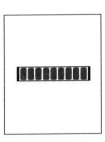

Hornback:\h0003293.pcx

Hornback:\h0003294.pcx

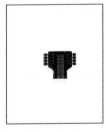

Hornback:\h0003295.pcx

Hornback:\h0003296.pcx

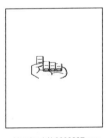

Hornback:\h0003297.pcx

Hornback:\h0003298.pcx

Hornback:\h0003299.pcx

Hornback:\h0003300.pcx

Hornback:\h0003301.pcx

Hornback:\h0003302.pcx

Hornback:\h0003303.pcx

Hornback:\h0003304.pcx

Hornback:\h0003305.pc

Hornback:\h0003306.pcx

Hornback:\h0003307.pcx

Hornback:\h0003308.pcx

Hornback:\h0003309.pc

Hornback:\h0003310.pcx

Hornback:\h0003311.pcx

Hornback:\h0003312.pcx

Hornback:\h0003313.pc

Hornback:\h0003314.pcx

Hornback:\h0003315.pcx

Hornback:\h0003316.pcx

Hornback:\h0003317.pc

Hornback:\h0003318.pcx

Hornback:\h0003319.pcx

Hornback:\h0003320.pcx

Hornback:\h0003321.pcx

Hornback:\h0003322.pcx

Hornback:\h0003323.pcx

Hornback:\h0003324.pcx

Hornback:\h0003325.pcx

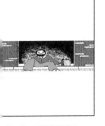

Hornback:\h0003326.pcx

Hornback:\h0003327.pcx

Hornback:\h0003328.pcx

Hornback:\h0003329.pcx

Hornback:\h0003330.pcx

Hornback:\h0003331.pcx

Hornback:\h0003332.pcx

Hornback:\h0003333.pcx

Hornback:\h0003334.pcx

Hornback:\h0003335.pcx

Hornback:\h0003336.pcx

Hornback:\h0003337.pc

Hornback:\h0003338.pcx

Hornback:\h0003339.pcx

Hornback:\h0003340.pcx

Hornback:\h0003341.pc

Hornback:\h0003342.pcx

Hornback:\h0003343.pcx

Hornback:\h0003344.pcx

Hornback:\h0003345.pc

Hornback:\h0003346.pcx

Hornback:\h0003347.pcx

Hornback:\h0003348.pcx

Hornback:\h0003349.pc

Hornback:\h0003350.pcx

Hornback:\h0003351.pcx

Hornback:\h0003352.pcx

Hornback:\h0003353.pcx

Hornback:\h0003354.pcx

Insects:\i0003355.pcx

Insects:\i0003356.pcx

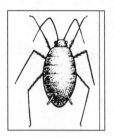

Insects:\i0003357.pcx

Insects:\i0003358.pcx

Insects:\i0003359.pcx

Insects:\i0003360.pcx

Insects:\i0003361.pcx

Insects:\i0003362.pcx

Insects:\i0003363.pcx

Insects:\i0003364.pcx

Insects:\i0003365.pcx

Insects:\i0003366.pcx

Insects:\i0003367.pcx

Insects:\i0003368.pcx

Insects:\i0003369.pcx

Insects:\i0003370.pcx

Insects:\i0003371.pcx

Insects:\i0003372.pcx

Insects:\i0003373.pcx

Insects:\i0003374.pcx

Insects:\i0003375.pcx

Insects:\i0003376.pcx

Insects:\i0003377.pcx

Insects:\i0003378.pcx

Insects:\i0003379.pcx

Insects:\i0003380.pcx

Insects:\i0003381.pcx

Insects:\i0003382.pcx

Insects:\i0003383.pcx

Insects:\i0003384.pcx

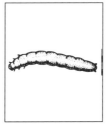

Insects:\i0003385.pcx

Insects:\i0003386.pcx

Insects:\i0003387.pcx

Insects:\i0003388.pcx

Insects:\i0003389.pcx

Insects:\i0003390.pcx

Insects:\i0003391.pcx

Insects:\i0003392.pcx

Insects:\i0003393.pcx

Insects:\i0003394.pcx

Insects:\i0003395.pcx

Insects:\i0003396.pcx

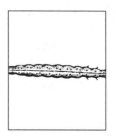

Insects:\i0003397.pcx

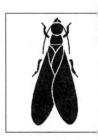

Insects:\i0003398.pcx

Insects:\i0003399.pcx

Insects:\i0003400.pcx

Insects:\i0003401.pcx

Insects:\i0003402.pcx

Insects:\i0003403.pcx

Insects:\i0003404.pcx

Insects:\i0003405.pcx

Insects:\i0003406.pcx

Insects:\i0003407.pcx

Insects:\i0003408.pcx

Insects:\i0003409.pcx

Insects:\i0003410.pcx

Insects:\i0003411.pcx

Insects:\i0003412.pcx

Insects:\i0003413.pcx

Insects:\i0003414.pcx

Insects:\i0003415.pcx

Insects:\i0003416.pcx

Insects:\i0003417.pcx

Insects:\i0003418.pcx

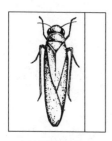

Insects:\i0003419.pcx

Insects:\i0003420.pcx

Insects:\i0003421.pcx

Insects:\i0003422.pcx

Insects:\i0003423.pcx

Insects:\i0003424.pcx

Insects:\i0003425.pcx

Insects:\i0003426.pcx

Insects:\i0003427.pcx

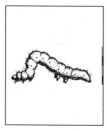

Insects:\i0003428.pcx

Insects:\i0003429.pcx

Insects:\i0003430.pcx

Insects:\i0003431.pcx

Insects:\i0003432.pcx

Insects:\i0003433.pcx

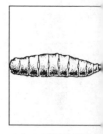

Insects:\i0003434.pcx

Insects:\i0003435.pcx

Insects:\i0003436.pcx

Insects:\i0003437.pcx

Insects:\i0003438.pcx

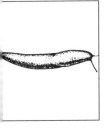

Insects:\i0003439.pcx

Insects:\i0003440.pcx

Insects:\i0003441.pcx

Insects:\i0003442.pcx

Insects:\i0003443.pcx

Insects:\i0003444.pcx

Insects:\i0003445.pcx

Insects:\i0003446.pcx

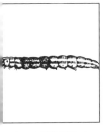

Insects:\i0003447.pcx

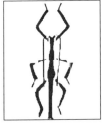

Insects:\i0003448.pcx

Insects:\i0003449.pcx

Insects:\i0003450.pcx

Insects:\i0003451.pcx

Insects:\i0003452.pcx

Insects:\i0003453.pcx

Insects:\i0003454.pcx

Insects:\i0003455.pcx

Insects:\i0003456.pcx

Insects:\i0003457.pcx

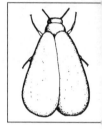

Insects:\i0003458.pcx

Insects:\i0003459.pcx

Jobs:\j0003460.pcx

Jobs:\j0003461.pcx

Jobs:\j0003462.pcx

Jobs:\j0003463.pcx

Jobs:\j0003464.pcx

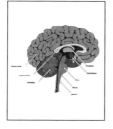

Jobs:\j0003465.pcx

Jobs:\j0003466.pcx

Jobs:\j0003467.pcx

Jobs:\j0003468.pcx

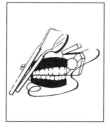

Jobs:\j0003469.pcx

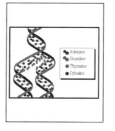

Jobs:\j0003470.pcx

Jobs:\j0003471.pcx

Jobs:\j0003472.pcx

Jobs:\j0003473.pcx

Jobs:\j0003474.pcx

Jobs:\j0003475.pcx

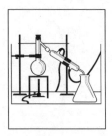

Jobs:\j0003477.pcx

Jobs:\j0003478.pcx

Jobs:\j0003479.pcx

Jobs:\j0003480.pcx

Jobs:\j0003481.pcx

Jobs:\j0003482.pcx

Jobs:\j0003483.pcx

Jobs:\j0003484.pcx

Jobs:\j0003485.pcx

Jobs:\j0003486.pcx

Jobs:\j0003487.pcx

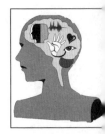

Jobs:\j0003488.pcx

Jobs:\j0003489.pcx

Jobs:\j0003490.pcx

Jobs:\j0003491.pcx

Jobs:\j0003492.pcx

Jobs:\j0003493.pcx

Jobs:\j0003494.pcx

Jobs:\j0003495.pcx

Jobs:\j0003496.pcx

Jobs:\j0003497.pcx

Jobs:\j0003498.pcx

Jobs:\j0003499.pcx

Jobs:\j0003500.pcx

Jobs:\j0003501.pcx

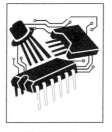

Jobs:\j0003502.pcx

Jobs:\j0003503.pcx

Maps:\m0003504.pcx

Maps:\m0003505.pcx

Maps:\m0003506.pcx

Maps:\m0003507.pcx

Maps:\m0003508.pcx

Maps:\m0003509.pcx

Maps:\m0003510.pcx

Maps:\m0003511.pcx

Maps:\m0003512.pcx

Maps:\m0003513.pcx

Maps:\m0003514.pcx

Maps:\m0003515.pcx

Maps:\m0003516.pcx

Maps:\m0003517.pcx

Maps:\m0003518.pcx

Maps:\m0003519.pcx

Maps:\m0003520.pcx

Maps:\m0003521.pcx

Maps:\m0003522.pcx

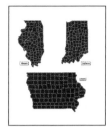

Maps:\m0003523.pcx

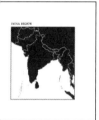

Maps:\m0003524.pcx

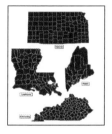

Maps:\m0003525.pcx

Maps:\m0003526.pcx

Maps:\m0003527.pcx

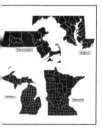

Maps:\m0003528.pcx

Maps:\m0003529.pcx

Maps:\m0003530.pcx

Maps:\m0003531.pcx

Maps:\m0003532.pcx

Maps:\m0003533.pcx

Maps:\m0003534.pcx

Maps:\m0003535.pcx

Maps:\m0003536.pcx

Maps:\m0003537.pcx

Maps:\m0003538.pcx

Maps:\m0003539.pcx

Maps:\m0003540.pcx

Maps:\m0003541.pcx

Maps:\m0003542.pcx

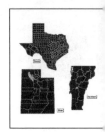

Maps:\m0003543.pcx

Maps:\m0003544.pcx

Maps:\m0003545.pcx

Maps:\m0003546.pcx

Maps:\m0003547.pcx

Maps:\m0003548.pcx

Maps:\m0003549.pcx

Maps:\m0003550.pcx

Maps:\m0003551.pcx

Maps:\m0003552.pcx

Maps:\m0003553.pcx

Maps:\m0003554.pcx

Maps:\m0003555.pcx

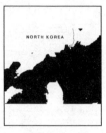

Maps2:\m0003676.pcx

Maps2:\m0003677.pcx

Maps2:\m0003678.pcx

Maps2:\m0003679.pcx

Maps2:\m0003680.pcx

Maps2:\m0003681.pcx

Maps2:\m0003682.pcx

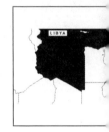

Maps2:\m0003683.pcx

Maps2:\m0003684.pcx

Maps2:\m0003685.pcx

Maps2:\m0003686.pcx

Maps2:\m0003687.pcx

Maps2:\m0003688.pcx

Maps2:\m0003689.pcx

Maps2:\m0003690.pcx

Maps2:\m0003691.pcx

Maps2:\m0003692.pcx

Maps2:\m0003693.pcx

Maps2:\m0003694.pcx

Maps2:\m0003695.pcx

Maps2:\m0003696.pcx

Maps2:\m0003697.pcx

Maps2:\m0003698.pcx

Maps2:\m0003699.pcx

Maps2:\m0003700.pcx

Maps2:\m0003701.pcx

Maps2:\m0003702.pcx

Maps2:\m0003703.pcx

Maps2:\m0003704.pcx

Maps2:\m0003705.pcx

Maps2:\m0003706.pcx

Maps2:\m0003707.pcx

Maps2:\m0003708.pcx

Maps2:\m0003709.pcx

Maps2:\m0003710.pcx

Maps2:\m0003711.pcx

Maps2:\m0003712.pcx

Maps2:\m0003713.pcx

Maps2:\m0003714.pcx

Maps2:\m0003715.pcx

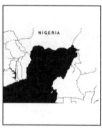

Maps2:\m0003716.pcx

Maps2:\m0003717.pcx

Maps2:\m0003718.pcx

Maps2:\m0003719.pcx

Maps2:\m0003720.pcx

Maps2:\m0003721.pcx

Maps2:\m0003722.pcx

Maps2:\m0003723.pcx

Maps2:\m0003724.pcx

Maps2:\m0003725.pcx

Maps2:\m0003726.pcx

Maps2:\m0003727.pcx

Maps2:\m0003728.pcx

Maps2:\m0003729.pcx

Maps2:\m0003730.pcx

Maps2:\m0003731.pcx

Maps2:\m0003732.pcx

Maps2:\m0003733.pcx

Maps2:\m0003734.pcx

Maps2:\m0003735.pcx

Maps2:\m0003736.pcx

Maps2:\m0003737.pcx

Maps2:\m0003738.pcx

Maps2:\m0003739.pcx

Maps2:\m0003740.pcx

Maps2:\m0003741.pcx

Maps2:\m0003742.pcx

Maps2:\m0003743.pcx

Maps2:\m0003744.pcx

Maps2:\m0003745.pcx

Maps2:\m0003746.pcx

Maps2:\m0003747.pcx

Maps2:\m0003748.pcx

Maps2:\m0003749.pcx

Maps2:\m0003750.pcx

Maps2:\m0003751.pcx

Maps2:\m0003752.pcx

Maps2:\m0003753.pcx

Maps2:\m0003754.pcx

Maps2:\m0003755.pcx

Maps2:\m0003756.pcx

Maps2:\m0003757.pcx

Maps2:\m0003758.pcx

Maps2:\m0003759.pcx

Maps2:\m0003760.pcx

Maps2:\m0003761.pcx

Maps2:\m0003762.pcx

Maps2:\m0003763.pcx

Maps2:\m0003764.pcx

Maps2:\m0003765.pcx

Maps2:\m0003766.pcx

Maps2:\m0003767.pcx

Maps2:\m0003768.pcx

Maps2:\m0003769.pcx

Maps2:\m0003770.pcx

Maps2:\m0003771.pcx

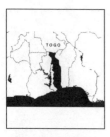

Maps2:\m0003772.pcx

Maps2:\m0003773.pcx

Maps2:\m0003774.pcx

Maps2:\m0003775.pcx

Maps2:\m0003776.pcx

Maps2:\m0003777.pcx

Maps2:\m0003778.pcx

Maps2:\m0003779.pcx

Maps2:\m0003780.pcx

Maps2:\m0003781.pcx

Maps2:\m0003782.pcx

Maps2:\m0003783.pcx

Maps2:\m0003784.pcx

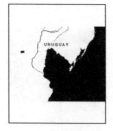

Maps2:\m0003785.pcx

Maps2:\m0003786.pcx

Maps2:\m0003787.pcx

Maps2:\m0003788.pcx

Maps2:\m0003789.pcx

Maps2:\m0003790.pcx

Maps2:\m0003791.pcx

Maps2:\m0003792.pcx

Maps2:\m0003793.pcx

Maps2:\m0003794.pcx

Maps2:\m0003795.pcx

Maps2:\m0003796.pcx

Maps2:\m0003797.pcx

Maps2:\m0003798.pcx

Maps2:\m0003799.pcx

Maps2:\m0003800.pcx

Maps2:\m0003801.pcx

Maps3:\m0003556.pcx

Maps3:\m0003557.pcx

Maps3:\m0003558.pcx

Maps3:\m0003559.pc

Maps3:\m0003560.pcx

Maps3:\m0003561.pcx

Maps3:\m0003562.pcx

Maps3:\m0003563.pc

Maps3:\m0003564.pcx

Maps3:\m0003565.pcx

Maps3:\m0003566.pcx

Maps3:\m0003567.pc

Maps3:\m0003568.pcx

Maps3:\m0003569.pcx

Maps3:\m0003570.pcx

Maps3:\m0003571.pc

Maps3:\m0003572.pcx

Maps3:\m0003573.pcx

Maps3:\m0003574.pcx

Maps3:\m0003575.pcx

Maps3:\m0003576.pcx

Maps3:\m0003577.pcx

Maps3:\m0003578.pcx

Maps3:\m0003579.pcx

Maps3:\m0003580.pcx

Maps3:\m0003581.pcx

Maps3:\m0003582.pcx

Maps3:\m0003583.pcx

Maps3:\m0003584.pcx

Maps3:\m0003585.pcx

Maps3:\m0003586.pcx

Maps3:\m0003587.pcx

Maps3:\m0003588.pcx

Maps3:\m0003589.pcx

Maps3:\m0003590.pcx

Maps3:\m0003591.pc

Maps3:\m0003592.pcx

Maps3:\m0003593.pcx

Maps3:\m0003594.pcx

Maps3:\m0003595.p

Maps3:\m0003596.pcx

Maps3:\m0003597.pcx

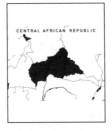

Maps3:\m0003598.pcx

Maps3:\m0003599.p

Maps3:\m0003600.pcx

Maps3:\m0003601.pcx

Maps3:\m0003602.pcx

Maps3:\m0003603.p

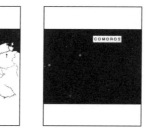

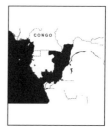

Maps3:\m0003604.pcx

Maps3:\m0003605.pcx

Maps3:\m0003606.pcx

Maps3:\m0003607.pcx

Maps3:\m0003608.pcx

Maps3:\m0003609.pcx

Maps3:\m0003610.pcx

Maps3:\m0003611.pcx

Maps3:\m0003612.pcx

Maps3:\m0003613.pcx

Maps3:\m0003614.pcx

Maps3:\m0003615.pcx

Maps3:\m0003616.pcx

Maps3:\m0003617.pcx

Maps3:\m0003618.pcx

Maps3:\m0003619.pcx

Maps3:\m0003620.pcx

Maps3:\m0003621.pcx

Maps3:\m0003622.pcx

Maps3:\m0003623.pc

Maps3:\m0003624.pcx

Maps3:\m0003625.pcx

Maps3:\m0003626.pcx

Maps3:\m0003627.p

Maps3:\m0003628.pcx

Maps3:\m0003629.pcx

Maps3:\m0003630.pcx

Maps3:\m0003631.p

Maps3:\m0003632.pcx

Maps3:\m0003633.pcx

Maps3:\m0003634.pcx

Maps3:\m0003635.p

Maps3:\m0003636.pcx

Maps3:\m0003637.pcx

Maps3:\m0003638.pcx

Maps3:\m0003639.pcx

Maps3:\m0003640.pcx

Maps3:\m0003641.pcx

Maps3:\m0003642.pcx

Maps3:\m0003643.pcx

Maps3:\m0003644.pcx

Maps3:\m0003645.pcx

Maps3:\m0003646.pcx

Maps3:\m0003647.pcx

Maps3:\m0003648.pcx

Maps3:\m0003649.pcx

Maps3:\m0003650.pcx

Maps3:\m0003651.pcx

Maps3:\m0003652.pcx

Maps3:\m0003653.pcx

Maps3:\m0003654.pcx

Maps3:\m0003655.pc

Maps3:\m0003656.pcx

Maps3:\m0003657.pcx

Maps3:\m0003658.pcx

Maps3:\m0003659.p

Maps3:\m0003660.pcx

Maps3:\m0003661.pcx

Maps3:\m0003662.pcx

Maps3:\m0003663.p

Maps3:\m0003664.pcx

Maps3:\m0003665.pcx

Maps3:\m0003666.pcx

Maps3:\m0003667.p

Maps3:\m0003668.pcx

Maps3:\m0003669.pcx

Maps3:\m0003670.pcx

Maps3:\m0003671.pcx

Maps3:\m0003672.pcx

Maps3:\m0003673.pcx

Maps3:\m0003674.pcx

Maps3:\m0003675.pcx

Marine:\m0003802.pcx

Marine:\m0003803.pcx

Marine:\m0003804.pcx

Marine:\m0003805.pc

Marine:\m0003806.pcx

Marine:\m0003807.pcx

Marine:\m0003808.pcx

Marine:\m0003809.pc

Marine:\m0003810.pcx

Marine:\m0003811.pcx

Marine:\m0003812.pcx

Marine:\m0003813.p

Marine:\m0003814.pcx

Marine:\m0003815.pcx

Marine:\m0003816.pcx

Marine:\m0003817.p

Marine:\m0003818.pcx

Marine:\m0003819.pcx

Marine:\m0003820.pcx

Marine:\m0003821.pcx

Marine:\m0003822.pcx

Marine:\m0003823.pcx

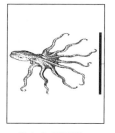

Marine:\m0003825.pcx

Marine:\m0003826.pcx

Marine:\m0003827.pcx

Marine:\m0003828.pcx

Marine:\m0003829.pcx

Marine:\m0003830.pcx

Marine:\m0003831.pcx

Marine:\m0003832.pcx

Marine:\m0003833.pcx

Marine:\m0003834.pcx

Marine:\m0003835.pcx

Marine:\m0003836.pcx

Marine:\m0003837.pcx

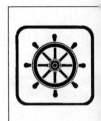

Marine:\m0003838.pcx

Marine:\m0003839.pcx

Marine:\m0003840.pcx

Marine:\m0003841.pcx

Marine:\m0003842.pcx

Marine:\m0003843.pcx

Marine:\m0003844.pcx

Marine:\m0003845.pcx

Marine:\m0003846.pcx

Marine:\m0003847.pcx

Medical:\m0003848.pcx

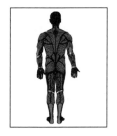

Medical:\m0003849.pcx

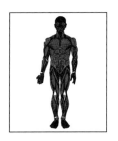

Medical:\m0003850.pcx

Medical:\m0003851.pcx

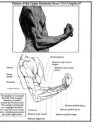

Medical:\m0003852.pcx

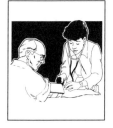

Medical:\m0003853.pcx

Medical:\m0003854.pcx

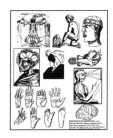

Medical:\m0003855.pcx

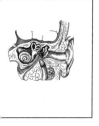

Medical:\m0003856.pcx

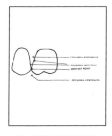

Medical:\m0003857.pcx

Medical:\m0003858.pcx

Medical:\m0003859.pcx

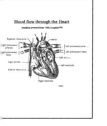

Medical:\m0003860.pcx

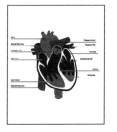

Medical:\m0003861.pcx

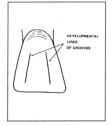

Medical:\m0003862.pcx

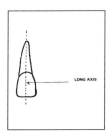

Medical:\m0003863.pcx

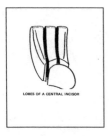

Medical:\m0003864.pcx

Medical:\m0003865.pcx

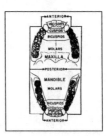

Medical:\m0003866.pcx

Medical:\m0003867.pcx

Medical:\m0003868.pcx

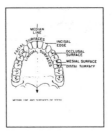

Medical:\m0003869.pcx

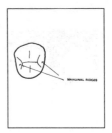

Medical:\m0003870.pcx

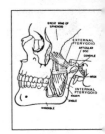

Medical:\m0003871.pcx

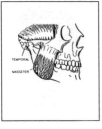

Medical:\m0003872.pcx

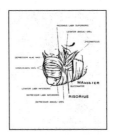

Medical:\m0003873.pcx

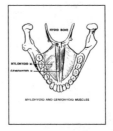

Medical:\m0003874.pcx

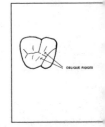

Medical:\m0003875.pcx

Medical:\m0003876.pcx

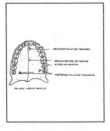

Medical:\m0003877.pcx

Medical:\m0003878.pcx

Medical:\m0003879.pcx

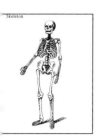

Medical:\m0003880.pcx

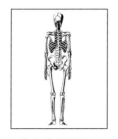

Medical:\m0003881.pcx

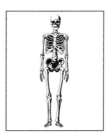

Medical:\m0003882.pcx

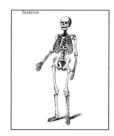

Medical:\m0003883.pcx

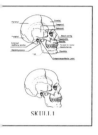

Medical:\m0003884.pcx

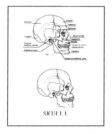

Medical:\m0003885.pcx

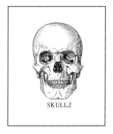

Medical:\m0003886.pcx

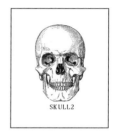

Medical:\m0003887.pcx

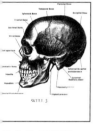

Medical:\m0003888.pcx

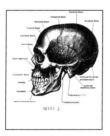

Medical:\m0003889.pcx

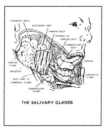

Medical:\m0003890.pcx

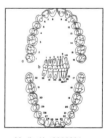

Medical:\m0003891.pcx

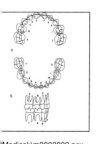

Medical:\m0003892.pcx

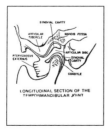

Medical:\m0003893.pcx

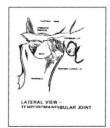

Medical:\m0003894.pcx

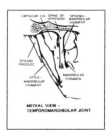

Medical:\m0003895.pcx

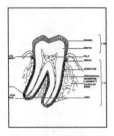

Medical:\m0003896.pcx

Medical:\m0003897.pcx

Medical:\m0003898.pcx

Medical:\m0003899.pc

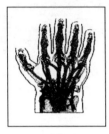

Medical:\m0003900.pcx

Military:\m0003901.pcx

Military:\m0003902.pcx

Military:\m0003903.pcx

Military:\m0003904.pcx

Military:\m0003905.pcx

Military:\m0003906.pcx

Military:\m0003907.pcx

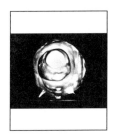

Military:\m0003908.pcx

Military:\m0003909.pcx

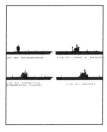

Military:\m0003910.pcx

Military:\m0003911.pcx

Military:\m0003912.pcx

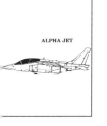

Military:\m0003913.pcx

Military:\m0003914.pcx

Military:\m0003915.pcx

Military:\m0003916.pcx

Military:\m0003917.pcx

Military:\m0003918.pcx

Military:\m0003919.pcx

Military:\m0003920.pcx

Military:\m0003921.pcx

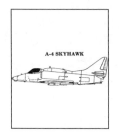

Military:\m0003922.pcx

Military:\m0003923.pcx

Military:\m0003924.pcx

Military:\m0003925.pcx

Military:\m0003926.pcx

Military:\m0003927.pcx

Military:\m0003928.pcx

Military:\m0003929.pcx

Military:\m0003930.pcx

Military:\m0003931.pcx

Military:\m0003932.pcx

Military:\m0003933.pcx

Military:\m0003934.pcx

Military:\m0003935.pcx

Military:\m0003936.pcx

Military:\m0003937.pcx

Military:\m0003938.pcx

Military:\m0003939.pcx

Military:\m0003940.pcx

Military:\m0003941.pcx

Military:\m0003942.pcx

Military:\m0003943.pcx

Military:\m0003944.pcx

Military:\m0003945.pcx

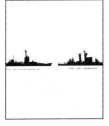

Military:\m0003946.pcx

Military:\m0003947.pcx

Military:\m0003948.pcx

Military:\m0003949.pcx

Military:\m0003950.pcx

Military:\m0003951.pcx

Military:\m0003952.pcx

Military:\m0003953.pcx

Military:\m0003954.pcx

Military:\m0003955.pcx

Military:\m0003956.pcx

Military:\m0003957.pcx

Military:\m0003958.pcx

Military:\m0003959.pcx

Military:\m0003960.pcx

Military:\m0003961.pcx

Military:\m0003962.pcx

Military:\m0003963.pcx

Military:\m0003964.pcx

Military:\m0003965.pcx

Military:\m0003966.pcx

Military:\m0003967.pcx

Military:\m0003968.pcx

Military:\m0003969.pcx

Military:\m0003970.pcx

Military:\m0003971.pcx

Military:\m0003972.pcx

Military:\m0003973.pcx

Military:\m0003974.pcx

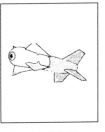

Military:\m0003975.pcx

Military:\m0003976.pcx

Military:\m0003977.pcx

Military:\m0003978.pcx

Military:\m0003979.pcx

Military:\m0003980.pcx

Military:\m0003981.pcx

Military:\m0003982.pcx

Military:\m0003983.pcx

Military:\m0003984.pcx

Military:\m0003985.pcx

Military:\m0003986.pcx

Military:\m0003987.pcx

Military:\m0003988.pcx

Military:\m0003989.pcx

Military:\m0003990.pcx

Military:\m0003991.pcx

Military:\m0003992.pcx

Military:\m0003993.pcx

Military:\m0003994.pcx

Military:\m0003995.pcx

Military:\m0003996.pcx

Military:\m0003997.pcx

Military:\m0003998.pcx

Military:\m0003999.pcx

Military:\m0004000.pcx

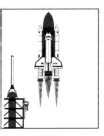

Military:\m0004001.pcx

Military:\m0004002.pcx

Military:\m0004003.pcx

Military:\m0004004.pcx

Military:\m0004005.pcx

Military:\m0004006.pcx

Military:\m0004007.pcx

Military:\m0004008.pcx

Military:\m0004009.pcx

Military:\m0004011.pcx

Military:\m0004012.pcx

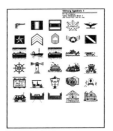

Military:\m0004013.pcx

Military:\m0004014.pcx

Military:\m0004015.pcx

Military:\m0004016.pcx

Military:\m0004017.pcx

Military:\m0004018.pcx

Military:\m0004019.pcx

Military:\m0004020.pcx

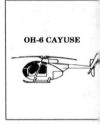

Military:\m0004021.pcx

Military:\m0004022.pcx

Military:\m0004023.pcx

Military:\m0004024.pcx

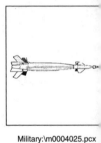

Military:\m0004025.pcx

Military:\m0004026.pcx

Military:\m0004027.pcx

Military:\m0004028.pcx

Military:\m0004029.pcx

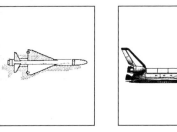

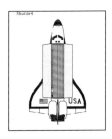

Military:\m0004030.pcx Military:\m0004031.pcx Military:\m0004032.pcx Military:\m0004033.pcx

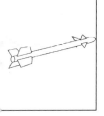

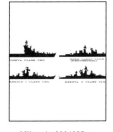

Military:\m0004034.pcx Military:\m0004035.pcx Military:\m0004036.pcx Military:\m0004037.pcx

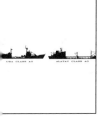

Military:\m0004038.pcx Military:\m0004039.pcx Military:\m0004040.pcx Military:\m0004041.pcx

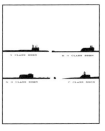

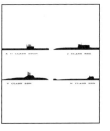

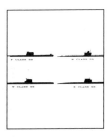

Military:\m0004042.pcx Military:\m0004043.pcx Military:\m0004044.pcx Military:\m0004045.pcx

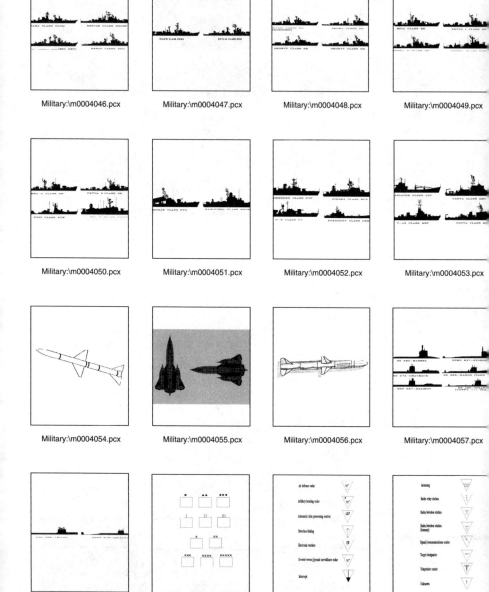

Military:\m0004046.pcx

Military:\m0004047.pcx

Military:\m0004048.pcx

Military:\m0004049.pcx

Military:\m0004050.pcx

Military:\m0004051.pcx

Military:\m0004052.pcx

Military:\m0004053.pcx

Military:\m0004054.pcx

Military:\m0004055.pcx

Military:\m0004056.pcx

Military:\m0004057.pcx

Military:\m0004058.pcx

Military:\m0004059.pcx

Military:\m0004060.pcx

Military:\m0004061.pcx

Military:\m0004062.pcx

Military:\m0004063.pcx

Military:\m0004064.pcx

Military:\m0004065.pcx

Military:\m0004066.pcx

Military:\m0004067.pcx

Military:\m0004068.pcx

Military:\m0004069.pcx

Military:\m0004070.pcx

Military:\m0004071.pcx

Military:\m0004072.pcx

Military:\m0004073.pcx

Military:\m0004074.pcx

Military:\m0004075.pcx

Military:\m0004076.pcx

Military:\m0004077.pcx

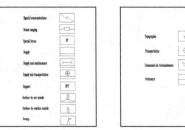

Military:\m0004078.pcx

Military:\m0004079.pcx

Military:\m0004080.pcx

Military:\m0004081.pcx

Military:\m0004082.pcx

Military:\m0004083.pcx

Military:\m0004084.pcx

Military:\m0004085.pcx

Military:\m0004086.pcx

Military:\m0004087.pcx

Military:\m0004088.pcx

Military:\m0004089.pcx

Military:\m0004090.pcx

Military:\m0004091.pcx

Military:\m0004092.pcx

Military:\m0004093.pc:

Military:\m0004094.pcx   Military:\m0004095.pcx

Misc:\m0004096.pcx

Misc:\m0004097.pcx

Misc:\m0004098.pcx

Misc:\m0004099.pcx

Misc:\m0004100.pcx

Misc:\m0004102.pcx

Misc:\m0004103.pcx

Misc:\m0004104.pcx

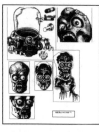

Misc:\m0004105.pcx

Misc:\m0004106.pcx

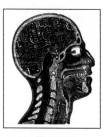

Misc:\m0004107.pcx

Misc:\m0004108.pcx

Misc:\m0004109.pcx

Misc:\m0004110.pcx

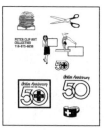

Misc:\m0004111.pcx

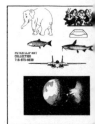

Misc:\m0004112.pcx

Misc:\m0004113.pcx

Misc:\m0004114.pcx

Misc:\m0004115.pcx

Misc:\m0004116.pcx

Misc:\m0004117.pcx

Misc:\m0004118.pcx

Misc:\m0004119.pcx

Misc:\m0004120.pcx

Misc:\m0004121.pcx

Misc:\m0004122.pcx

Misc:\m0004123.pcx

Misc:\m0004124.pcx

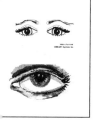

Misc:\m0004125.pcx

Misc:\m0004126.pcx

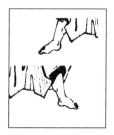

Misc:\m0004127.pcx

Misc:\m0004128.pcx

Misc:\m0004129.pcx

Misc:\m0004130.pcx

Misc:\m0004131.pcx

Misc:\m0004132.pcx

Misc:\m0004133.pcx

Misc:\m0004134.pcx

Misc:\m0004135.pcx

Misc:\m0004136.pcx

Misc:\m0004137.pcx

Misc:\m0004138.pcx

Misc:\m0004139.pcx

Misc:\m0004140.pcx

Misc:\m0004141.pcx

Misc:\m0004142.pcx

Misc:\m0004143.pcx

Misc:\m0004144.pcx

Misc:\m0004145.pcx

Misc:\m0004146.pcx

Misc:\m0004147.pcx

Misc:\m0004148.pcx

Misc:\m0004149.pcx

Misc:\m0004150.pcx

Misc:\m0004151.pcx

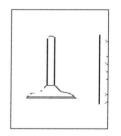

Misc:\m0004152.pcx

Misc:\m0004153.pcx

Misc:\m0004154.pcx

Misc:\m0004155.pcx

Misc:\m0004156.pcx

Misc:\m0004157.pcx

Misc:\m0004158.pcx

Misc:\m0004159.pcx

Misc:\m0004160.pcx

Misc:\m0004161.pcx

Misc:\m0004162.pcx

Misc:\m0004163.pcx

Misc:\m0004164.pcx

Misc:\m0004165.pcx

Misc:\m0004166.pcx

Misc:\m0004167.pcx

Misc:\m0004168.pcx

Misc:\m0004169.pcx

Misc:\m0004170.pcx

Misc:\m0004171.pcx

Misc:\m0004172.pcx

Misc:\m0004173.pcx

Misc:\m0004174.pcx

Misc:\m0004175.pcx

Misc:\m0004176.pcx

Misc:\m0004177.pcx   Misc:\m0004178.pcx

Music:\m0004179.pcx

Music:\m0004180.pcx

Music:\m0004181.pcx

Music:\m0004182.pcx

Music:\m0004183.pcx

Music:\m0004184.pcx

Music:\m0004185.pcx

Music:\m0004186.pcx

Music:\m0004187.pcx

Music:\m0004189.pcx

Music:\m0004190.pcx

Music:\m0004191.pcx

Music:\m0004192.pcx

Music:\m0004193.pcx

Music:\m0004194.pcx

Music:\m0004195.pc

Music:\m0004196.pcx

Music:\m0004197.pcx

Music:\m0004198.pcx

Music:\m0004199.pcx

Music:\m0004200.pcx

Music:\m0004201.pcx

Music:\m0004202.pcx

Music:\m0004203.pcx

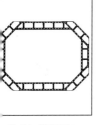

Music:\m0004204.pcx

Music:\m0004205.pcx

Music:\m0004206.pcx

Music:\m0004207.pcx

Music:\m0004208.pcx

Music:\m0004209.pcx

Music:\m0004210.pcx

Music:\m0004211.pcx

Music:\m0004212.pcx

Music:\m0004213.pcx

Music:\m0004214.pcx

Music:\m0004215.pcx

Music:\m0004216.pcx

Music:\m0004217.pcx

Music:\m0004218.pcx

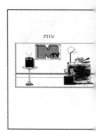

Music:\m0004219.pcx

Music:\m0004220.pcx

Music:\m0004221.pcx

Music:\m0004222.pcx

Music:\m0004223.pcx

Music:\m0004224.pcx

Music:\m0004225.pcx

Music:\m0004226.pcx

Music:\m0004227.pcx

Music:\m0004228.pcx

Music:\m0004229.pcx

Music:\m0004230.pcx

Music:\m0004231.pcx

Music:\m0004232.pcx

Music:\m0004233.pcx

Music:\m0004234.pcx

Music:\m0004235.pcx

Music:\m0004236.pcx

Music:\m0004237.pcx

Music:\m0004238.pcx

Music:\m0004239.pcx

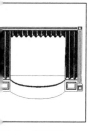

Music:\m0004240.pcx

Music:\m0004241.pcx

Music:\m0004242.pcx

Music:\m0004243.pcx

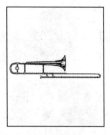

Music:\m0004244.pcx

Music:\m0004245.pcx

Music:\m0004246.pcx

Music:\m0004247.pc

Music:\m0004248.pcx

Music:\m0004249.pcx

Music:\m0004250.pcx

Music:\m0004251.pc

Music:\m0004252.pcx

Music:\m0004253.pcx

Oldfas:\o0004254.pcx

Oldfas:\o0004255.pcx

Oldfas:\o0004256.pcx

Oldfas:\o0004257.pcx

Oldfas:\o0004258.pcx

Oldfas:\o0004259.pcx

Oldfas:\o0004260.pcx

Oldfas:\o0004261.pcx

Oldfas:\o0004262.pcx

Oldfas:\o0004263.pcx

Oldfas:\o0004264.pcx

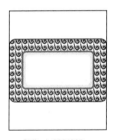

Oldfas:\o0004265.pcx

Oldfas:\o0004266.pcx

Oldfas:\o0004267.pcx

Oldfas:\o0004268.pcx

Oldfas:\o0004269.pcx

Oldfas:\o0004270.pcx

Oldfas:\o0004271.pcx

Oldfas:\o0004272.pcx

Oldfas:\o0004273.pc

Oldfas:\o0004274.pcx

Oldfas:\o0004275.pcx

Oldfas:\o0004276.pcx

Oldfas:\o0004277.pc

Oldfas:\o0004278.pcx

Oldfas:\o0004279.pcx

Oldfas:\o0004280.pcx

Oldfas:\o0004281.pc

Oldfas:\o0004282.pcx

Oldfas:\o0004283.pcx

Oldfas:\o0004284.pcx

Oldfas:\o0004285.pc

Oldfas:\o0004286.pcx

Oldfas:\o0004287.pcx

Oldfas:\o0004288.pcx

Oldfas:\o0004289.pcx

Oldfas:\o0004290.pcx

Oldfas:\o0004291.pcx

Oldfas:\o0004292.pcx

Oldfas:\o0004293.pcx

Oldfas:\o0004294.pcx

Oldfas:\o0004295.pcx

Oldfas:\o0004296.pcx

Oldfas:\o0004297.pcx

Oldfas:\o0004298.pcx

Oldfas:\o0004299.pcx

Oldfas:\o0004300.pcx

Outdoor:\o0004301.pcx

Outdoor:\o0004302.pcx

Outdoor:\o0004303.pcx

Outdoor:\o0004304.pc

Outdoor:\o0004305.pcx

Outdoor:\o0004306.pcx

Outdoor:\o0004307.pcx

Outdoor:\o0004308.p

Outdoor:\o0004309.pcx

Outdoor:\o0004310.pcx

Outdoor:\o0004311.pcx

Outdoor:\o0004312.p

Outdoor:\o0004313.pcx

Outdoor:\o0004314.pcx

Outdoor:\o0004315.pcx

Outdoor:\o0004316.p

Outdoor:\o0004317.pcx

Outdoor:\o0004318.pcx

Outdoor:\o0004319.pcx

Outdoor:\o0004320.pcx

Outdoor:\o0004321.pcx

Outdoor:\o0004322.pcx

Outdoor:\o0004323.pcx

Outdoor:\o0004324.pcx

Outdoor:\o0004325.pcx

Outdoor:\o0004326.pcx

Outdoor:\o0004327.pcx

Outdoor:\o0004328.pcx

Outdoor:\o0004329.pcx

Outdoor:\o0004330.pcx

Outdoor:\o0004333.pcx

Outdoor:\o0004334.pcx

Outdoor:\o0004335.pcx

Outdoor:\o0004336.pcx

Outdoor:\o0004337.pcx

Outdoor:\o0004338.pc

Outdoor:\o0004339.pcx

Outdoor:\o0004340.pcx

Outdoor:\o0004341.pcx

Outdoor:\o0004342.pc

Outdoor:\o0004343.pcx

Outdoor:\o0004344.pcx

People1:\p0004345.pcx

People1:\p0004346.pcx

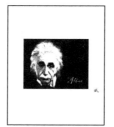

People1:\p0004347.pcx

People1:\p0004348.pcx

People1:\p0004349.pcx

People1:\p0004350.pcx

People1:\p0004351.pcx

People1:\p0004352.pcx

People1:\p0004353.pcx

People1:\p0004354.pcx

People1:\p0004355.pcx

People1:\p0004356.pcx

People1:\p0004357.pcx

People1:\p0004360.pcx

People1:\p0004361.pcx

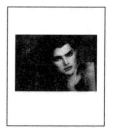

People1:\p0004362.pcx

People1:\p0004363.pcx

People1:\p0004364.pcx

People1:\p0004365.pcx

People1:\p0004366.pc

People1:\p0004367.pcx

People1:\p0004368.pcx

People1:\p0004369.pcx

People1:\p0004370.p

People1:\p0004371.pcx

People1:\p0004372.pcx

People1:\p0004373.pcx

People1:\p0004374.p

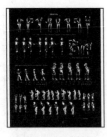

People1:\p0004375.pcx

People1:\p0004376.pcx

People1:\p0004377.pcx

People1:\p0004379.p

People1:\p0004380.pcx

People1:\p0004381.pcx

People1:\p0004382.pcx

People1:\p0004383.pcx

People1:\p0004384.pcx

People1:\p0004385.pcx

People1:\p0004386.pcx

People1:\p0004387.pcx

People1:\p0004388.pcx

People1:\p0004389.pcx

People1:\p0004390.pcx

People1:\p0004391.pcx

People1:\p0004392.pcx

People1:\p0004393.pcx

People1:\p0004394.pcx

People1:\p0004395.pcx

People1:\p0004396.pcx

People1:\p0004397.pcx

People1:\p0004398.pcx

People1:\p0004399.pc

People1:\p0004400.pcx

People1:\p0004401.pcx

People1:\p0004402.pcx

People1:\p0004403.pc

People1:\p0004404.pcx

People1:\p0004405.pcx

People1:\p0004406.pcx

People1:\p0004407.pc

People1:\p0004408.pcx

People1:\p0004409.pcx

People1:\p0004410.pcx

People1:\p0004411.pc

People1:\p0004412.pcx

People1:\p0004413.pcx

People1:\p0004414.pcx

People1:\p0004415.pcx

People1:\p0004416.pcx

People1:\p0004417.pcx

People1:\p0004418.pcx

People1:\p0004419.pcx

People1:\p0004421.pcx

People1:\p0004423.pcx

People1:\p0004424.pcx

People1:\p0004425.pcx

People1:\p0004426.pcx

People1:\p0004427.pcx

People1:\p0004428.pcx

People1:\p0004429.pcx

People1:\p0004430.pcx

People1:\p0004431.pcx

People1:\p0004432.pcx

People1:\p0004433.pcx

People1:\p0004434.pcx

People1:\p0004435.pcx

People1:\p0004438.pcx

People1:\p0004439.pcx

People1:\p0004440.pcx

People1:\p0004443.pcx

People1:\p0004444.pcx

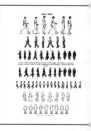

People1:\p0004445.pcx

People1:\p0004446.pcx

People1:\p0004447.pcx

People1:\p0004448.pcx

People1:\p0004449.pcx

People1:\p0004450.pcx

People1:\p0004451.pcx

People1:\p0004452.pcx

People1:\p0004453.pcx

People1:\p0004455.pcx

People1:\p0004456.pcx

People1:\p0004457.pcx

People1:\p0004458.pcx

People1:\p0004459.pcx

People1:\p0004460.pcx

People1:\p0004461.pcx

People1:\p0004462.pcx

People1:\p0004463.pcx

People1:\p0004464.pcx

People1:\p0004465.pcx

People1:\p0004466.pcx

People1:\p0004468.pcx

People1:\p0004470.pcx

People1:\p0004471.pcx

People1:\p0004472.pcx

People1:\p0004473.pcx

People1:\p0004474.pcx

People1:\p0004475.pcx

People1:\p0004476.pcx

People1:\p0004477.pcx

People1:\p0004478.pcx

People1:\p0004479.pcx

People1:\p0004480.pcx

People1:\p0004481.pcx

People1:\p0004482.pcx

People1:\p0004483.pcx

People1:\p0004484.pcx

People1:\p0004485.pcx

People1:\p0004486.pcx

People1:\p0004487.pcx

People1:\p0004488.pcx

People1:\p0004489.pcx

People1:\p0004490.pcx

People1:\p0004491.pcx

People1:\p0004492.pcx

People1:\p0004493.pcx

People1:\p0004494.pcx

People1:\p0004495.pcx

People1:\p0004496.pcx

People1:\p0004497.pcx

People1:\p0004498.pcx

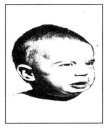

People1:\p0004499.pcx

People1:\p0004500.pcx

People1:\p0004501.pcx

People1:\p0004503.pcx

People1:\p0004504.pcx

People1:\p0004505.pcx

People1:\p0004506.pcx

People1:\p0004507.pcx

People1:\p0004508.pcx

People1:\p0004509.pcx

People1:\p0004510.pcx

People1:\p0004511.pcx

People1:\p0004512.pcx

People1:\p0004513.pcx

People1:\p0004514.pcx

People1:\p0004515.pcx

People1:\p0004516.pcx

People1:\p0004517.pcx

People1:\p0004518.pcx

People1:\p0004519.pcx

People1:\p0004520.pcx

People1:\p0004521.pcx

People1:\p0004522.pcx

People1:\p0004523.pcx

People1:\p0004524.pcx

People1:\p0004525.pcx

Punch:\punch001.pcx

Punch:\punch002.pcx

Punch:\punch003.pcx

Punch:\punch004.pcx

Punch:\punch005.pcx

Punch:\punch006.pcx

Punch:\punch007.pcx

Punch:\punch008.pcx

Punch:\punch009.pcx

Punch:\punch010.pcx

Punch:\punch011.pcx

Punch:\punch012.pcx

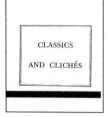

Punch:\punch013.pcx

Punch:\punch014.pcx

Punch:\punch015.pcx

Punch:\punch016.pcx

Punch:\punch017.pcx

Punch:\punch018.pcx

Punch:\punch019.pcx

Punch:\punch020.pcx

Punch:\punch021.pcx

Punch:\punch022.pcx

Punch:\punch023.pcx

Punch:\punch024.pcx

Punch:\punch025.pcx

Punch:\punch026.pcx

Punch:\punch027.pcx

Punch:\punch028.pcx

Punch:\punch029.pcx

Punch:\punch030.pcx

Punch:\punch031.pcx

Punch:\punch032.pcx

Punch:\punch033.pcx

Punch:\punch034.pcx

Punch:\punch035.pcx

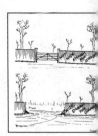

Punch:\punch036.pcx

Punch:\punch037.pcx

Punch:\punch038.pcx

Punch:\punch039.pcx

Punch:\punch040.pcx

Punch:\punch041.pcx

Punch:\punch042.pcx

Punch:\punch043.pcx

Punch:\punch044.pcx

Punch:\punch045.pcx

Religion:\r0004526.pcx

Religion:\r0004527.pcx

Religion:\r0004528.pcx

Religion:\r0004529.pcx

Religion:\r0004530.pcx

Religion:\r0004531.pcx

Religion:\r0004532.pcx

Religion:\r0004533.pcx

Religion:\r0004534.pcx

Religion:\r0004535.pcx

Religion:\r0004536.pcx

Religion:\r0004537.pcx

Religion:\r0004538.pcx

Religion:\r0004539.pcx

Religion:\r0004540.pcx

Religion:\r0004541.pcx

Religion:\r0004542.pcx

Religion:\r0004543.pcx

Religion:\r0004544.pcx

Religion:\r0004545.pc

Religion:\r0004546.pcx

Religion:\r0004547.pcx

Religion:\r0004548.pcx

Religion:\r0004549.pc

Religion:\r0004550.pcx

Religion:\r0004551.pcx

Religion:\r0004552.pcx

Religion:\r0004553.pc

Religion:\r0004554.pcx

Religion:\r0004555.pcx

Religion:\r0004556.pcx

Religion:\r0004557.pc

Religion:\r0004558.pcx

Religion:\r0004559.pcx

Religion:\r0004560.pcx

Religion:\r0004561.pcx

Religion:\r0004562.pcx

Religion:\r0004563.pcx

Religion:\r0004564.pcx

Religion:\r0004565.pcx

Religion:\r0004566.pcx

Religion:\r0004567.pcx

Religion:\r0004568.pcx

Religion:\r0004569.pcx

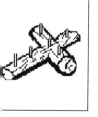

Religion:\r0004570.pcx

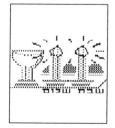

Religion:\r0004571.pcx

Religion:\r0004572.pcx

Religion:\r0004573.pcx

THE LORD
HATH COME

Religion:\r0004574.pcx

COME
ONTO ME

Religion:\r0004575.pcx

Religion:\r0004576.pcx

COUNT YOU
BLESSINGS

Religion:\r0004577.pcx

Religion:\r0004578.pcx

Religion:\r0004579.pcx

Religion:\r0004580.pcx

Religion:\r0004581.pc

THOU SHALL
NOT CURSE

Religion:\r0004582.pcx

Religion:\r0004583.pcx

Discipleship

Religion:\r0004584.pcx

Religion:\r0004585.pc

THY WILL
BE DONE

Religion:\r0004586.pcx

Easter

Religion:\r0004587.pcx

EVENING
SERVICES

Religion:\r0004588.pcx

KEEP
THE FAITH

Religion:\r0004589.p

Religion:\r0004590.pcx

Religion:\r0004591.pcx

Religion:\r0004592.pcx

Religion:\r0004593.pcx

Religion:\r0004594.pcx

Religion:\r0004595.pcx

Religion:\r0004596.pcx

Religion:\r0004597.pcx

Religion:\r0004598.pcx

Religion:\r0004599.pcx

Religion:\r0004600.pcx

Religion:\r0004601.pcx

Religion:\r0004602.pcx

Religion:\r0004603.pcx

Religion:\r0004604.pcx

Religion:\r0004605.pcx

Religion:\r0004606.pcx

Religion:\r0004607.pcx

Religion:\r0004608.pcx

Religion:\r0004609.pc:

Religion:\r0004610.pcx

Religion:\r0004611.pcx

Religion:\r0004612.pcx

Religion:\r0004613.pc

Religion:\r0004614.pcx

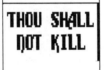

Religion:\r0004615.pcx

Religion:\r0004616.pcx

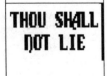

Religion:\r0004617.pc

Religion:\r0004618.pcx

Religion:\r0004619.pcx

Religion:\r0004620.pcx

Religion:\r0004621.p

Religion:\r0004622.pcx

Religion:\r0004623.pcx

Religion:\r0004624.pcx

Religion:\r0004625.pcx

Religion:\r0004626.pcx

Religion:\r0004627.pcx

Religion:\r0004628.pcx

Religion:\r0004629.pcx

Religion:\r0004630.pcx

Religion:\r0004631.pcx

Religion:\r0004632.pcx

Religion:\r0004633.pcx

Religion:\r0004634.pcx

Religion:\r0004635.pcx

Religion:\r0004636.pcx

Religion:\r0004637.pcx

Religion:\r0004638.pcx

Religion:\r0004639.pcx

Religion:\r0004640.pcx

Religion:\r0004641.pcx

Religion:\r0004642.pcx

Religion:\r0004643.pcx

Religion:\r0004644.pcx

Religion:\r0004645.pc

Religion:\r0004646.pcx

Religion:\r0004647.pcx

Religion:\r0004648.pcx

Religion:\r0004649.pc

Religion:\r0004650.pcx

Religion:\r0004651.pcx

Religion:\r0004652.pcx

Religion:\r0004653.pc

Religion:\r0004654.pcx

Religion:\r0004655.pcx

Religion:\r0004656.pcx

Religion:\r0004657.pcx

Religion:\r0004658.pcx

Religion:\r0004659.pcx

Religion:\r0004660.pcx

Religion:\r0004661.pcx

Religion:\r0004662.pcx

Religion:\r0004663.pcx

Religion:\r0004664.pcx

Religion:\r0004665.pcx

Religion:\r0004666.pcx

Religion:\r0004667.pcx

Religion:\r0004668.pcx

Religion:\r0004669.pcx

Religion:\r0004670.pcx

Religion:\r0004671.pcx

Religion:\r0004672.pcx

Religion:\r0004673.pcx

Religion:\r0004674.pcx

Religion:\r0004675.pcx

Religion:\r0004676.pcx

Religion:\r0004677.pc

Religion:\r0004678.pcx

Religion:\r0004679.pcx

Religion:\r0004680.pcx

Religion:\r0004681.pc

Religion:\r0004682.pcx

Religion:\r0004683.pcx

Religion:\r0004684.pcx

Religion:\r0004685.pc

Religion:\r0004686.pcx

Religion:\r0004687.pcx

REMEMBER THE SABBATH

Religion:\r0004688.pcx

REPENT AND BE SAVED

Religion:\r0004689.pcx

Light Your World

Religion:\r0004690.pcx

SENIORS

Religion:\r0004691.pcx

GO AND SIN NO MORE

Religion:\r0004692.pcx

Religion:\r0004693.pcx

PRAY FOR US SINNERS

Religion:\r0004694.pcx

Bible Study

Religion:\r0004695.pcx

SUNDAY SCHOOL

Religion:\r0004696.pcx

SUNRISE SERVICES

Religion:\r0004697.pcx

CHURCH SUPPER

Religion:\r0004698.pcx

SUPPORT THE CHURCH

Religion:\r0004699.pcx

TEACH ME O LORD

Religion:\r0004700.pcx

TEACH ME O LORD

Religion:\r0004701.pcx

Religion:\r0004702.pcx

Religion:\r0004703.pcx

Religion:\r0004704.pcx

Religion:\r0004705.pc

Religion:\r0004706.pcx

Religion:\r0004707.pcx

Religion:\r0004708.pcx

Religion:\r0004709.pc

Religion:\r0004710.pcx

Religion:\r0004711.pcx

Religion:\r0004712.pcx

Religion:\r0004713.pc

Religion:\r0004714.pcx

Religion:\r0004715.pcx

Season:\s0004716.pcx

Season:\s0004717.pcx

Season:\s0004718.pcx

Season:\s0004719.pcx

Season:\s0004720.pcx

Season:\s0004721.pcx

Season:\s0004722.pcx

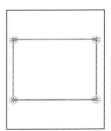

Season:\s0004723.pcx

Season:\s0004724.pcx

Season:\s0004725.pcx

Season:\s0004726.pcx

Season:\s0004727.pcx

Season:\s0004728.pcx

Season:\s0004729.pcx

Season:\s0004730.pcx

Season:\s0004731.pcx

Season:\s0004732.pcx

Season:\s0004733.pcx

Season:\s0004734.pcx

Season:\s0004735.pc

Season:\s0004736.pcx

Season:\s0004737.pcx

Season:\s0004738.pcx

Season:\s0004739.pc

Season:\s0004740.pcx

Season:\s0004741.pcx

Season:\s0004742.pcx

Season:\s0004743.pc

Season:\s0004744.pcx

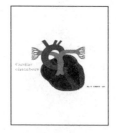

Season:\s0004745.pcx

Season:\s0004746.pcx

Season:\s0004747.pc

Season:\s0004748.pcx

Season:\s0004749.pcx

Season:\s0004750.pcx

Season:\s0004751.pcx

Season:\s0004752.pcx

Season:\s0004753.pcx

Season:\s0004754.pcx

Season:\s0004755.pcx

Season:\s0004756.pcx

Season:\s0004757.pcx

Season:\s0004758.pcx

Season:\s0004759.pcx

Season:\s0004760.pcx

Season:\s0004761.pcx

Season:\s0004762.pcx

Season:\s0004763.pcx

Season:\s0004764.pcx

Season:\s0004765.pcx

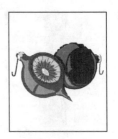

Season:\s0004766.pcx

Season:\s0004767.pcx

Season:\s0004768.pcx

Season:\s0004769.pcx

Season:\s0004770.pcx

Season:\s0004771.pc

Season:\s0004772.pcx

Season:\s0004773.pcx

Season:\s0004774.pcx

Season:\s0004775.pc

Season:\s0004776.pcx

Season:\s0004777.pcx

Season:\s0004778.pcx

Season:\s0004779.pc

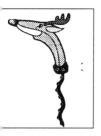

Season:\s0004780.pcx

Season:\s0004781.pcx

Season:\s0004782.pcx

Season:\s0004783.pcx

Season:\s0004784.pcx

Season:\s0004785.pcx

Season:\s0004786.pcx

Season:\s0004787.pcx

Season:\s0004788.pcx

Season:\s0004789.pcx

Season:\s0004790.pcx

Season:\s0004791.pcx

Season:\s0004792.pcx

Season:\s0004793.pcx

Season:\s0004794.pcx

Season:\s0004795.pcx

Season:\s0004796.pcx

Season:\s0004797.pcx

Season:\s0004798.pcx

Season:\s0004799.pcx

Season:\s0004800.pcx

Season:\s0004801.pcx

Season:\s0004802.pcx

Season:\s0004803.pc

Season:\s0004804.pcx

Season:\s0004805.pcx

Season:\s0004806.pcx

Season:\s0004807.pc

Season:\s0004808.pcx

Season:\s0004809.pcx

Season:\s0004810.pcx

Season:\s0004811.pc

Season:\s0004812.pcx

Sheets:\s0004813.pcx

Sheets:\s0004815.pcx

Sheets:\s0004816.pcx

Sheets:\s0004817.pcx

Sheets:\s0004818.pcx

Sheets:\s0004820.pcx

Sheets:\s0004821.pcx

Sheets:\s0004822.pcx

Sheets:\s0004824.pcx

Sheets:\s0004825.pcx

Sheets:\s0004826.pcx

Sheets:\s0004827.pcx

Sheets:\s0004828.pcx

Sheets:\s0004829.pcx

Sheets:\s0004830.pcx

Sheets:\s0004831.pc

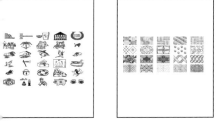

Sheets:\s0004832.pcx

Sheets:\s0004833.pcx

Sheets:\s0004834.pcx

Sheets:\s0004835.pcx

Sheets:\s0004836.pcx

Sheets:\s0004837.pcx

Sheets:\s0004838.pcx

Sheets:\s0004839.pcx

Sheets:\s0004840.pcx

Sheets:\s0004841.pcx

Sheets:\s0004842.pcx

Sheets:\s0004843.pcx

Sheets:\s0004844.pcx

Sheets:\s0004845.pcx

Sheets:\s0004846.pcx

Sheets:\s0004847.pcx

Sheets:\s0004848.pcx

Sheets:\s0004849.pcx

Sheets:\s0004850.pcx

Sheets:\s0004851.pcx

Sheets:\s0004852.pcx

Sheets:\s0004853.pcx

Sheets:\s0004854.pcx

Sheets:\s0004855.pcx

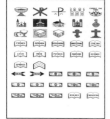

Sheets:\s0004856.pcx

Sheets:\s0004857.pcx

Sheets:\s0004858.pcx

Sheets:\s0004859.pcx

Sheets:\s0004860.pcx

Sheets:\s0004861.pcx

Sheets:\s0004862.pcx

Sheets:\s0004863.pcx

Sheets:\s0004864.pcx

Sheets:\s0004865.pcx

Sheets:\s0004866.pcx

Sheets:\s0004867.pcx

Sheets:\s0004868.pcx

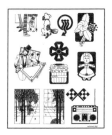

Sheets:\s0004869.pcx

Sheets:\s0004870.pcx

Sheets:\s0004871.pcx

Sheets:\s0004872.pcx

Sheets:\s0004873.pcx

Sheets:\s0004874.pcx

Sheets:\s0004875.pcx

Sheets:\s0004876.pcx

Sheets:\s0004877.pcx

Sheets:\s0004878.pcx

Sheets:\s0004879.pcx

Signs:\s0004880.pcx

Signs:\s0004881.pcx

Signs:\s0004882.pcx

Signs:\s0004883.pcx

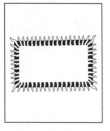

Signs:\s0004884.pcx

Signs:\s0004885.pcx

Signs:\s0004886.pcx

Signs:\s0004887.pcx

Signs:\s0004888.pcx

Signs:\s0004889.pcx

Signs:\s0004890.pcx

Signs:\s0004891.pcx

Signs:\s0004892.pcx

Signs:\s0004893.pcx

Signs:\s0004894.pcx

Signs:\s0004895.pcx

Signs:\s0004896.pcx

Signs:\s0004897.pcx

Signs:\s0004898.pcx

Signs:\s0004899.pcx

Signs:\s0004900.pcx

Signs:\s0004901.pcx

Signs:\s0004902.pcx

Signs:\s0004903.pcx

Signs:\s0004904.pcx

Signs:\s0004905.pcx

Signs:\s0004906.pcx

Signs:\s0004907.pcx

Signs:\s0004908.pcx

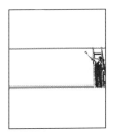

Signs:\s0004909.pcx

Signs:\s0004910.pcx

Signs:\s0004911.pcx

Signs:\s0004912.pcx

Signs:\s0004913.pcx

Signs:\s0004914.pcx

Signs:\s0004915.pcx

Signs:\s0004916.pcx

Signs:\s0004917.pcx

Signs:\s0004918.pcx

Signs:\s0004919.pcx

Signs:\s0004920.pcx

Signs:\s0004921.pcx

Signs:\s0004922.pcx

Signs:\s0004923.pcx

Signs:\s0004924.pcx

Signs:\s0004925.pcx

Signs:\s0004926.pcx

Signs:\s0004927.pcx

Signs:\s0004928.pcx

Signs:\s0004929.pcx

Signs:\s0004930.pcx

Signs:\s0004931.pcx

Signs:\s0004932.pcx

Signs:\s0004933.pcx

Signs:\s0004934.pcx

Signs:\s0004935.pcx

Signs:\s0004936.pcx

Signs:\s0004937.pcx

Signs:\s0004938.pcx

Signs:\s0004939.pcx

Signs:\s0004940.pcx

Signs:\s0004941.pcx

Signs:\s0004942.pcx

Signs:\s0004943.pcx

Signs:\s0004944.pcx

Signs:\s0004945.pcx

Signs:\s0004946.pcx

Signs:\s0004947.pcx

Signs:\s0004948.pcx

Signs:\s0004949.pcx

Signs:\s0004950.pcx

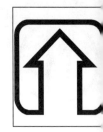

Signs:\s0004951.pcx

Signs:\s0004952.pcx

Signs:\s0004953.pcx

Signs:\s0004954.pcx

Signs:\s0004955.pcx

Space:\s0004956.pcx

Space:\s0004957.pcx

Space:\s0004958.pcx

Space:\s0004959.pcx

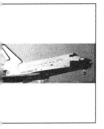

Space:\s0004960.pcx

Space:\s0004961.pcx

Space:\s0004962.pcx

Space:\s0004963.pcx

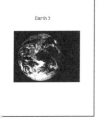

Space:\s0004964.pcx

Space:\s0004965.pcx

Space:\s0004966.pcx

Space:\s0004967.pcx

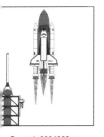

Space:\s0004968.pcx

Space:\s0004969.pcx

Space:\s0004970.pcx

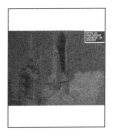

Space:\s0004971.pcx

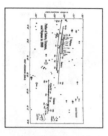

Space:\s0004972.pcx

Space:\s0004973.pcx

Space:\s0004974.pcx

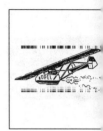

Space:\s0004975.pcx

Space:\s0004976.pcx

Space:\s0004977.pcx

Space:\s0004978.pcx

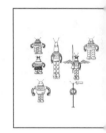

Space:\s0004979.pcx

Space:\s0004981.pcx

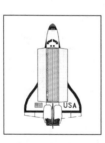

Space:\s0004982.pcx

Space:\s0004983.pcx

Space:\s0004984.pcx

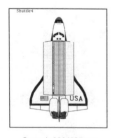

Space:\s0004985.pcx

Space:\s0004986.pcx

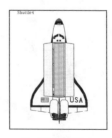

Space:\s0004987.pcx

Space:\s0004988.pcx

Space:\s0004989.pcx

Space:\s0004990.pcx

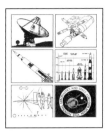

Space:\s0004991.pcx

Space:\s0004992.pcx

Space:\s0004993.pcx

Space:\s0004994.pcx

Space:\s0004995.pcx

Space:\s0004996.pcx

Sport:\s0004997.pcx

Sport:\s0004998.pcx

Sport:\s0004999.pcx

Sport:\s0005000.pcx

Sport:\s0005001.pcx

Sport:\s0005002.pcx

Sport:\s0005003.pcx

Sport:\s0005004.pcx

Sport:\s0005005.pcx

Sport:\s0005006.pcx

Sport:\s0005007.pcx

Sport:\s0005008.pcx

Sport:\s0005009.pcx

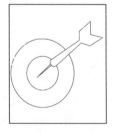

Sport:\s0005010.pcx

Sport:\s0005011.pcx

Sport:\s0005012.pcx

Sport:\s0005013.pcx

Sport:\s0005014.pcx

Sport:\s0005015.pcx

Sport:\s0005016.pcx

Sport:\s0005017.pcx

Sport:\s0005018.pcx

Sport:\s0005019.pcx

Sport:\s0005020.pcx

Sport:\s0005021.pcx

Sport:\s0005022.pcx

Sport:\s0005023.pcx

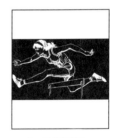

Sport:\s0005024.pcx

Sport:\s0005025.pcx

Sport:\s0005026.pcx

Sport:\s0005027.pcx

Sport:\s0005028.pcx

Sport:\s0005029.pcx

Sport:\s0005030.pcx

Sport:\s0005031.pcx

Sport:\s0005032.pcx

Sport:\s0005034.pcx

Sport:\s0005035.pcx

Sport:\s0005036.pcx

Sport:\s0005037.pcx

Sport:\s0005038.pcx

Sport:\s0005039.pcx

Sport:\s0005040.pcx

Sport:\s0005041.pcx

Sport:\s0005042.pcx

Sport:\s0005043.pcx

Sport:\s0005044.pcx

Sport:\s0005045.pcx

Sport:\s0005046.pcx

Sport:\s0005047.pcx

Sport:\s0005048.pcx

Sport:\s0005049.pcx

Sport:\s0005050.pcx

Sport:\s0005051.pcx

Sport:\s0005052.pcx

Sport:\s0005053.pcx

Sport:\s0005054.pcx

Sport:\s0005055.pcx

Sport:\s0005056.pcx

Sport:\s0005057.pcx

Sport:\s0005058.pcx

Sport:\s0005059.pcx

Sport:\s0005060.pcx

Sport:\s0005061.pcx

Sport:\s0005062.pcx

Sport:\s0005063.pcx

Sport:\s0005064.pcx

Symbols:\s0005065.pcx

Symbols:\s0005066.pcx

Symbols:\s0005067.pcx

Symbols:\s0005068.pcx

Symbols:\s0005069.pcx

Symbols:\s0005070.pcx

Symbols:\s0005071.pcx

Symbols:\s0005072.pcx

Symbols:\s0005073.pcx

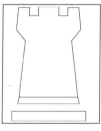

Symbols:\s0005074.pcx

Symbols:\s0005075.pcx

Symbols:\s0005076.pcx

Symbols:\s0005077.pcx

Symbols:\s0005078.pcx

Symbols:\s0005079.pcx

Symbols:\s0005080.pcx

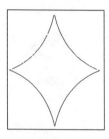

Symbols:\s0005081.pcx

Symbols:\s0005082.pcx

Symbols:\s0005083.pcx

Symbols:\s0005084.pc

Symbols:\s0005085.pcx

Symbols:\s0005086.pcx

Symbols:\s0005087.pcx

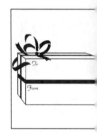

Symbols:\s0005088.p

Symbols:\s0005089.pcx

Symbols:\s0005090.pcx

Symbols:\s0005091.pcx

Symbols:\s0005092.p

Symbols:\s0005093.pcx

Symbols:\s0005094.pcx

Symbols:\s0005095.pcx

Symbols:\s0005096.p

Symbols:\s0005097.pcx

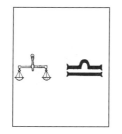

Symbols:\s0005098.pcx

Symbols:\s0005099.pcx

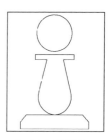

Symbols:\s0005100.pcx

Symbols:\s0005101.pcx

Symbols:\s0005102.pcx

Symbols:\s0005103.pcx

Symbols:\s0005104.pcx

Symbols:\s0005105.pcx

Symbols:\s0005106.pcx

Symbols:\s0005107.pcx

Symbols:\s0005108.pcx

ymbols:\s0005109.pcx

Symbols:\s0005110.pcx

Symbols:\s0005111.pcx

Symbols:\s0005112.pcx

Symbols:\s0005113.pcx

Symbols:\s0005114.pcx

Symbols:\s0005115.pcx

Symbols:\s0005116.p

Symbols:\s0005117.pcx

Symbols:\s0005118.pcx

Symbols:\s0005119.pcx

Symbols:\s0005120.p

Symbols:\s0005121.pcx

Tools:\t0005122.pcx

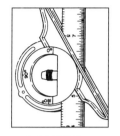

Tools:\t0005123.pcx

Tools:\t0005124.pcx

Tools:\t0005125.pcx

Tools:\t0005126.pcx

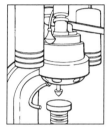

Tools:\t0005127.pcx

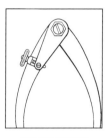

Tools:\t0005128.pcx

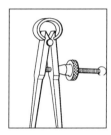

Tools:\t0005129.pcx

Tools:\t0005130.pcx

Tools:\t0005131.pcx

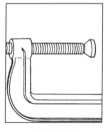

Tools:\t0005132.pcx

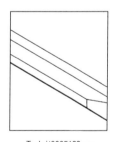

Tools:\t0005133.pcx

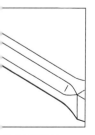

Tools:\t0005134.pcx

Tools:\t0005135.pcx

Tools:\t0005136.pcx

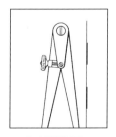

Tools:\t0005137.pcx

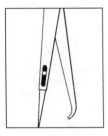

Tools:\t0005138.pcx

Tools:\t0005139.pcx

Tools:\t0005140.pcx

Tools:\t0005141.pcx

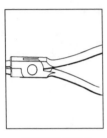

Tools:\t0005142.pcx

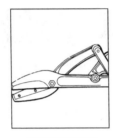

Tools:\t0005143.pcx

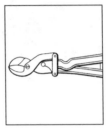

Tools:\t0005144.pcx

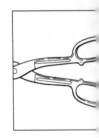

Tools:\t0005145.pcx

Tools:\t0005146.pcx

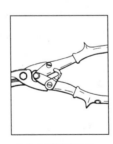

Tools:\t0005147.pcx

Tools:\t0005148.pcx

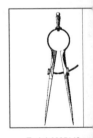

Tools:\t0005149.pcx

Tools:\t0005150.pcx

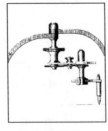

Tools:\t0005151.pcx

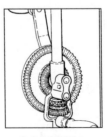

Tools:\t0005152.pcx

Tools:\t0005153.pc

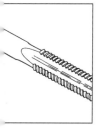

Tools:\t0005154.pcx

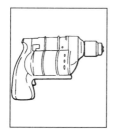

Tools:\t0005155.pcx

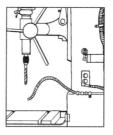

Tools:\t0005156.pcx

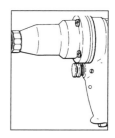

Tools:\t0005157.pcx

Tools:\t0005158.pcx

Tools:\t0005159.pcx

Tools:\t0005160.pcx

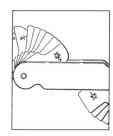

Tools:\t0005161.pcx

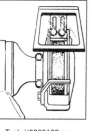

Tools:\t0005162.pcx

Tools:\t0005163.pcx

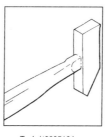

Tools:\t0005164.pcx

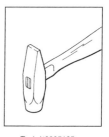

Tools:\t0005165.pcx

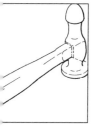

Tools:\t0005166.pcx

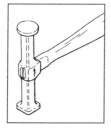

Tools:\t0005167.pcx

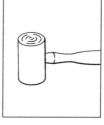

Tools:\t0005168.pcx

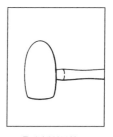

Tools:\t0005169.pcx

Tools:\t0005170.pcx

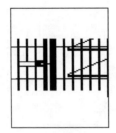

Tools:\t0005171.pcx

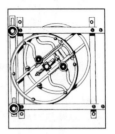

Tools:\t0005172.pcx

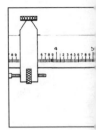

Tools:\t0005173.pcx

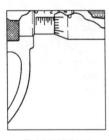

Tools:\t0005174.pcx

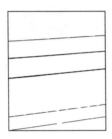

Tools:\t0005175.pcx

Tools:\t0005176.pcx

Tools:\t0005177.pcx

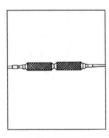

Tools:\t0005178.pcx

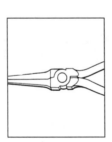

Tools:\t0005179.pcx

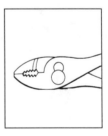

Tools:\t0005180.pcx

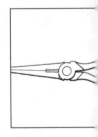

Tools:\t0005181.pcx

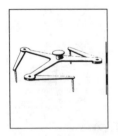

Tools:\t0005182.pcx

Tools:\t0005183.pcx

Tools:\t0005184.pcx

Tools:\t0005185.pcx

Tools:\t0005186.pcx

Tools:\t0005187.pcx

Tools:\t0005188.pcx

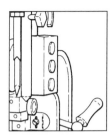

Tools:\t0005189.pcx

Tools:\t0005190.pcx

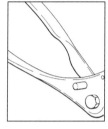

Tools:\t0005191.pcx

Tools:\t0005192.pcx

Tools:\t0005193.pcx

Tools:\t0005194.pcx

Tools:\t0005195.pcx

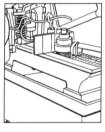

Tools:\t0005196.pcx

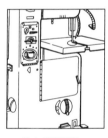

Tools:\t0005197.pcx

Tools:\t0005198.pcx

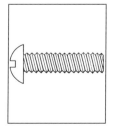

Tools:\t0005199.pcx

Tools:\t0005200.pcx

Tools:\t0005201.pcx

Tools:\t0005202.pcx

Tools:\t0005203.pcx

Tools:\t0005204.pcx

Tools:\t0005205.pcx

Tools:\t0005206.pcx

Tools:\t0005207.pcx

Tools:\t0005208.pcx

Tools:\t0005209.pcx

Tools:\t0005210.pcx

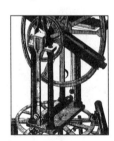

Tools:\t0005211.pcx

Tools:\t0005212.pcx

Tools:\t0005213.pcx

Tools:\t0005214.pcx

Tools:\t0005215.pcx

Tools:\t0005216.pcx

Tools:\t0005217.pc

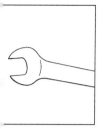

Tools:\t0005218.pcx

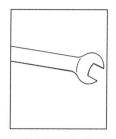

Tools:\t0005219.pcx

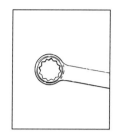

Tools:\t0005220.pcx

Tools:\t0005221.pcx

Tools:\t0005222.pcx

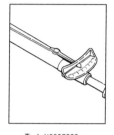

Tools:\t0005223.pcx

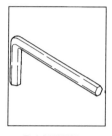

Tools:\t0005224.pcx

Transpor:\t0005225.pcx

Transpor:\t0005226.pcx

Transpor:\t0005227.pcx

Transpor:\t0005228.pcx

Transpor:\t0005229.pcx

Transpor:\t0005230.pcx

Transpor:\t0005231.pcx

Transpor:\t0005232.pcx

Transpor:\t0005233.pcx

Transpor:\t0005234.pcx

Transpor:\t0005235.pcx

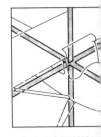

Transpor:\t0005236.pc

Transpor:\t0005237.pcx

Transpor:\t0005238.pcx

Transpor:\t0005239.pcx

Transpor:\t0005240.pc

Transpor:\t0005241.pcx

Transpor:\t0005243.pcx

Transpor:\t0005244.pcx

Transpor:\t0005245.pcx

Transpor:\t0005246.pcx

Transpor:\t0005247.pcx

Transpor:\t0005248.pcx

Transpor:\t0005249.pcx

Transpor:\t0005250.pcx

Transpor:\t0005251.pcx

Transpor:\t0005252.pcx

Transpor:\t0005253.pcx

Transpor:\t0005254.pcx

Transpor:\t0005255.pcx

Transpor:\t0005256.pcx

Transpor:\t0005257.pcx

Transpor:\t0005258.pcx

Transpor:\t0005259.pcx

Transpor:\t0005260.pcx

Transpor:\t0005261.pcx

Transpor:\t0005262.pcx

Transpor:\t0005263.pcx

Transpor:\t0005264.pcx

Transpor:\t0005265.pc

Transpor:\t0005266.pcx

Transpor:\t0005267.pcx

Transpor:\t0005268.pcx

Transpor:\t0005269.pc

Transpor:\t0005270.pcx

Transpor:\t0005271.pcx

Transpor:\t0005272.pcx

Transpor:\t0005273.pc

Transpor:\t0005274.pcx

Transpor:\t0005275.pcx

Transpor:\t0005276.pcx

Transpor:\t0005277.pcx

Transpor:\t0005278.pcx

Transpor:\t0005279.pcx

Transpor:\t0005280.pcx

Transpor:\t0005281.pcx

Transpor:\t0005282.pcx

Transpor:\t0005283.pcx

Transpor:\t0005284.pcx

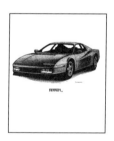

Transpor:\t0005285.pcx

Transpor:\t0005286.pcx

Transpor:\t0005287.pcx

Transpor:\t0005288.pcx

Transpor:\t0005289.pcx

Transpor:\t0005290.pcx

Transpor:\t0005291.pcx

Transpor:\t0005292.pcx

Transpor:\t0005293.pc

Transpor:\t0005294.pcx

Transpor:\t0005295.pcx

Transpor:\t0005296.pcx

Transpor:\t0005297.p

Transpor:\t0005298.pcx

Transpor:\t0005299.pcx

Transpor:\t0005300.pcx

Transpor:\t0005301.p

Transpor:\t0005302.pcx

Transpor:\t0005303.pcx

Transpor:\t0005304.pcx

Transpor:\t0005305.p

Transpor:\t0005306.pcx

Transpor:\t0005307.pcx

Transpor:\t0005308.pcx

Transpor:\t0005309.pcx

Transpor:\t0005310.pcx

Transpor:\t0005311.pcx

Transpor:\t0005312.pcx

Transpor:\t0005313.pcx

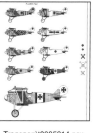

Transpor:\t0005314.pcx

Transpor:\t0005315.pcx

Transpor:\t0005316.pcx

Transpor:\t0005318.pcx

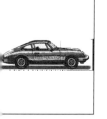

Transpor:\t0005319.pcx

Transpor:\t0005320.pcx

Transpor:\t0005321.pcx

Transpor:\t0005322.pcx

Transpor:\t0005323.pcx

Transpor:\t0005324.pcx

Transpor:\t0005325.pcx

Transpor:\t0005326.pcx

Transpor:\t0005327.pcx

Transpor:\t0005328.pcx

Transpor:\t0005329.pcx

Transpor:\t0005330.pcx

Transpor:\t0005331.pcx

Transpor:\t0005332.pcx

Transpor:\t0005333.pcx

Transpor:\t0005335.pcx

Transpor:\t0005336.pcx

Transpor:\t0005337.pcx

Transpor:\t0005338.pcx

Transpor:\t0005339.pcx

Transpor:\t0005340.pcx

Transpor:\t0005341.pcx

Transpor:\t0005342.pcx

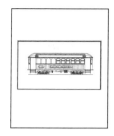

Transpor:\t0005343.pcx

Transpor:\t0005344.pcx

Transpor:\t0005345.pcx

Transpor:\t0005346.pcx

Transpor:\t0005347.pcx

Transpor:\t0005348.pcx

Transpor:\t0005349.pcx

Transpor:\t0005350.pcx

Transpor:\t0005351.pcx

Transpor:\t0005352.pcx

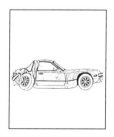

Transpor:\t0005353.pcx

Transpor:\t0005354.pcx

Transpor:\t0005355.pcx

Transpor:\t0005356.pcx

Travel:\t0005357.pcx

Travel:\t0005358.pcx

Travel:\t0005359.pcx

Travel:\t0005360.pcx

Travel:\t0005361.pcx

Travel:\t0005362.pcx

Travel:\t0005363.pcx

Travel:\t0005364.pcx

Travel:\t0005365.pcx

Travel:\t0005366.pcx

Travel:\t0005367.pcx

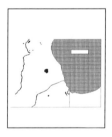

Travel:\t0005368.pcx

Travel:\t0005369.pcx

Travel:\t0005370.pcx

Travel:\t0005371.pcx

Travel:\t0005372.pcx

Travel:\t0005373.pcx

Travel:\t0005374.pcx

Travel:\t0005375.pcx

Travel:\t0005376.pcx

Travel:\t0005377.pcx

Travel:\t0005378.pcx

Travel:\t0005379.pcx

Travel:\t0005380.pc

Travel:\t0005381.pcx

Travel:\t0005382.pcx

Travel:\t0005383.pcx

Travel:\t0005384.pcx

Travel:\t0005385.pcx

Travel:\t0005386.pcx

Travel:\t0005387.pcx

Travel:\t0005388.pc

Travel:\t0005389.pcx

Travel:\t0005390.pcx

Travel:\t0005391.pcx

Travel:\t0005392.pcx

Travel:\t0005393.pcx

Travel:\t0005394.pcx

Travel:\t0005395.pcx

Travel:\t0005396.pcx

Travel:\t0005397.pcx

Travel:\t0005398.pcx

Travel:\t0005399.pcx

Travel:\t0005400.pcx

Travel:\t0005401.pcx

Travel:\t0005403.pcx

Travel:\t0005404.pcx

Travel:\t0005405.pcx

Travel:\t0005406.pcx

Travel:\t0005407.pcx

Travel:\t0005408.pcx

Travel:\t0005409.pcx

Travel:\t0005410.pcx

Travel:\t0005411.pcx

Travel:\t0005412.pcx

Travel:\t0005413.pc

Travel:\t0005414.pcx

Travel:\t0005415.pcx

Travel:\t0005416.pcx

Travel:\t0005417.pc

Travel:\t0005418.pcx

Travel:\t0005419.pcx

Travel:\t0005420.pcx

Travel:\t0005421.pc

Travel:\t0005422.pcx

Travel:\t0005423.pcx

Travel:\t0005424.pcx

Travel:\t0005425.pcx

Travel:\t0005426.pcx

Travel:\t0005427.pcx

Trees:\t0005428.pcx

Trees:\t0005429.pcx

Trees:\t0005430.pcx

Trees:\t0005431.pcx

Trees:\t0005432.pcx

Trees:\t0005433.pcx

Trees:\t0005434.pcx

Trees:\t0005435.pcx

Trees:\t0005436.pcx

Trees:\t0005437.pcx

Trees:\t0005438.pcx

Trees:\t0005439.pc

Trees:\t0005440.pcx

Trees:\t0005441.pcx

Trees:\t0005442.pcx

Trees:\t0005443.pc

Trees:\t0005444.pcx

Trees:\t0005445.pcx

Trees:\t0005446.pcx

Trees:\t0005447.pcx

Trees:\t0005448.pcx

Trees:\t0005449.pcx

Trees:\t0005450.pcx

Trees:\t0005451.pcx

Trees:\t0005452.pcx

Trees:\t0005453.pcx

Trees:\t0005454.pcx

Trees:\t0005455.pcx

Trees:\t0005456.pcx

Trees:\t0005457.pcx

Trees:\t0005458.pcx

Trees:\t0005459.pcx

Trees:\t0005460.pcx

Trees:\t0005461.pcx

Trees:\t0005462.pcx

Trees:\t0005463.pcx

Trees:\t0005464.pcx

Trees:\t0005465.pcx

Trees:\t0005466.pcx

Trees:\t0005467.pcx

Trees:\t0005468.pcx

Trees:\t0005469.pcx

Trees:\t0005470.pcx

Trees:\t0005471.pcx

Trees:\t0005472.pcx

Trees:\t0005473.pcx

Trees:\t0005474.pcx

Trees:\t0005475.pcx

Trees:\t0005476.pcx

Trees:\t0005477.pcx

Trees:\t0005478.pcx

Trees:\t0005479.pcx

Trees:\t0005480.pcx

Trees:\t0005481.pcx

Trees:\t0005482.pcx

Trees:\t0005483.pcx

Trees:\t0005484.pcx

Trees:\t0005485.pcx

Trees:\t0005486.pcx

Trees:\t0005487.pcx

Trees:\t0005488.pcx

Trees:\t0005489.pcx

Trees:\t0005490.pcx